MISCELLANIES

OF

GEORGIA,

Historical, Biographical, Descriptive, Etc.

BY

ABSALOM H. CHAPPELL.

IN THREE PARTS.

PART I.

JAMES F. MEEGAN,
ATLANTA, GA.
1874

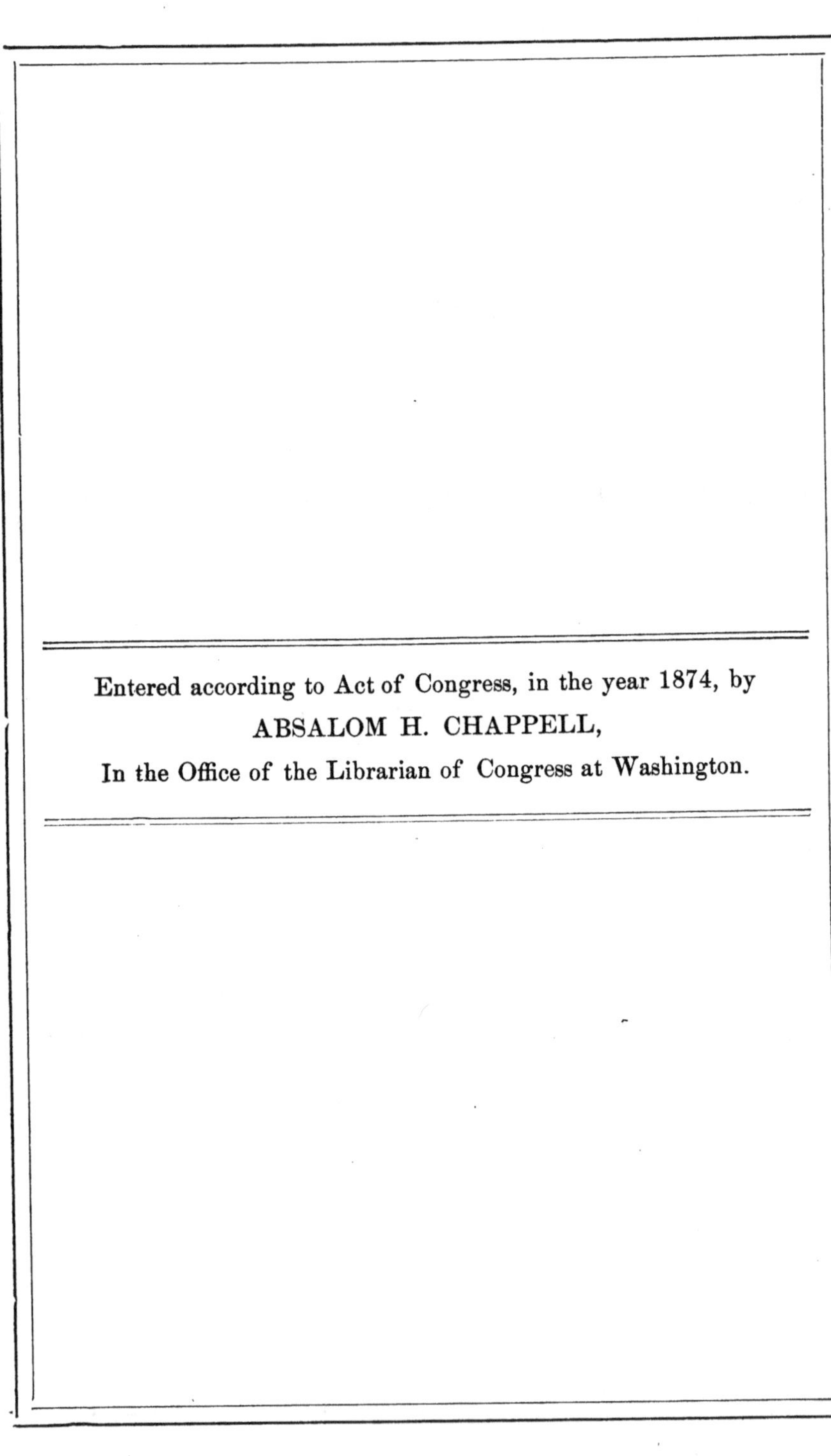

TO THE

HON. HENRY R. HARRIS,

MEMBER OF CONGRESS FROM GEORGIA,

TO WHOM THESE SHEETS ARE BEHOLDEN FOR SEEING THE LIGHT,

THEY ARE INSCRIBED

BY HIS KINSMAN AND FRIEND,

THE AUTHOR.

PROEME.

I have gotten beyond the Scriptural term of years allotted to man on earth. I have outlived my three score and ten. But although old age is fully upon me, I do not as yet feel its weight. Deep in the mid winter of life, I have not as yet felt its chill. I am sensible of no decline of physical health or mental alacrity, or warmth of heart. At no period have I enjoyed more consciously that great blessing, a sound mind in a sound body. In this respect I sometimes almost feel entitled to lay claim to what Cicero lauds in his immortal work *De Senectute:* Eam senectutem quæ fundamentis adolesentiæ constituta est:—*That old age which is built on the foundations of youth.* Where these are sound and well laid, both mind and body are apt to bear up bravely under a pretty heavy superstructure of years, and to acquire hardness and strength, rather than incur premature decay from time.

Whilst, however, sustaining thus well the weight of age, I cannot help at the same time feeling how near my end really is. To me the horizon of life no longer recedes as I advance. It stands still and awaits me, and I must soon reach it and disappear beneath it from earthly view. But I recoil not from the near seen event. God has been pleased to grant me a length of years beyond the common lot. It saddens me to think how little good use I have made of them, how much I have been wanting to Him my Maker, to myself and to my kind. Yet I have some comfort in the reflection, that though I have fallen very short of my duty and of what I might and should have done in my day and generation, still I have striven throughout life, and I trust not ineffectually, against the downward tendencies of my poor human nature and have sought to keep my soul erect and aspiring towards God and Heaven, and may I not humbly hope that when it shall pass from earth, it will be received into that celestial home for which it yearns.

I have reached a stage at which the mind has ceased to dwell over-fondly on things of the Present. Rather do I find myself inclining more and more to ruminate on my long, multifarious Past, and to ponder on the short, precarious future lying before me. Day by day I feel more strongly that the little time I have left is quite too little, in my actual circumstances, for any important worldly effort or effect, and every day I long, with growing solicitude and misgiving for somewhat to do or attempt, that may promise to rescue my remaining days from the stigma of an inane and useless existence.

Were I in the zenith or not too far beyond the zenith of life, I would disregard the ruin war has brought upon me and set to work untiringly to retrieve my fortunes; to which end I would have but to repeat, to live over again my past life, and upon the simple principle that like causes, if they have but time to operate, will produce like effects, I would be sanguine of being able to replace the lost fruits of the past with another ample store. But I have neither time nor strength left for this repetition,—for planting and cultivating such another, or indeed any other crop. My downfall has come upon me too late in life to admit of recuperation, and there is no alternative for me but to sit and die amidst its ruins. But still I would not sit idle and be utterly useless in the dear little circle which confines me. I would fain keep my mind bright and elastic and worthily at work in some way to the very last, if it were but for my own sake;—and for the sake of the beloved ones involved in my impoverishment and to whom I can no longer bequeath money or money's worth, I would fain leave something behind me, which, if I can but be happy in its delivery, may be, if not a compensation, at least a consolation—something that will be precious to their hearts when I am gone, and I pray Heaven, solidly profitable to them for time and for eternity.

Behold here, why and for whom the impulse to write first seized me! Aye, it was for the loving hearts and partial eyes of those to whom nothing that relates to me or proceeds from me, can ever be devoid of interest! It was for those to whom I feel that I am ever the same, though fortune is no longer my friend, but has deserted me, and now instead of her, age and poverty are my companions, grimly escorting me to an humble grave which no marble will adorn or iron inclose. But little to me, marble tomb or iron inclosure. For I shall rest in thy bosom, Georgia!—thy skies over me, thine earth and air above and around me, thy sons and daughters, from generation to generation, side by side with me, and on thy maternal lap, beneath thy sacred, conscious sod, I shall sleep proudly, though sorrowfully, forever sensible of thy nobleness and worth, forever mourning thy wrongs and ruin. A son's strong love for thee unites with a father's for his children to impel my pen, and it may be I have seen and known and heard enough, and felt and thought enough about thee and thine, to make some things that pen shall trace not wholly uninteresting to thy true children too.

CHAPTER I.

THE OCONEE WAR.

In the first year of the present century, the Oconee river, three miles from which I was then born, in Hancock county, was still the dividing line between a powerful, ever aggressive Anglo-American civilization on its eastern side, and the immemorial Indian barbarism which reigned as yet all the way from its western bank to the shores of the Pacific. But my, then clear and beautiful, native stream, on whose bright bosom, with its glorious garniture of towering, overhanging trees in their rich autumnal attire, I first gazed enraptured as the light canoe bore me, a child, swiftly across its placid, broad-seeming wave, safe in a mother's encircling arms and a father's skilled rowing hands, was not destined to retain much longer the distinction of being so important a boundary. The relentless tide of the white man's insatiable land-greed was already beating heavily against it, and soon swept over it, and in less than another year the red man was pressed back another and to him sad remove towards the setting sun. For it was the very next spring, in the month of April, 1802, that the Federal Government entered into the famous compact with Georgia, long celebrated in her annals, known as the Articles of Agreement and Cession, by which Georgia ceded to the United States the whole of her territory lying between her present western boundary and the Mississisppi river, comprising nearly all of what now constitutes the two great States of Alabama and Mississippi. In return for which, besides a million and a quarter to be paid in money, the United States also stipulated to extinguish for Georgia the aboriginal title to all the lands still occupied by the Indians within her thus reduced limits. And before the end of the year the National Administration, heedful of the obligation it had taken upon itself, hastened to take the first step in discharging it, by purchasing of the Muscogee or Creek Nation the fertile and beautiful tract of country spreading out west from the Oconee river to the Ocmulgee.

At this period, not twenty years had yet elapsed since Georgia had gotten from the Creeks and Cherokees the whole region, of which Hancock was only a very small part, commencing far down on the Altamaha, and lying first between that great river and the Ogeechee, and then between the Ogeechee and the Oconee, all the way up to their sources, and from thence across, between lines nearly parallel, to the Savannah and the Tugalo:—A region nearly equal in extent, and more than equal in value and fertility, to all of organized Georgia as then existing; a fact strongly showing what an important stride towards future development and greatness the State made when she effected that enlargement of her bounds, and how sagacious our predecessors of that day were in seizing the opportunity of effecting it, which presented itself at the triumphant close of the Revolutionary war; up to which time all this country had remained in the hands of the Indians, Georgia having previously acquired from them no more than a narrow strip along the sea-board from the Savannah to the St. Mary's, and another narrow strip running up between the Savannah and the Ogeechee, comprehending all Wilkes county as originally constituted. Both the Creeks and Cherokees had sided and fought with Great Britain against us, during the Revolutionary war, and having failed with her and been left by her to their fate, they necessarily incurred the fate of the vanquished, and Georgia, as the victor, having them at her mercy, dictated such terms of peace as suited her, and obtained the large cession of lands above mentioned. But the terms were too hard upon the Indians for a sincere and solid peace, and it turned out, as might have been foreseen, to be a hollow and unreal one. Treaties of peace were, indeed, made, but they brought no peace. They only terminated one war to sow the seeds and pave the way for another.

The Cherokees being comparatively weak and unwarlike and destitute of any very able and ambitious leadership among themselves, the lands also derived from them being of much less extent and value, the trouble our ancestors had with them never became so very formidable, and was much more easily composed.

Not so with the Creeks. They were by far the most numerous, powerful and warlike of all the Indian tribes in North America, and their name had gotten, during the Revolutionary war, to strike terror around every hearthstone in Georgia. To them, moreover, had belonged the lower, and the larger and more valuable portion of our new acquisitions. Cherishing still the rancors of past hostility, chafing under what they deemed the enormous price exacted for peace, and inspired by a supreme chief* of consummate abilities, ambition and influence, and especially animated by hatred of Georgia, they utterly refused to acquiesce in the cession which a portion of their head men had made at Augusta in 1783, and resorted to arms against it and to resist our occupation of the ceded lands. In the irregular, desultory manner of savage warfare, they kept up for many years a struggle, frequently relaxed, sometimes even intermitted, yet always overhanging and threatening to break out in fresh incursions and outrages. The Georgians, nevertheless, or Virginians, as the Indians called them, thronged in great numbers and undeterred, into the contested territory and pitched their settlements wherever they best liked, upon soil which they were liable every moment to have to defend with their lives. They lived, of course, in perpetual peril, and were compelled to be always in arms and on the alert. It would not be too strong to say of the infancy of this part of the State that it was baptised

*Alexander McGillivray.

in the blood of men, women and children. The reliance for defence was in part on a very few United States troops, garrisoned here and there along the Oconee river, and on volunteer horsemen organized under State authority, in small bands, regularly officered, always ready to take the saddle, indeed most of the time in it, and actively traversing the country in all directions, attacking, repelling, pursuing, intimidating—to whose aid upon emergency all the fighting men rushed from their houses and fields at a moment's warning. All this, however, would not have sufficed without the help of other means, and as the best other means in their power, the different settlements took a somewhat military character, and might indeed have been not inaptly termed semi-military colonies. By their own voluntary labor the people of each neighborhood, when numerous enough, built what was dignified as a fort, a strong wooden stockade or block-house, entrenched, loop-holed, and surmounted with lookouts at the angles. Within this rude extemporised fortress ground enough was enclosed to allow room for huts or tents for the surrounding families when they should take refuge therein—a thing which continually occurred; and, indeed, it was often the case, that the Fort became a permanent home for the women and children, while the men spent their days in scouring the country, and tilling, with their slaves, lands within convenient reach; at night betaking themselves to the stronghold for the society and protection of their families, as well as for their own safety. Well do I remember the large, level old field in my maternal grandfather's plantation, which in my early boyhood, was still noted as having been the site of one of those forts. Also the creek near by took its name from the Fort, and was and is still called Fort Creek. My grand-father, however, a fresh emigrant from Virginia, did not like this mode of life for his wife and children, and established them for two years to the east of the Ogeechee in what was then Columbia county, whilst he with his negroes cleared land, made crops and faced the Indians in Hancock, or rather in what was then Washington county. For in February, 1784, the Legislature, acting upon the treaties to which I have alluded, made at Augusta the year previous, passed a law throwing open to settlers the whole of the new acquired country from the Altamaha to the mountains, and forming it into two vast counties, Washington and Franklin, whose huge size was afterwards, from time to time, diminished by carving out new counties, among them Hancock. Thus Washington and Franklin, originally twin, coterminous counties, became disparted, and now an hundred intervening miles lie between them. But no length of time or width of space will ever dissociate the great and venerable names they bear.

CHAPTER II.

THE OCONEE WAR CONTINUED.

This rancorous Indian broil lasted with many vicissitudes and various degrees of violence for some dozen years before it was finally extinguished by the treaty of Colraine in June, 1796. All the while too it was intimately complicated with an obstinate territorial quarrel between the United States and Spain, growing out of their conflicting claims of sovereignty to the entire Indian country west of the Chattahoochee: Spain claiming as her own all the region occupied by the Creeks and other tribes between that river and the Mississippi, upon the ground of having reconquered the province of West Florida from Great Britain during the Revolutionary war,—which re-conquest, as contended by her, covered all that country at least, if not much more. From this antagonistic Spanish claim sprang Spanish tamperings with the Indians against us, the result from which, and from the hard, injurious treatment the Indians thought they had received from Georgia by the treaty of Augusta and the seizure of the Oconee lands, was that the Creek nation precipitately, in 1784, transferred to Spain in preference to the United States that allegiance or rather adherence that had just dropped from the vanquished hands of Great Britain. Their Supreme Chief, McGillivray, greatly incensed by said treaty of Augusta and the proceedings of Georgia thereon, hastened to Pensacola as both sovereign and ambassador, and formed with the creatures of Spain there what was called a treaty of Alliance and Friendship, subjecting his people and country absolutely to the Spanish yoke and sceptre. It is impossible to peruse this document without being amazed at the excessive subjugation it stipulates, so unlike anything in our Indian treaties, and the conviction seizes upon the mind that a villainous fraud was practised by the Spaniards on McGillivray in the translation of it to him. For he was a stranger at that time to their language, though master both with his tongue and pen of ours. It can hardly be doubted that he became aware afterwards of the atrocious cheat that had been perpetrated upon him. But he hid the disparaging discovery in his own proud, politic bosom, at the same time silently ignoring and annulling by all his action the false, unstipulated matter foisted by the Spaniards into the treaty.* For he was altogether too shrewd to make proclamation of his having been their dupe; a thing which would have damaged him deeply

**American State Papers—Foreign Affairs—Vol.* 1, *p.* 278.—Where this extraordinary treaty will be found at length signed by McGillivray alone on the part of the Indians. In the treaty is contained a statement that McGillivray was made acquainted with its contents by "a literal and exact translation which was reduced by Don Juan Joseph Duforrett, Captain of the militia of Louisiana and Interpreter of the English Idiom for his Majesty in said Province." The *existence* of this treaty soon became a fact well known, and was, indeed, never intended to be concealed. That its *precise character and contents*, however, were kept secret for a long time is apparent from a diplomatic letter of our Commissioners in Spain, Messrs. Short and Carmichael, addressed to the Madrid Government in August, 1792, wherein, replying to a note of the Spanish Minister bringing forward the pretensions of Spain under that treaty, they say that its contents had never been made known to them, and therefore they could say nothing in respect to it.—*American State Papers—Foreign Affairs—Vol.* 1, *page* 276.

with his own people, besides forcing upon him a breach with the Spaniards as the only alternative to his own loss of honor.

But although foul towards the Indians, both in what it contained and the manner of its obtainment, the treaty of Pensacola undoubtedly had the effect of attaching the Spaniards closely to them as our enemies: not that they avowed themselves as such and openly took the field against us. It suited their ends better to stand masked behind the Indians, and to instigate, sustain and exasperate them in their hostilities and depredations. Hence, during the period after the Revolutionary war that the old Continental Confederation was still subsisting as the only tie between the States, Georgia was all the while harassed by a huge two-fold trouble pressing upon her conjointly—an Indian trouble and a Spanish—and so thoroughly were these troubles conjoined that it was quite impossible to manage the nearer and more immediately perilous one, that with the Indians, with any success separately from its Spanish adjunct, from which it mainly drew its mischievous energies and means of annoyance. And yet this latter—*the Spanish one*—though so potent in its effects against us, was not only locally distant and beyond the arm's reach of the State, but was also politically outside of her jurisdiction, belonging, with the general mass of our foreign affairs, exclusively to the authorities of the Confederation.*

---

*Whilst Georgia during the Confederation always exercised a jurisdiction both of war and peace in Indian Affairs, which was never controverted by the United States, yet she was careful not to exercise it in any manner that might embarrass the United States in the conducting of the great territorial dispute with Spain. Hence, although the Legislature in 1785, by way of asserting the title of the State and protesting against the adverse Spanish claim, passed an act creating the county of Bourbon, extending from the mouth of the Yazoo down the Mississippi to the 31st parallel, and as far eastwardly "as the lands reached which in that District had been at any time relinquished by the Indians," and which lands the Spaniards were taking steps to occupy and settle, yet Georgia stopped short with simply creating the county of Bourbon on her statute book, taking no proceedings of any kind under the law, and in 1788 quietly repealed it, because she saw that her attempting to carry it into execution would be

It is not surprising that the State got along poorly with a task for which she was thus disabled at once by *its* distraction and her own want of strength. She did her best, however, confining herself to the Indian part of it, while the Confederation, through that eminent statesman, John Jay, as minister and secretary for Foreign Affairs, worried to quite as little purpose with the Spanish part.

Georgia, in her sphere, exerted herself not only in efforts of fighting and skirmishing, but also in a good deal of finesse and negotiation with the Indians. Her first essay in the last-mentioned way, after the opening of hostilities, was in the year 1785, and it resulted in the treaty of Galphinton, which, as to boundaries simply, reiterated the treaty of Augusta with a further cession of a considerable breadth of land between the Altamaha and the St. Mary's, which went by the name of Talassee or Talahassee.* Within another

likely to increase the difficulties of the United States in their diplomatic strife with Spain touching that and all the other territory then in dispute between the two countries.—*For the Bourbon County Act and its repeal, see Watkins' Digest of the Laws of Georgia*—304, 371.

* "Tallassee" is the name applied to this country by our Legislature in the Act of December 28th, 1794.—*Watkins' Digest*, 551—*See same Act, American State Papers, Indian Affairs, Vol. 1st*, 551, 552. In various other places in the State Papers where mention is made of this country, it is called Talassee. But Mr. Jefferson in his annual message to Congress of December, 1802, calls it the Tallahassee country. In old Indian times of the last century the name belonged to the largest and most important of the political Districts into which the Creek, or, as it is styled in the treaty of Pensacola, the Tallapouchee nation was divided. It is the first named District in that treaty, and is mentioned there as consisting of four towns. It undoubtedly embraced at that time an area much larger than the Galphinton cession. All, indeed, of South Eastern Georgia, except the old counties of Glynn and Camden, and the larger part, if not the whole of Southern and Southwestern Georgia, was comprehended in it; much likewise of Middle Florida—a fact recognized by the Floridians in the name they have bestowed on their capital. The Indians seem to have been greatly attached as well to the name as to that part of their country that bore it. Hence, McGillivray christened his chief residence on the Coosa "Little Tallassee," and the beautiful spot at the foot of the first falls of the Tallapoosa river was called Tallassee,—a name it bears to this day. "Galphinton" was a famous old Indian trading post on the Ogeechee some dozen miles below Louisville. "Shoulderbone" is the great creek of Hancock county.—*For the Treaties, see Watkins, and Marbury & Crawford's Digests.*

year another treaty was needed, and in 1786 that of Shoulderbone was made reaffirming the cessions of Augusta and Galphinton. All three of these treaties were transactions of Georgia alone with the Indians. The United States was neither a party to them nor had anything to do with them, and their effect was rather to deepen and exasperate than to extinguish or appease enmity. The Indians charged that they were sheer frauds, contrived by Georgia with persons of their tribe falsely pretending to have authority to treat. After much investigation at a subsequent period by Commissioners of the United States, a conclusion favorable to the fairness and authenticity of these treaties was reached.* The main thing, undoubtedly, which impaired them in Indian eyes was the expecting of aid from Spain in resisting them, and the belief that Georgia would be unable to enforce them against the combined Indian and Spanish opposition. For savages, not unlike civilized people, are very much inclined, when under the influence of strong passions or interests, to trample on good faith and the sanctity of compacts, unless deterred by the dread which superior power on the adverse side is apt to inspire. Hence hostilities continued to rage, not the less, perhaps even the more, on account of these abortive attempts at pacification; and there is no telling what might not have been the disastrous upshot, had not the new Federal Constitution been adopted, and under it a new government started in 1789 for our young Federal Republican nation, strong enough to inspire the Indians with a salutary fear, and clothed with the whole war-making and treaty-making power; and also with the absolute control over all Indian as well as all foreign affairs. By this wise and happy concentration, all the reins over the subject, as well in its Indian as its Spanish aspect, were gathered into one great, commanding, national grasp, and were from thenceforth handled in unison, and with abundant judgment, skill and success.

For from the very outset of his administration, Washing-

**American State Papers—Indian Affairs, Vol. 1st*, 616.

ton, from his lofty stand point at the head of the Goverment, and with his large, well-poised, well-braced mind, long versed in great, perilous and perplexed affairs, surveyed the whole field, and kept it clearly beneath his eye. He saw in all their magnitude and complication, the difficulties of the case with which he had to deal, and set about overcoming them with characteristic wisdom, justice and statesmanship. He found the negotiations in which the defunct Government of the Confederation had been engaged with Spain in an exceedingly unpromising state, nor were the prospects in that quarter much bettered during the first years of his own governance. For Spain was at that period still one of the proudest, most powerful and self-sufficient monarchies of the world, and had evidently made up her mind to yield nothing and exact everything in this dispute with a new-born, poor and feeble country. And certainly she was not far wrong in supposing the United States were at that time in no condition for taking strong measures against her, and she feared not to impinge upon the very confines of insolence in some of her diplomatic passages with us.

Seeing, therefore, no near or flattering prospect of getting rid of the Indian war and its numerous attendant ills by sapping the Spanish foundation on which it mainly stood, Washington proceeded very soon to address himself in the most direct and effectual manner to the Indians themselves. He determined to try what could be done to dissolve their Spanish ties and bring them under an American Protectorate. To this end he resorted to the best and most hopeful means. Early in 1790 he dispatched from New York, then the Federal capital, a distinguished and singularly suitable man, well known to him, Col. Marinus Willet, upon a confidential mission into the Creek nation, accredited to McGillivray. Colonel Willet's instructions were to prevail on McGillivray and the other great Chiefs to send a delegation, headed by McGillivray himself, to New York to confer and treat with Washington, face to face. The mission was successful, and Col. Willet returned to New York accompanied by McGillivray and his head men, representing the more hostile element of the nation. It was undoubtedly the most important and imposing Indian embassy that ever visited our Government, and they were received and treated every where along the route and in New York with extraordinary distinction and attention. They remained a good while in that city. Many conferences and talks were held, and the result was the treaty of New York, concluded on the 7th of August, 1790, negotiated by Gen. Knox, Secretary at War, under the immediate eye and direction of Washington. By its stipulations the Creeks accepted fully the protection of the United States to the exclusion of Spain and all other powers, and bound themselves not to enter into any treaty or compact with any of the States or any individuals or foreign country. They also agreed to abide by the Altamaha and Oconee as their dividing line, following the latter stream along its westernmost branch to its source. Our Government, on its part, restored to them the Tallassee country, and also guaranteed the same and all their remaining lands to them forever against all the world. A treaty more cardinal, consequential, and even revolutionary in its character, could hardly be imagined. Upon it as upon a hinge, the Creek nation swung around completely and at once into those natural relations with the United States which its interests dictated, but which had been passionately rejected at the close of the Revolutionary war for a Spanish alliance and subjugation. It was undoubtedly in gross conflict with the treaty of Pensacola, and it could not but have the effect of creating an early crisis of the most decisive kind between Spain and the United States, whilst it certainly involved the Creeks themselves in a position not a little embarrassing between those two powers.

It was a compact, however, on the whole not less wise and well considered than highly important, and having been concluded and solemnly perfected by the signatures of Gen. Knox and twenty-four great Chiefs, and the attestation of the Indian National Interpreter and several of our own most distinguished men, the work of the Creek delegation was done; and now, loaded with presents and assurances of friendship, they were ready with their train of attendants to depart for their far distant Southern hunting grounds. But their long and diversified ambassadorial tour from the heart of their own country over land to New York through so many States, towns and cities was destined to be strikingly contrasted by the character of the homeward journey that was in store for them, by the monotonous, though deeply impressive sea voyage arranged for them by Washington over ten parallels of latitude from New York to St. Mary's,—a mode of returning they were led to prefer by certain politic ideas as well as by somewhat of curiosity. For they wished for some ocular knowledge of that mighty ocean to which McGillivray had been long attracting their thoughts by saying they ought to have a free trading outlet to it at the mouth of the St. Mary's,—and especially were they desirous of seeing and knowing for themselves that oft commended harbor and outlet. Hence, mainly their disposition to go home by water, for little cared they for the considerations of mere greater ease and expedition that were held out to them. Old Neptune, well pleased, grew serene at beholding them, and greeted with smiles that beamed over the ocean his strange new visitants—nature's erect, still unsubdued sons and stoic lords of the woods. And well might he look graciously on the novel and interesting array they presented to his view. For never before or since, in all his reign, has it been given him, nor may he hope it will ever be given him again, to lift his storm-quelling Trident aloft over his liquid realm in propitious behalf of such another cargo of travelers on its billowy bosom as these stern, turbaned, plaided, buskined heroes and kings of the new world's yet unviolated wilds, their hearts full of homage to himself, and their aspect filling with wonderment his Tritons and Nereides and all his other subject "blue haired" deities of the deep.

Arrived at St. Mary's they quitted without regret the noble sea ship, which it was certain nevertheless they would always remember with admiring love and honor, and, transferred to smaller craft, wended their way slowly up the tortuous river to the famous old frontier Indian trading post of Colraine. And now they soon stood once more on that beloved ancestral soil which they had just recovered back to their nation, large, level-lying Tallassee, a land of pine trees and the cypress, dismal emblem of death, though itself so impervious to decay; of the hardy perennial wire-grass, nutritious to cattle and deer; of ever-green oaks, and the also ever-green stately magnolia, glorious in the middle and high upper air, its aspiring branches and lofty top resplendent with grand, shining, aromatic white flowers; a land, too, abounding in game of the forest and fish and wild fowl; swarming with the honey bee likewise with its generous stores of mellifluous wealth wonderously elaborated from millions of woodland leaves and blossoms; and scarcely less alive with wolves, wild cats, bears and tigers;* washed along its Northern border by the broad, poetic Altama,† swamp-

*"Tigers" was the name formerly given to panthers in this part of Georgia, and is still their name in East Florida.

†"Altama" is Goldsmith's poetic contraction for the Altamaha, formed by the confluence of the Oconee and Ocmulgee. *See* his beautiful poem of "The Deserted Village" written more than an hundred years ago, at a time when the emigration of the virtuous poor from Great Britain to the young colony of Georgia was at its height. The tide of emigration had been setting, when the poem was written, very strongly to the lower banks of the Altamaha, and among the emigrants there were not a few who ultimately rose to fortune and founded families and left names which are a pride and honor to the State. Here are the fine lines—which our great river, and its scenery and reputation—called forth in a strain graphic and powerful, though in some respects exaggerated and erroneous:

"Ah, no! To distant climes, a dreary scene,
Where half the convex world intrudes between,
Through torrid tracts with fainting steps they go,
Where wild Altama murmurs to their woe.
Far different there from all that charmed before,
The various terrors of that horrid shore:
Those blazing suns that dart a downward ray,
And fiercely shed intolerable day;
Those matted woods where birds forget to sing,
But silent bats in drowsy clusters cling;
Those pois'nous fields with rank luxuriance crown'd,
Where the dark scorpion gathers death around;
Where at each step the stranger fears to wake

engloomed river, lonely and austere, recoiling from the sea, reluctant and sad to be so far estranged alike in space, in scenery, and in name from all its sweet highland springs; whilst on the other, its southern side, the Immaculate Virgin Mother's sacred stream laved it with unfailing waters, ever distilling from the vast and secret Okeefeenokee.*

The rattling terrors of the vengeful snake;
Where crouching tigers wait their hapless prey,
And savage men more murd'rous still than they;
While oft in whirls the mad tornado flies,
Mingling the ravag'd landscape with the skies.
Far different these from every former scene,
The cooling brook, the grassy vested green,
The breezy covert of the warbling grove,
That only shelter'd thefts of harmless love."

The river's name pronounced in the usual manner with a light accent on the first syllable and a full, strong one on the last, thus *Awl-ta-ma-haw*, sounds very like an Indian word; and yet quite surely it is not of Indian, but of Spanish parentage. It is an interesting fact, reflecting light on the first exploration of the State, and clearing up a part of its history otherwise obscure, that so many of the Atlantic rivers of Georgia have the Spanish stamp on their names,—as the St. Mary's, the Great and Little St. Illa, the Altamaha, and last, and if possible, plainest of all, the Savannah. For no one can ascend that stream from the sea, or stand on the edge of the bluff, which the city occupies, or on the top of its ancient Exchange, (which may fire, and war, and tempest, and the tooth of time, and the felon hand of improvement long spare,) and overlook the vast expanse of flat lands that spread out on both sides of the river, forming in winter a dark, in summer a green, in autumn a saffron contrast to its bright, intersecting waters, without knowing at once that from these plains, these savannas, the river got its name, derived from the Spanish language and the Spanish word *sabanna*,—and that it was baptized with the christian, though not saintly name it bears, by Spanish discoverers just as certainly as the great grassy planes in South America owed their name of Savannas to the same national source. The case of the Altamaha is equally free from doubt, though not so self-evident on the first glance. It comes from the old, now disused Spanish word *Altamia*, pronounced *Altameeah*, signifying a deep earthen plate or dish of whatever form; a name naturally enough suggested by the character and aspect, deep, broad, still, of the lower end of the river, probably the only part the Spaniards had seen when they christened it, and which doubtless looked to them much like a hugh, longitudinal dish kept brimful rather by stagnation of its waters and impulse from the sea than by large, everflowing supplies from an unknown interior.

* The Okeefeenokee far outsizes all the swamps of the world. Even that great Serbonian Bog, celebrated by Milton,

"Betwixt Damiata and Mount Cassius old
Where armies whole have sunk!"

was small in comparison. In old times when Morse's earlier editions were still authority in the Geography of the United States, three hundred miles was

The stalwart, taciturn Chiefs rejoiced to traverse anew, with noiseless footfall, the great woody expanse, now profaned and denaturalized by railroads, then only threaded by the tiny, interminable Indian trail, for which no tree had to be felled or earth removed; and they exulted to know it again as their country's unquestioned domain, reclaimed from the Galphinton cession and grasp of Georgia by that treaty of New York which their talks had demanded and their hands had signed.

But just as was their exultation and important as was the the territory they had regained, their wild countrymen were far from being satisfied. They had gotten back very much, it was true, but not much more than one-half, in supposed value at least, of what they had eagerly insisted upon and expected. Nor were the Georgians better content. Nothing indeed could more strikingly show how difficult and malignant the state of things was, and how stubborn were the obstacles which Spanish interference with the Indians and the bitter temper of Georgia towards them threw in the way, than the fact that the combined names of Washington and McGillivray, corroborated by the strong necessities of the case and the plainest dictates of policy, availed not to render the treaty acceptable to either side. The Georgians, although they had gotten by it the whole of the so much coveted Oconee country, recalcitrated because it retroceded to the Indians the above named Tallassee country between the Altamaha and St. Mary's, and also because of its perpetual guarantee to them of all their remaining unceded territory. And although the Indians had gotten this guar-

the supposed circumference of the Okeefeenokee. Modern scepticism has lessened it one-half, I believe; but it is mere guess work. Its impenetrable recesses defy the compass and chain, and its outer boundary if not immeasurable, has at least never been measured. The St. Mary's is not the only river it feeds. It is also the birth place of the Suwanee, a river flowing into the Gulf, the present name of which is a corruption of the Spanish San Juan, *Anglice*, St. John. The St. Johns of the English and of this day was the St. Matheo of the Spaniards.—*Bancroft's Hist. U. S., Vol.* 1, *p.* 61. It may well enhance our sense of the grandeur of the Okeefeenokee that it should be the matrix of two such rivers as the St. Mary's and the Suwanee.

antee, of which they were so desirous, and had also gotten back the Tallassee country on which they laid so much stress as an indispensable winter hunting ground, and likewise on account of its convenience to the sea, by the short navigation of the St. Mary's, yet they were ill-humored because they did not also get back the rich gore of land in the fork of the Oconee and Apalachee. Indeed, McGillivray acquiesced most reluctantly in this feature of omission in the treaty, and gave fair notice at the time of the dissatisfaction it would cause in his nation. Under all these circumstances the treaty led not to an entire restoration of peace, to not much more indeed than a feverish lull of the war. Depredations and occasional outbreaks of hostility continued to occur and to impart an uneasy ill-natured threatening aspect to our Creek Indian affairs.

Washington, than whom no man ever understood better the art of temporizing wisely or knew better when the precise moment to strike and for decisive action had come, was in no hurry by precipitating things, to endanger the chances which he saw brightening for the propitious settlement of the whole trouble, Spanish and Indian, at one time and by one blow. For now the French Revolution had broken out, and Spain and most of the powers of Europe began soon to be drawn within its vortex or to tremble on its verge, aghast at its fierce gyrations and direful portents. Meantime, Washington kept alive his negotiations and grew more positive and urgent as the clouds thickened around Spain in Europe. Yet he was free from hot haste. For he saw that the mighty chapter of accidents which God alone peruses and overrules was now in rapid evolution and likely to throw forth opportunities felicitous for his country in this and other important matters. So he persisted in biding his time and nursing the negotiation, notwithstanding the impatient pressure upon him from Georgia for greater energy and celerity in his measures. At length the European distresses and perils of Spain reached a crisis so urgent and menacing as made her feel it madness to enhance her other ills by our enmity, and convinced her how utterly hopeless it was to continue to press longer her vast territorial pretensions against us, under the very shadow of our gigantic and now thrifty and rapidly growing young Republic. In the midst of this crisis, well knowing as she did, that the claim of the United States was one that could by no possibility ever be surrendered whilst men and muskets remained to us, she made a merit of the necessity which it was useless for her longer to resist, and in October, 1795, entered into the treaty of San Lorenzo, ceding to us all her claims on this side of the Mississippi to the north of the 31st parallel and west of the Chattahoochee. At the same time confirming the old boundary from the confluence of that river with the Flint eastwardly to the mouth of the St. Mary's, thus surrendering, on account of the distresses of her own situation, what she never would have yielded up to a sense of our rights; a loss little memorable, however, by the side of the stupendous sacrifice she was soon afterwards forced to make of her immense and splendid Province of Louisiana to the boundless ambition and rapacity of France.

With this cession by Spain of her cherished claim to all the Indian Territory that had been in contest between herself and the United States, went her pretensions to a protectorate and sovereignty over the Indians themselves which were founded solely on that claim. The Indians were therefore now left to themselves and to us without any chance of foreign aid or exposure to foreign interference or instigation for the future. Every consequence desirable on our side followed now easily and almost of course. The root of mischief had been exterminated. Friendly tempers and dispositions on the part of the Indians towards us had only to be duly courted and cultivated on our part in order to insure their rapid development and growth. Soon the fruit of a permanent Indian peace was fully in our reach, inviting our grasp, and ready to drop into our hands as the natural sequel of the happy Spanish adjustment that had taken place. It had required nearly the whole length of Washington's

Administration from its first year to its last to bring things to this point,—to manage and successfully settle this its great Southern Spanish-Indian trouble. But he finally brought it to an auspicious termination. By the treaty of Colraine, concluded as we have seen in the summer of 1796, the last year of the last term of his Presidency, the boundaries stipulated at New York were recognized and reaffirmed, and the seal was put to a longed-for and lasting peace, and our horizon cleared at length of every boding Indian cloud. For both Georgians and Indians had by this time become educated and reconciled to those boundaries and were never again disposed to quarrel about them; a temper of mind in a large degree induced by Washington's immense weight of character with both sides, and by their natural feeling of submission to the grandeur of the power, which he represented and wielded. All which however might have failed of such early and full effect on the Indians, but for the disheartening fact which stared them in the face, that the territory to the east of the Oconee and its prongs for which they had been contending, was already hopelessly lost to them, having become, during the contention, filled up and occupied by a population more than able and intensely determined to hold and defend it against them forever.

CHAPTER III.

ALEXANDER McGILLIVRAY.

Thus long have I, yielding to a just love and partiality for the section of Georgia in which I was born and in which the bones of my forefathers repose, lingered and dwelt on the troublous and important interval of time which elapsed from its first acquisition and settlement down to its final pacification. And, moreover, it is a portion of the history of the State well worthy, on its own account, to be recalled and remembered, for it records a great step,—a striking epoch in her progress and development. But it is impossible not to be conscious that the scenes and events of that period have had their full day on the world's stage and in men's minds, and now not only have they passed off from both, but there is no longer a generation living whose blood could be made to tingle at their recital. And yet to me, long accustomed to cherish dearly the memories and traditions of my native soil, it has often seemed that in this protracted, fitful, frontier war for the lordship of the Oconee lands, there was much in regard both to the actors and the things enacted on which the mind might dwell not unrewarded, and which Georgians at least ought not willingly to let go down to oblivion.

Particularly has it struck me that connected with this war there was a signal circumstance, which rendered it exceptional and ennobled it among Indian wars. The proud fact, I mean, that it was the theatre on which was conspicuously displayed one of those infrequent, extraordinary characters that history loves to contemplate, and which, however they may specially belong to some one people, sect or class, during their active, living career, become the large and general property of mankind when dead.

Such a character was Alex. McGillivray, by all odds the foremost man of Indian blood and raising that Anglo-America has ever seen ; one who was universally allowed and felt in his day to be the very soul of the Creek nation, which was almost absolutely swayed by his genius and will. And be it remembered, that it was not a petty, confined tribe that was thus swayed by him, and swayed, too, in a manner and with an ability which struck enlightened civilized observers with admiration, but a wide extended Indian commonwealth, exulting in thousands of fearless warriors and an hundred organized towns, all under their respective Chiefs,* overspreading a region far greater than all Georgia now is. McGillivray was Supreme Chief of the whole, freely elevated to that height by his fierce countrymen because of his superior qualities and merits, aided also by some considerable advantages of family and connection. He made himself effectively felt all the while throughout his wild domains and the surrounding parts. His entire country lay within the chartered bounds of Georgia and Florida, and the absorbing study and struggle of his life, after our Revolutionary war, was how to save it from the territorial greed of Georgia,—a danger from which he early augured that ruin to his nation, which long after his death was so fully realized. Peace or war with us he clearly saw was alike perilous to his country, and he would gladly have kept her away as well from our caresses as from our hostilities, for they both always equally menaced her integrity, looking as they invariably did, to still other treaties and other surrenders of land. Fully sensible of the difficulty and peril of his country's situation, he glanced keenly around in every direction for extrication and support. There is no doubt that he had formed and was seeking to accomplish the scheme of an intimate and permanent confederation of the

**American State Papers, Indian Affairs, Vol. 1st, p.* 15; *Gen. Knox's Report of July 6th*, 1789.

four great Southern tribes, the Creeks, Cherokees, Choctaws and Chickasaws, of which he would undoubtedly have become the head alike in fact and in form. He turned his attention also to Florida and Spain, and became an apt diplomatist and negotiator with the Spanish authorities in Pensacola, Mobile and New Orleans, and our own national archives abound in proof how well he acquitted himself in all his transactions and correspondence with our public fuctionaries and commissioners.*

Col. Seagrove, United States Agent among the Creeks, and other minor national officials, as well as the Georgians generally of that day, used oddly enough to inveigh against him for what they called his duplicity. The charge, it must be admitted, was not purely fictitious, though certainly not very reasonable or just in the quarter from whence it came. What right have the strong to cast such a reproach on the weak, whom they are seeking to oppress and dispossess by sheer means of greater force? And yet it is the standing reproach, which in all ages, the *vis major*, superior, overbearing power has been wont to hurl at the feeble, whenever they have happened to be troublesomely successful in employing what is stigmatized as artifice and cunning for their defense and safety. Undoubtedly in the circumstances, in which McGillivray saw himself placed, threatened by Georgia and the United States on the one hand, treacherously embraced and instigated by Spain on the other, both powers an entire overmatch for his own country, he must needs have abandoned that country's cause to ruin or resorted to somewhat of duplicity for her sake, that is to say, he was compelled to play adroitly between the two dreaded powers. In such a situation duplicity changed its nature and became, as practised by him, a high, patriotic virtue, the only one, indeed, which he could make count for much against two such hollow friends and real rival enemies as he had too much reason to fear they both were. Accordingly he deserves no censure from us or from anybody, because, incensed and alarmed at

*See 1st Vol. *American State Papers on Indian Affairs—passim.*

the deep incision made into his territory by our fathers at the close of the Revolutionary war, he hastened to throw himself into the arms of Spain as a security and resentment alike against Georgia and the United States. After continuing firm for a number of years to this enforced Spanish preference, learning from his own keen observation, as well as from all the antecedents of Spain in America, what abundant cause there was to be distrustful of her, he oscillated back towards the United States, attracted by the great confidence inspired by the character of Washington, by the concentration of all power over Indian affairs in the Federal Government, and by the better terms and stipulations now held out from our side to his own and all other Indian tribes. Yet it is obvious that in taking this great turn which culminated so quickly in the treaty of New York, he was far from contemplating any breach with Spain. For he deemed it his policy to keep a strong, though latent hold on her as a safeguard against the United States, whom, nevertheless, he was bent on attaching as a friend, and holding, moreover, as a guarantor of the territory of the Indians against all the world, Spain included.

In the meantime, as already mentioned, he was scheming to construct a grand confederacy of the four great Southern tribes which might serve as a bulwark to the whole of them against the grasping designs of both the United States and Spain. It is not extravagant to say that the most consummate political genius could hardly have devised anything better or more suited to the circumstances than this, his plan, in its entirety. Had he lived to bring it to perfection and launch it into operation, there is no telling how much it might have changed the whole character and current of our subsequent Indian relations and history, and prevented many disastrous Indian (and perhaps also Spanish) events that afterwards took place. It might even have been that the Creeks, Cherokees, Choctaws and Chickasaws, instead of dwindling away, as they now seem likely to do, unhappy exotics in their compulsory Trans-Mississippi homes, would have become, under his auspices, one grand, consolidated, Indian commonwealth, rooted and flourishing permanently on their beloved ancestral soil, and destined finally perhaps to full, fraternal incorporation into our mighty American system of States. Such at least was the consummation which, it is known and recorded, this great Muscogee patriot and statesman had conceived and suggested in regard to his own particular tribe.

Behold here the magnanimous hopes that flattered McGillivray and occupied his thoughts and fired his ambition! But he was arrested by death in the midst of these high and beneficent machinations, and at a time, too, when he was apparently under a cloud. If his life had been prolonged, time would probably, however, have vindicated his strategy and his control over events, and it is likely that a brighter sun and a broader and more brilliant horizon would have beamed out upon him than he had ever known. With endowments such as distinguished him, with such a prestige as he had with the Indians of his own and all the neighboring tribes, and his strong, easy influence over them, fortune could hardly have continued lastingly untractable towards him. His authority with his people had a vitality which reached beyond his life. Whilst the tone of the Creek nation went down considerably from the time of his death, yet for years afterwards the subtle influence that had long emanated from him and ruled in Creek affairs, survived him and continued to be felt. Particularly was it an element along with the name of Washington and other causes that gradually led his countrymen to become reconciled to the long distasteful treaty of New York, for which he was responsible as its almost sole negotiator and author on the Indian side,—his brother Chiefs having been not much more than machines in his hands in that great piece of Indian diplomacy.

If ever there shall arise a weird pen fitted to deal with such a subject, it will find in this man's character and career a theme full of inspiration and demanding all its power. The fabled centaur of antiquity, that marvelous conception of the human, united with the equine form and nature, was but a fiction, though one full of richest meaning. The scarcely less wonderful union of the civilized with the savage man in Alexander McGillivray was a hard, tangible reality, the most felicitous compound of the kind ever seen. Both by lineage and education he was heir to the two natures, which co-existed in him seemingly without conflict and with great force and harmony of development. In youth he had what Washington and Franklin had, a common English education, sufficient to enable him as them in after life to impress on all men a strong sense of the greatness which nature had bestowed, and which fortune and circumstances exercised to the utmost and brought out fully to the world's view. The shrewdness, the robust sense and crude force of the Scotch Highland Chieftain were blended in him with calm Indian subtlety and intensity, and the innate dignity of the Muscogee warrior statesman. He had great ambition, great abilities, and what is most of all, and the true imperial sign of greatness, he had great power of influencing and controlling men on a large scale and in great affairs. What an outgrowth of civilization on what a stock of barbarism! Like most very strong natures, he was strong at once by his virtues and talents, which were great and many, and by his vices, which were few but telling, though not deformed by Indian ferocity, (for he was a stranger to the thirst for blood, and his breast was the seat of humanity) whilst all his qualities, good and bad, were apt to his situation and the necessities of the part he had to play. It has been said, more daringly than reverently or truly, that it took nature a gestation of a thousand years to produce a Napoleon Bonaparte. The great mother of us all ought not to be thus slurred in order to add to the renown of one of her sons. But this much is certainly true: Long intervals often occur without witnessing any of those extraordinary conjunctures, which are necessary to the production and manifestation of great and extraordinary men, and it is not by any means probable that the world will soon again have the opportunity of beholding the like of General McGillivray. For to this end, there must happen the coupling of another man such as him with a fortune and circumstances as peculiar and extraordinary as his, and which, acting on him, made him what he was and blest him, moreover, with a felicity seldom the lot of the great among barbarians, that of being well handed down in civilized records, and consequently rightly known to civilized people—the only arbiters of fame and custodians of glory. Yet let it not be supposed that his good fortune in this regard, though marked, was perfect and entire. In the mention of it, therefore, there must be some reserve. History has not been enabled to present him fully. She has only preserved and spread before us the last half, or it may be less than the last half, of his public active career. When she first takes him up and makes him her theme, to-wit: at the opening of the Creek troubles with Georgia, soon after the Revolutionary war, he was already in the maturity of his greatness, and at the pinnacle of power. Of the length of time he had been there, of the steps and means, by which he had risen so high, and the talents and conduct by which he had sustained and illustrated himself in that elevation, there is not, there never was, any record, so far as I have been able to find out, and all tradition in relation thereto, has long since either perished or become apocryphal, except the general fact of his having at one time served under his father as a deputy in the British Indian Agency during the Revolutionary war—with the titular rank of a British Colonel.*

His father was a Georgian, Lacklan McGillivray, who came in early youth from Scotland and was among those, who, in the Revolutionary war, sided strongly with Great Britain. He was a leading Indian trader, a man of property and consequence, and his name appears in the acts of confiscation and banishment passed by Georgia. His mother was a principal Creek woman of striking personal charms,

**American State Papers, Indian Affairs, 2d Vol.*, 788.

heightened, it is said, by some French blood in her veins, and he himself was a Georgian born. The circumstances of his parentage and breeding would naturally have carried him into the ranks of the enemies of the State. But tradition and written accounts alike inform us that it was his father's banishment and the confiscation of his father's estate that envenomed his heart and filled it with deep, vindictive hatred of Georgia and her people. Notwithstanding which, Georgia may well feel some pride that such a man was her son, whom destiny, not his own fault or crime, made her enemy. For he who devotes himself ably, patriotically, unflinchingly and untiringly in the higher and more perilous spheres of service to the cause of his country's salvation, unimportant though that country may be in the world's mouth or mind, merits the homage of mankind and even of those against whom he has devoted himself in such a cause.

He died on the 17th of February, 1793, a peaceful death on civilized soil, whilst a visitor at Pensacola among those Spanish friends and allies with whom he had long been accustomed to work and plot against us, whom at the same time he too shrewdly understood, and too profoundly fathomed, not to see that there was reason why he should watch them closely and make a friend of the United States against them. And yet, as if fate had decreed that in everything and to the very last there should be something remarkable and out of the common course in regard to him, this man, whom nature and fortune had concurred to make great, dying there on Spanish soil, was spurned when dead by Spanish religion and denied burial in their sacred ground* by those who had courted and magnified him while living, and was left to be obscurely interred by private and profane hands in the garden of his Scotch friend, Panton, the great Indian trader, where doubtless all trace of his grave has long since vanished, and the spot will be forever unknown, which inhumes the once famous and potential Alexander

**American State Papers, Indian Affairs, Vol.* 1, 382.

McGillivray. What a contrast to the treatment of the aged and distinguished Choctaw Chief Pushmataha, who, dying at Washington in 1824, not only found an honored grave in the Congressional burying ground with monumental stone and inscription, but whose dying wish, "when I am gone, let the big guns be fired over me," was touchingly fulfilled by the booming of minute guns from Capitol Hill, the roar of cannon over his grave and all the accompanying pomps and glories of a grand and crowded public funeral.* But the indignant shade of McGillivray was not left long disconsolate under this poor Spanish slight. Precious amends came soon to soothe and requite. The news of his death, traveling by way of the Havana and Baltimore, reached Washington in the latter city en route to Mount Vernon to enjoy there a few days' repose from the toils of the Presidency. That great nature which ever discerned and honored sterling worth and true nobility of mind and character wherever they existed, in whomsoever of human found, had recognized these qualities in McGillivray and felt his kindred to himself. He felt consequently his death, and on arriving at Mount Vernon wrote to Gen. Knox informing him of the event and calling the deceased their friend. When we remember what ample and identical opportunities Gen. Washington and Gen. Knox had both had of knowing McGillivray well, and how chary Washington always was of praise, and how few and chosen were the men to whom he ever applied the sympathetic phrase of friend, this simple spontaneous testimonial from the greatest of Americans to the illustrious Muscogee Chief goes to the heart and arrests the mind by its high value and touching significance.†

History too often slights and neglects to record many minor things about which posterity feels curious and would gladly be informed touching distinguished and important personages. The Heroditus of Alabama has, however, avoided this fault in the case of McGillivray, and has grati-

Col. McKenny's Indian Lives and Portraits; Title, Pushmataha.

†*Spark's Life and Writings of Washington, Vol. 10, p. 335.*

fied us fully in regard to his person, appearance, manners and other outward circumstances. He describes him as "six feet high, spare made and remarkably erect in person and carriage. His eyes were large, dark and piercing. His forehead was so peculiarly shaped that the old Indian countrymen often spoke of it. It commenced expanding at the eyes and widened considerably at the top of his head. It was a bold, lofty forehead. His fingers were long and tapering, and he wielded a pen with the greatest rapidity. His face was handsome and indicative of quick thought and much sagacity. Unless interested in conversation he was disposed to be taciturn, but even then was polite and respectful. When a British Colonel he dressed in the British uniform, and when in the Spanish service he wore the military dress of that country. When Washington bestowed on him the honorary rank and title of a Brigadier-General, he sometimes wore the uniform of the American army, but never in the presence of the Spaniards. His usual dress was a mixture of the Indian and American garb. He always traveled with two servants, David Francis, a half-breed, and Paro, a negro. He was the owner at his death of sixty negroes, three hundred head of cattle and a large stock of horses. He had good houses at the Hickory Grounds and Little Tallassee, where he entertained free of charge distinguished Government Agents and persons traveling through his extensive dominions. Like all other men he had his faults. He was ambitious, crafty and rather unscrupulous, yet he possessed a good heart and was polite and hospitable. For ability and sagacity he had few superiors."*

It is impossible not to be struck with McGillivray's cranial development as here given: It is the very ideal of the sculptor for a head pregnant and alive with combined intellectual and moral power. If any man wants to be well satisfied on this point, let him go and gaze on the bust of the young Augustus by the Kentucky artist, Harte, which I saw at the Louisville Exposition in the fall of 1872.

Pickett's History of Alabama, Vol. 2, Ch. 24, p. 142, 143.

CHAPTER IV.

GENERAL ELIJAH CLARK.

And on our own, the civilized side, there was also a prominent representative character, whom we should not overlook; a leading, sterling, nobly meritorious, yet unhappily before the end of his career, a somewhat erring soldier and patriot, whom it would be wrong and incomplete to quit the Oconee war without noticing and honoring, and whom at the same time it is impossible to recollect without some feeling of melancholy.

If I were asked what man in those uneasy, perilous times was most formidable to the savage foe, most serviceable to the exposed frontier, most unsparing of himself, ever foremost in doing or attempting whatever he saw was best for the security and advancement of the State; who, whilst he lived, always made himself strongly felt wherever he took part, and who, now when we look back, continues still to be seen in the mind's eye stalking sternly, with his armor on, across the troublous space he once so bravely filled in our dim, historic past; his stalwart, war-hardened form, yet dominant on the theatre where he was so long wont at different periods to suffer, fight and strive for Georgia, not against the Indians only, but against the British Tories also; my prompt answer would be that General Clark, the elder, Elijah Clark, the father, was that man. I designate him thus because, distinguished as he was himself, no Georgian, who lived half a century ago, could possibly recall him without remembering instantly that it was his good fortune to be further felicitously distinguished, by having a son, also a General, who during a long striking career courted and acquired great eminence, both personal and official, and honorably illustrated, if he did not augment the name he inherited, leaving it more intensely imprinted at least, if not higher enrolled on Fame's proud catalogue. Thus much one, who was never his political friend, drops in passing, as a spontaneous tribute to the memory of that strong charactered, most remarkable man, General Clark, the son, about whom his fellow citizens were too long and fiercely divided in his life-time to have become fully reconciled since his death, now about forty years ago. That reconciliation, will not, if ever, be perfect till its cause shall be pleaded at the bar of an entirely new generation.

General Elijah Clark was indebted in no small degree, to the fact of his residence in Wilkes county, on the then upper border of the State, for his great conspicuousness in our past Revolutionary Indian troubles. Had he lived on the seaboard or anywhere else far down the country, it is almost certain that his part in those scenes would not have been so important, stirring and incessant; neither would he probably have become involved, as a consequence partly at least of his connection with them, in those more than questionable doings, which in his latter years drew down condemnation for him from the highest and best quarters, and which have furnished a handle to a recent historian for reflecting altogether too injuriously on his name and fame.* Residing, however, as he did, in the immediate neighborhood of the Indian hostilities and depredations, he could not but be aroused by them to continual vigilance and activity. Moreover, the very high military reputation which he had won and brought out of the Revolutionary war, made him the man, to whom all the upper new settlements looked as the most competent of leaders and the most fearless of fighters. Hence the universal voice of men, women and children conspired with his own patriotic and pugnacious qualities and impulses to bring him to the front in every emergency of much danger and anxiety. On such occasions at his bugle

*Steven's History of Georgia, Vol. 2, p. 404, 405, 406.

call, there never failed to come trooping to him from the freshly cleared fields and still uncleared forests, bands of armed men, at the head of whom he would repel incursions, and pursue and punish the flying foe even in the distant recesses of his wild woods.

The most signal battle in this whole war, that of Jack's Creek, in what was then Indian territory, but is now Walton county, was fought by him in the year 1787, in this way.* It is striking to read his report of this battle to Gov. Matthews. No mention is made in it of his having a son in the battle, though with a just paternal pride, commingled with a proper delicacy, he emphasizes together the gallantry and conduct of Col. Freeman and Major Clark, and baptizes the thereto nameless little stream, on which the battle was fought, by simply saying that it was called Jack's Creek—a name then but just bestowed by admiring comrades in arms in compliment to the exploits and bravery of the General's youthful son on the occasion. Long, very long after that son had ceased to be young and the frosts of winter were on his warlike and lofty brow, thousands and thousands of old Georgians used to love still to repeat the name of Jack Clark without prefix of either Governor or General, and to remember him too as the hero of the well fought and important, though now it would be deemed, tiny battle of Jack's Creek. For in those days of hourly dread and peril, to be forward and valiant in defending the settlements from the

---

* *White's Statistics* 581 ; *Historical Collections* 672. —White in his Statistics of Georgia dignifies this battle no little by saying that the Indians were commanded by McGillivray; a great mistake, which White himself tacitly acknowledges by wholly omitting any such statement in the account he gives of the battle in his subsequent and more labored work, "The Historical Collections of Georgia." Moreover, if a fact that would have added so much to the *eclat* of the battle and victory, had really existed, Gen. Clark would hardly have left it out of his official report of the battle to Gov. Matthews. And yet Gen. Clark says nothing about it. McGillivray's forte and function to which he always confined himself was that of being the great statesman and supreme magistrate at the helm of his nation, not a leader of the petty bands by which Indian warfare was waged.

Indian tomahawk and scalping knife was a sure road to everybody's lasting admiration and gratitude.

The sudden, irregular calls thus made by the old General to armed attack and pursuit of the Indians, and the prompt, rushing obedience the rural new settlers invariably yielded him, were merely occasional things, it is true, but they occurred often enough and were successful enough to make the General feel what power he had among the people and to familiarize and endear his exercises of that power to the people. But destiny, which had hitherto been forced into being his friend by his irresistable valor and energy, and by his ardent, uniform adherence to a right conduct in all things, began at length to be his enemy and to impel him into some improper and ill-starred, though not ill-meant courses. His first error was his lending himself to the scheme of the unmannerly, mischief-making French Minister, Genet; his next, that of setting on foot the Oconee Rebellion, as it was called; missteps, both of which, were owing rather to accidental circumstances existing at that particular time, than to any intentional wrong doing on his part. For the Indian war, which, although not entirely quashed as yet by the New York treaty, was by its influence greatly crippled and reduced in magnitude, no longer presented a sufficient field for the restless, bellicose passions which it had nurtured. These passions not having died out proportionately with the war, were still alive and smouldering in many adventurous bosoms, among others in Gen. Clark's, at the date of Genet's arrival in the United States, in the Spring of 1793, and engaging in his insurrectionary tamperings against the foreign policy of our Government. The French insanity, which had already seized strongly on the country, now rapidly spread and increased. Most generally, however, it found vent only in a wordy fray intended to influence the Government and to drive it from its neutral policy into a belligerency on the French side. But Gen. Clark was by all his temperament, training and habits, a man of emphatic deeds and substantial daring, and when the French wild-fire reached him, it ignited a nature which wanted but opportunity to break out into action, and enlisted a man, who felt assured that his standard, once raised, would bring a numerous body of daring, war-loving spirits of the South and West around him. Hence sprang those two marring and reprehensible incidents of his life above noticed, namely, his complicity with Genet in his schemes, and then, as an offshoot therefrom, his Oconee irregularity. For it would be the sheerest misnomer to call it a rebellion. And as those incidents are both matters which have been greatly misunderstood and mishandled to the no little detriment of Gen. Clark's name, a name dear to Georgia and which she is bound ever to overwatch and protect with grateful guardianship, I purpose by a faithful and succinct account to set them both in a clear and true light.

SECTION II.

Genet was the first envoy to the United States from regicide, Revolutionary France. Worthy to represent such a crew as Robespierre and the Jacobins, he came drunk, with the wild, unschooled spirit of liberty, which in his own country was then newly broken loose from the despotism of ages and was insanely exultant there still over the ruins of an old and the chaos of a new order of things. From the moment of his landing on our shores, he showed himself the very impersonation of diplomatic fanaticism, wrong-headedness and indecency, and entered at once on what was evidently a predetermined course of criminal, unneighborly intermeddling and agitation. He seemed bent on signalizing his embassy by every audacity and impropriety that could tend to throw our country into mad excitement and precipitate it as an accessory into the fiery whirlpool of French wars and quarrels. How successful he was in kindling the flames of popular fury and stirring up the people against their own Government for its firm, immovable stand against him and his machinations, forms one of the most extraordinary passages in American history. To such height did things get that the elder Adams in his writings speaks of the multitude in Philadelphia, (which had now become the seat of the General Government) as ripe for dethroning Washington himself.*

Genet was artful as well as bold and unscrupulous. This he evinced clearly from the moment of his appointment. Sailing from France in a ship under his own orders, he directed his voyage to Charleston, a port very distant from the seat of Government, and after landing there on the 8th of April, 1793, and tarrying for awhile, busied in illicit, inflammatory intrigues, he consumed weeks, devoted to similar objects, in his journey from thence overland to Philadelphia, where he arrived on the 16th of May, and whither the news of his evil practices had long preceded him.† No where, however, on his whole route did he meet with greater encouragement than in South Carolina. The large, very influential French Hugenot element in the lower part of that State responded to him promptly with assurances that went beyond mere expressions of sympathy. Indeed, a strong feeling of French consanguinity added force there to the universally prevalent sentiment of gratitude to France as our generous Revolutionary ally. Hence the people's hearts warmed readily to his appeals. He was greatly emboldened. A reckless French enthusiasm that had already gotten wide hold now spread and grew more intense in all directions. It soon crossed the Savannah river. And nowhere either in or out of Georgia did it seize upon a man more ardently prepared to be carried away by it than Gen. Clark. For all his feelings, his whole nature was strong, and with all his strength and soul he sympathized with France in her struggle for liberty, and paid back with every breath what he felt to be the impayable debt of love and gratitude his country owed her, for her aid in our great Revolutionary contest. Genet was not long in finding him

*Jno. Adams' Life and Writings, Vol. 8, 279.

†American State Papers, For. Re. Vol. 1, p. 167, 168.

out and learning all about him, and he eagerly pitched upon him as a man eminently suited in all respects, and especially by his great military prestige in the South, to become the leader in the military operations which it was his object to set on foot against the neighboring Spanish dominions, and which looked to nothing less than the seizure of the Floridas and reconquest of Louisiana mainly by means of American arms seduced to that illegal service. He thought that the pending war between France and Spain and the French epidemic now pervading the United States presented a fine opportunity for this purpose. Particularly was his heart set on the recovery of Louisiana, that vast region the loss of which, by the treaty of Paris of 1763, had never ceased to lie bitterly on the French stomach. Aside from the zeal for France by which he was fired, he burned with the personal ambition and thirsted intensely for the personal glory of exploiting this great achievement for his nation. And for the chance of it, he hesitated not to sacrifice all ambassadorial decorum, as well as to outrage our country's laws and neutrality, and endanger her peaceful relations and important pending negotiations with Spain.

This last consideration, however, was far from being any drawback with Gen. Clark. It rather impelled than deterred him. Nothing would have suited him better than war with Spain.. For he hated her hardly less than he loved France, and he felt that she well deserved all his hatred as being already and for years past the venomous enemy of the United States, and especially of Georgia, groundlessly, as he thought, seeking to rob her of a vast territory, at the same time meanly screening herself behind the Indians and insidiously instigating them against us. It was his deliberate conviction that in taking up arms against her, though under French colors, he was acquitting himself patriotically to his own country. He accordingly refused not the high command which was tendered him.* Commissions, also, for

* Both Stevens in history of Georgia and White in his statistics tell us he was commissioned a Major-General in the French service with a pay of $10,00

subordinate officers were placed in his hands in blank,—money and means were likewise furnished him, though in too limited an amount for the greatness of the enterprise. His authority was everywhere recognized by the adventurers whom Genet, his agents and emissaries succeeded in starting up and enlisting. From the banks of the Ohio to those of the Oconee and St. Mary's, his orders were obeyed in the making of preparations and getting up armaments, and men thronged from both South Carolina and Georgia to his points of rendezvous on the two latter streams,† fired at once by the splendor of the project and the renown of the leader. But mark! there was no movement whatever, actual or contemplated, against the Indians or their lands either within the chartered limits of Georgia or anywhere else. Nor did the Indians manifest any hostility towards the adventurers, trespassers, though they were on their hunting grounds. For it seems to have been made to be well understood by them that the whole aim was against the provinces of Spain, from whom the Indians, especially in parts remote from the Spanish border, were gradually becoming estranged since the treaty of New York, and were now still more disposed to be weaned when they were told there was a prospect of the restoration of the French as their neighbors, to whom they always had more liking than either to the Spaniards or Anglo-Americans. Indeed, the French made it their study to cultivate the favor of the Indians, who were even solicited to join in the enterprise. In every way it was sought to make fair weather with them with a view to the march of troops through their country on the proposed errand of Spanish invasion, while other forces recruited in the West

per annum; and there is no doubt of the fact. But when White further says that he was solicited by *two* great European powers to enter their service, it is giving him a little too much trans-Atlantic military renown. The story is a figment, which, like the statement that McGillivray was the Indian commander whom Gen. Clark defeated at Jack's Creek, must be numbered among the pretty fables, parasitical mistletoes, that are perpetually growing out upon the sturdy oak of history, slowly robbing it of its life and truth.

†*American State Papers, Foreign Relations, Vol. 1st, pages* 455, 458, 459, 460.

were to descend the Ohio and Mississippi in boats to meet and cooperate with the French squadron that was held out as expected to come to their aid by sea.*

But all this elaborate scheming and ado ended in total failure, never ripening into such action as was contemplated, —never reaching the stage at which General Clark was to stand forth, truncheon in hand, conspicuous and avowed as the leader of the enterprise. Washington's administration was too strong, vigilant and active for Genet and the French party. Our obligations of neutrality toward Spain were fully maintained, and all attempts against her within our bounds were effectually suppressed. The most decided steps were taken against Genet personally. His recall was demanded, and every proper means used to impair in the meanwhile his ability for mischief. But soon his actual recall and the coming of his successor, the citizen Fauchet, in the Spring of 1794, broke down his influence and dashed all the plans and prospects of those who had become connected with him. *The consequences were disastrous to Gen. Clark.* He was left standing blank, resourceless, aimless, in the wilderness, with a few troops here and there on the Indian side of the line, whom the power of his name had brought together, but whose destined field of employment was now abruptly taken away. There they were on his hands, awaiting his orders and expecting the fulfillment of his promises, and the desperate fortunes and wreckless character of most of them strongly appealed to him to engage them in some other career in lieu of that just closed against them, even though it should be one still more irregular and exceptionable.

It was under these untoward circumstances consequent on the sudden wreck and abandonment, in the South at least, of the Genet scheme, that Gen. Clark and his men in May, 1794, began to turn their thoughts upon the Indian territory

*Pickett's History of Alabama, Vol. 2, p. 152, 153; Foreign Relations, Vol. 1, 455, 458, 459.

where already they saw themselves quartered in arms. Nor did they think long before they took the overstrong resolution of seizing upon the country and setting up for themselves there, with an independent Government of their own creation,—the rich Indian lands being the tempting prize on which they relied to attract the needful men and means to their standard. In taking this step they were sensible of no patriotic scruples or impediments ; for, to a man, they regarded the country as already lost to Georgia by the perpetual national guarantee that had in the New York treaty been made of it to her Indian enemies, and by the State's seemingly settled acquiescense in that guarantee. Thus acquitted to their own minds, they proceeded gravely and with all due form in their new movement of government-making, unabashed by the contrast between the grandeur of the thing they were attempting, and the pettiness of their numbers and resources. A written constitution was adopted; Gen. Clark was chosen civil and military chief, and the members of a body politic under the name of "The Committee of Safety" were chosen to exercise along with him law-making and other sovereign functions. Whether any name, or what name was bestowed on the infant State, or whether it expired without baptism, no record or tradition remains to tell. Nor is there any copy of the Constitution now to be found. But in the 1st volume of the American State Papers, on Indian Affairs, there is preserved a letter of Gen. Clark's, to the Committee of Safety, dated at Fort Advance, the 5th day of September, 1794, which places beyond doubt, the adoption of the Constitution and the other facts of organization as above stated.*

Thus ended Gen. Clark's connection with Genet's project for the invasion of the Spanish provinces; and thus it became changed into a suddenly conceived scheme of seizing on the Indian lands, on which he found himself quartered, and erecting there a new trans-Oconee State of his own and

*American State Papers, Indian Affairs, Vol. 1, pp. 500–501.

his men's. It is clear that in pursuing this course he acted under strong duress. The French impulse and support under which he had thus far been proceeding, had all at once failed him ; French means, to which he had all along been beholden, had stopped and were no longer at his bidding. Consequently, French ends could no longer be consulted by him, and the new turn he gave to things, far from being a wanton, was a logical conduct on his part. It was the natural glancing in a new and unintended direction of a ball that had been otherwise launched at first, but which by an intervening obstacle had been thwarted and turned from its original aim towards another object.

The development which has now been given of the course and ending of the Genet affair in the South and of the springing up of the so called Oconee rebellion therefrom, shows how widely both those matters are misunderstood and mistold in Stevens' History of Georgia. In that work the facts are strangely transposed and misarranged. The Oconee affair is related as having preceded and led to Gen. Clark's engaging in the French project, and this French project is set forth *not* as having given birth to the Oconee attempt, but as having been itself a misborn, profligate offspring therefrom.* Such dislocation and misplacement of facts is tantamount in the effect to gross misstatement and works not less wrong to Gen. Clark than to chronology. For although he cannot be pronounced free from blame for his connection with those affairs, yet the difference is vast in every point of view, moral, political, patriotic, between his having become involved in them in the manner I have detailed, and that charged by the historian, who represents the Oconee part of his conduct as an orignal, wanton aggression upon Indian rights and territory, carrying with it rebellion towards Georgia and the United States, and the French part of it as a lawless, fillibustering enterprise, into which he had desperately flung himself after his character, fortunes

*Stevens' *History of Georgia, Vol.* 2, . *p*440, 405, 406.

and prospects had been already deeply damaged by the Oconee criminality.

A very little attention to dates and the actual order of events would have prevented this harsh, wrong treatment of Gen. Clark. Let us see: Genet arrived in this country in the Spring of 1793. He commenced his intrigues immediately, and it was not long before we find Gen. Clark connected with him, busied in fitting out and freighting boats on the Ohio with warlike stores, in receiving and dispensing French funds and commissions, and concentrating armed men under the name of the French Legion beyond the Altamaha and Oconee on *Indian soil*; the same being also claimed as *foreign soil*, in order to give a pretext for saying that the preparations there made were no violation of the territory and neutrality of the United States.* Now towards these lawless doings the authorities and people of Georgia evinced no displeasure for many months,—none, indeed, so long as they wore only a French character and were marked by only a French destination against the Spanish provinces. But when, upon the miscarriage of the Genet project in 1794, that character and destination were exchanged for an aggressive seizure of Georgia's Indian territory,—then for the first time popular feeling began to rise against Gen. Clark. Gov. Matthews began then to see there was something wrong in his proceedings, and bethought himself of interfering and of denouncing and arresting what he was doing. The result was that before the end of autumn the whole Oconee scheme was crushed by the arm of Georgia, prompted and upheld by Washington, as the French Genet scheme had months before been defeated by the arm of Washington alone.

And then upon the back of all and as a clinching disproof if any were needed, comes the insuperable, silencing fact of the poverty of Gen. Clark and his Oconee adherents. It is notorious that they were poor, (as indeed were the people of Georgia generally at that day, though far less so than now)

**American State Papers, Foreign Relations, Vol.* 1, *p.* 311.

altogether too poor to have made it possible for him and his followers and supporters ever to have set on foot by any means of their own such an enterprise as this was ; an enterprise involving from the outset an Indian war and a heavy outlay. Whence it is apparent from the very impossibility of the thing, that it would not have been started at all but for the French means and preparations that were on hand for another very different purpose, and which, upon the failure of that purpose, were readily convertible to this new object.

Having set forth thus fully the manner of Gen. Clark's becoming involved in these, the only reprehensible affairs of his life, we feel warranted in pronouncing it such as must greatly soften censure, and conciliate kindly feelings towards him. And more especially in relation to that part of his conduct in which he was implicated with Genet and his schemes, may it be claimed that the bare statement of the facts is all that his case needs. To add any elaborate apology and vindication would be idle and supererogatory. For in that whole matter he but acted in sympathy and accordance with a powerful and certainly not discreditable national feeling of his day ; a feeling fiercely inflamed against despotism and in favor of liberty and France. And into whatever of mistake or fault he and his abetting countrymen may have fallen, it was error rather of degree than of principle. The undue lengths to which they allowed themselves to be transported were but the pardonable result of the over-ardent French enthusiasm then prevalent, and have long since been condoned by the freedom-loving part of mankind as belonging to that class of things in which, although Governments are obliged to frown and fulminate, yet history and opinion delight to be gracious and hasten to acquit, propitiated by the nobleness and magnanimity of which they savor and which shed a tinge of honor on human nature even in its lapses and misdeeds.

SECTION III.

But as no such proud palliation, closely akin to praise itself, can be pleaded for his Oconee doings, it behooves us to give them some further attention, from whence it will be seen that his memory so far from suffering by a strict scrutiny here will, on the contrary, come out therefrom cleared of much of obloquy and misconception,—cleared sufficiently at least to save from historic blight the rich wreath of honor, fame and public gratitude with which a life of heroic, self-sacrificing services to his country had entwined his brow.

I will not here insist again on the casual and almost coercive, involuntary manner in which he was led into that Oconee fault. Enough has been said on that topic—enough to show that the way and manner were such as greatly to lighten whatever blame there was. But somewhat else remains that makes in his favor; other facts and considerations there are which, although perhaps only apologetic in their nature, nevertheless weigh strongly for him. Let us look at them as they have come down to us and in the light of the times in which they occurred, rather than in the altered hue which the changing circumstances and opinions of four-score years may have imparted to them.

Then, as we have already shown in the preceding articles, violent animosity had long prevailed between the Creek Indians and Georgia. They became during the Revolutionary war our bitter enemies and the allies of the British. Vanquished in that great conflict, they entered at its close into a treaty of peace, friendship and territorial cession with us at Augusta in 1783, whereby we became the absolute owners of the Oconee country, which, however, we were not allowed to enjoy in peace. For they kept no faith, and during the very next year, not only raised the warwhoop again, but rushed into a Spanish alliance in order to strengthen themselves in their hostilities. Further, also, we have seen that in the course of another year they composed this war by entering into another treaty, that of Galphinton, by which another large cession of land being made, the Tallassee country became ours. Both at Augusta and Galphinton General Clark was one of the commissioners on the part of the State, and as such was a negotiator and signer of both these highly important treaties. In seeking and obtaining the Tallassee cession, he and our other leading men who cooperated with him, were less actuated by the prevailing land-greed of that period than by a sagacious statemanship, that looked to the means of a permanent preservation of peace with the Indians, which they knew could only be effected by cutting them off by a wide interval of territory, from Spanish neighborhood and instigation. Long afterwards, at the treaty of Fort Jackson in 1814, Gen. Jackson avowed himself governed by precisely the same policy in forcing the conquered Creeks to surrender a wide strip embracing this very Tallassee region, and stretching from Wayne and Camden counties to the Chattahoochee, all along the line of what was then still the Spanish province of East Florida. But that very policy of isolation from Spanish influence which Gen. Clark and all Georgia had so much at heart in 1785, and which made the Tallassee cession so important in their eyes, rendered it at the same time extremely obnoxious to the Spaniards, who consequently exerted their influence to make it odious to the Indians and to stimulate them to fiercer warfare than ever against us, indeed, to make it impossible there ever should be peace without the retrocession of that country. And so, notwithstanding the Galphinton treaty, and yet another hollow peace signed at Shoulderbone in November, 1786, the war ceased not, but was continued and kept up by the Indians with a virulence that prevented even any attempt at pacification from being at any time afterwards made between them and the Georgians.

In this state things were when the new Government of the United States was first launched in 1789, and Washington was called to the helm. His attention was very soon claimed by this war. On the 6th of the ensuing July, in a report made to him by his Secretary of War, Gen. Knox, it is emphatically noticed as "a serious war in which Georgia was engaged with the Creek Indians, that might become so combined and extended as to require the interference of the United States."* Up to this period all affairs whether of peace or war, and all treaties and negotiations with the Creek nation had been, under the old Confederation, left almost wholly to be managed by Georgia as a sort of *peculium* of her's—and the rather because all of that tribe to be found within the United States were located on the chartered soil of Georgia. But all this *peculium* of the State was now at an end. It terminated by the new national Government assuming to itself an exclusive and unlimited control over all Indian affairs and Indian territory, whether within a State's chartered limits or not. This it did under its war-making, its treaty-making and its commerce regulating powers, and by a stretch in construing the same, to which the people of Georgia never became heartily reconciled, but again and again protested against it by both word and deed as long as any Indian occupancy existed within her limits. The men that witnessed and took part in the bitter, fearful quarreling that grew up eventually out of this question of power over Indian matters, and at length got to be chronic between the State and the general Government, are now nearly all gone. But as long as any of them shall live, it will not be forgotten how intensely General Clark's sentiments on the subject continued to be cherished in Georgia for more than thirty years after his death, nor will there be any lack of a feeling of indulgence towards him in regard to the errors of conduct into which those principles largely helped to hurry him.

This full transference of the whole Indian jurisdiction into Federal hands was practically exemplified in the length to which the oft-mentioned treaty of New York went, buying, as it did from the Creek Indians, a promise of peace

**American State Papers, Indian Affairs, Vol.* 1, *p.* 15.

at the price of the retrocession of Tallassee and of a perpetual guarantee to them by the United States of all their territory, regardless of the paramount rights and sovereignty of Georgia.

And yet high as was the price thus paid to the Indians for their promise of peace, that promise was not kept. The better and more informed among the chiefs and warriors were, it is true, disposed to keep it, but they were unable to restrain another and a very large portion of their people who, instigated by the Spaniards, and dissatisfied with the treaty of New York, because it did not contain all the concessions they wanted, persisted in their hostile incursions and depredations on our exposed frontier.

Such, then, was the posture, in which the war of the Creeks against Georgia stood and presented itself to the view of Gen. Clark in 1794, when the sudden foundering of the Genet scheme left him on their soil in the very embarrassing and difficult situation which we have above described; and such the circumstances under which he felt that he would be guilty of no wrong towards these savages in treating them as enemies and turning his arms against them as such, since they were still every now and then reeking their hostilities on Georgia in spite of so many treaties of peace, that of New York among the rest. Nor did he feel, either, that he was at all criminal towards the United States in so doing, inasmuch as he was simply disregarding and seeking to force to a proper test things, which he fully believed to be unconstitutional in that treaty and in the Congressional legislation by which it was supported, namely, the retrocession and perpetual guarantee provisions which it contained. And still less did it seem to him that Georgia had any right to be angry at what he was doing, for the reason that by submitting to those injurious treaty provisions, she had in principle and in fact surrendered her territorial rights and sovereignty, and thereby not only abased herself, but despoiled her citizens of their great landed birthright, and consequently was no longer entitled to denounce such of them as should choose to cut loose from her, and by their own strength and daring occupy the fair regions of which she had allowed herself to be so unconstitutionally stripped and disseized in favor of her savage enemies.

It was these views strongly entertained that, added to the pressure of the peculiar and untoward circumstances in which he found himself suddenly placed, turned the scale with General Clark, and determined him to a conduct he had not previously contemplated, namely, that of raising provisionally and temporarily the standard of private, military adventure, for the conquest of the Creek lands as prize of war to himself and followers; flattering himself that the Government, State and Federal, having been seemingly supine in regard to his part in the Genet operations, would continue supine still, and that his fellow citizens, of whose general sympathy he had no doubt, would not only not take part against him but would rally to him in sufficient force of men and means to insure his success.

But he was doomed to utter disappointment. He had erred egregiously as to the manner in which his enterprise would be regarded and treated. Both as to the supineness of Government and the support of the people he had calculated amiss, and awoke to the discovery that war even against savages was a royal game sacred to sovereigns and their subalterns, and that the people, ever jealous of their *rights of property at least*, and ravenous of broad, rich acres, will not tamely permit lands they have been wont to consider as their own and their children's forever, to be ravished away by the sword of any adventurer, however beloved and honored he may have been. The consequence was that Gen. Clark was speedily overwhelmed by heavy public censure and total discomfiture. The national and State administrations acted in concert against him and soon put him down. Washington, wisely holding back, as was his wont, the heavy Federal arm wherever the authorities of the States were faithful and adequate to the suppression of disorders within their own bounds, acted only as the prompter of Gov. Matthews in this matter, who, with his Revolutionary laurels still green, soon to be tarnished, however, by the Yazoo infamy, was now honorably filling his second term in the Executive Chair. The Governor thundered out upon the obnoxious General, in a proclamation of the 28th of July, 1794, in which he denounces him under the name of Elijah Clark, Esquire, as a violator of the laws and of the Indian territory. Judge Walton also came out strongly against him, though in language of marked consideration and respect, in his charges to grand juries.* But fulminations of this kind turned out to be inadequate to the case, though they had a good conservative effect on the public mind. The next step was decisive. The citizen soldiery were called out, and to General Clark's surprise, and utter extinguishment of his hopes, (for he had flattered himself that they could not be gotten to march against him) they promptly obeyed the order. As the storm thickened around him and his prospects darkened, there were none that came to his succor. Even his host of friends in Georgia, devoted to him as they were personally, stood aloof and quietly witnessed his fall, sad and sanctioning. What an impressive proof that the great body of our people were even in that early, frontier state of society, a truly orderly, loyal, law abiding people. They might, indeed, have been too ready perhaps to seize upon the Creek lands with little or no tenderness for Indian rights, provided only it was done under regular governmental authority, and with assurance that the lands would be made to enure to the enrichment of them and their children and to the public good. But they were resolutely averse to any scheme of acquisition not strictly as a public measure by public means and on public account, and the more were they opposed to the proceeding attempted in this instance, because it was in the very teeth of a treaty made by Washington himself with the Indians, and which how muchsoever disliked and regretted by the State, she, in her sovereign capacity was, nevertheless, treating with a wise

**American State Papers, Indian Affairs, Vol.* 1, *p.* 497, 498, 499.

and patriotic, though reluctant obedience and respect, and consequently could not and would not countenance individuals even the most exalted in violating it.

It redounds to Gen. Clark's honor and atones not a little for whatever was wrong in his conduct, that no sooner was he aware in what a great error he had become entangled, and how impracticable a thing he had undertaken, than he abandoned it ere he had done any appreciable mischief or shed a drop of even Indian blood. Hence his movement turned out to be a shortlived affair of a few months only. It is, indeed, beyond doubt that he never for a moment harbored the thought of raising his hand against any but the already hostile Indians and their Spanish abettors, whom he might chance to encounter. This explains the ready, absolute submission, with which, on being assured that he and his men would be allowed to go unmolested, he at length struck his colors, disbanded his followers, and returned chagrined to his home in Wilkes county, on the approach of Generals Twiggs and Irwin, under the Governor's orders, with a body of the State militia against him. His proud, courageous, magisterial nature, that ever exulted in facing danger and grappling with it, refused not now to calm down and humble itself at the bidding and in the presence of his beloved Georgia in arms,—choosing rather to succumb to her than fight his countrymen, from whom he had expected sympathy and support, not opposition and resistance. His several posts were abandoned. The torch soon followed* and its traces were long to be seen. But now, I ween, there is a many a dweller along the storied Oconee who never even heard of Fort Advance or Fort Defiance, and the other less noted warlike coverts that of yore for one whole summer and far into the first autumnal month, scowled on the impassive, race-dividing stream, and frowned trebly from its western bank on Georgia, the Indians and the general Government.

**American State Papers, Indian Affairs, Vol.* 1st, *page* 499; *Stevens' History of Georgia, Vol.* 2, *p.* 404.

SECTION IV.

But rising above all other considerations in estimating the bearing of this matter on Gen. Clark's fame, comes the crucial question, what was his *mind and intention*, what the real, ulterior object he had in view? Was it, at bottom, good or bad, patriotic or unpatriotic? There is, I believe, nothing on record, or coming down to us by tradition, that furnishes an answer in terms to these questions. But there is enough in the known facts of the case, and in the whole of Gen. Clark's character and career, from which a satisfactory answer may be educed.

In order then to a right answer, it must be remembered that Gen. Clark was not only a superior military man and a most ardent patriot, but also that he had in him no little of the statesman and political strategist, such particularly as was suited to the circumstances and times and the theatre in which he had to act:—A fact evinced by the leading part he took from and after the Revolutionary war at Augusta, Galphinton, Shoulderbone and elsewhere, in and about councils, negotiations and treaties touching Indian affairs, (which were then by far the greatest, most difficult and trying branch of our political affairs,) in all of which he showed himself hardly less apt and efficient than in commanding armed men, fighting battles and conducting campaigns. To him it was painfully clear that Georgia, with the Oconee river as a permanent guaranteed boundary between herself and the Indians, could never attain to much prosperity and importance, but must always continue feeble and poor, with but little rank in the sisterhood of States in which she was embraced, and still less security against the formidable Indian hordes by which she was surrounded on every side, except along the Atlantic and the Savannah river. He had an intense conviction that the paramount point in her policy to which her attention should be directed, was her enlargement towards the West, over those fine regions forming at this time the heart of what is called Middle Georgia, and which, on being settled and becoming populous and powerful, would form barriers deterring Indian hostilities and incursions, instead of being tempting fields for them, as long, feeble lines of frontier, always were.

This strong conviction was, beyond doubt, an influential element in impelling him in the spring of 1794, to seize the opportunity which then courted him, of making himself master of the trans-Oconee country by means of the French resources and preparations to which he had fallen heir. Fully believing that no considerations of patriotism forbade, on the contrary, that they warranted him in such a step, he hesitated not to make avail of his French means, and his unpleasant predicament on Indian soil, to create an Indian crisis that would either force a cession or end in a conquest. The government which for this purpose he extemporised and which he could, surely, not have intended for a permanency, pretended to only such faculties as might enable it to succeed in attracting by its promises and protecting by its arms and arrangements, the adventurers and settlers who were indispensable to his plans, and to whom the great inducement to join his standard was to be, as in old feudal times, liberal allotments of land,—the most effective device ever yet tried of inflaming to the utmost the rage of conquest. Such is a broad outline of the vision which all the circumstances indicate as having floated in Gen. Clark's mind, terminating in his thoughts in the eventual re-absorption of himself and his followers back again into the bosom of Georgia, with all their fair lands and brave acquisitions. That somewhat of this nature was the upshot, the aim and end he contemplated is, in the highest degree, probable. His character and all that throws any light upon his intentions, point that way. Indeed what other course could there have finally been for him? None, certainly, unless we can suppose he intended to reproduce, under circumstances most unfavorable, that recent abortion, the State of Franklin, with whose throes of ill success and ultimate total failure, he was too well acquainted to be in any danger of being tempted to engage in any similar experiment.

On the whole then, we rest in the conclusion that nothing could be more wrong than to treat this Oconee error as a misdemeanor against patriotism, or as detracting seriously from a great public deserver's claims to be cherished and honored by his countrymen. Indeed, it was an error founded no little in Gen. Clark's extreme love of Georgia, and his resentment of what he deemed a great injury to her, although its main cause undoubtedly was the very difficult, embarrassing situation, in which he was involved, and to which we have so fully adverted. No thought of rebellion, no sentiment of disloyalty ever entered his breast. Although throwing himself decidedly, as he did, in collision at once with the United States and Georgia, yet his eventual action showed that his design was nothing more nor worse than to exert a right undeniable to every citizen, whilst certainly it is one only to be exercised upon great consideration and with a deep conscientious sense of responsibility,—the right, namely, of disregarding and taking issue upon and bringing to the test any unconstitutional law or treaty,—especially when having a tendency so formidable as that of planting permanently on the chartered soil of the State a powerful savage nation under the pupilage and protection of the general Government. Such was the principle on which Gen. Clark acted, fully acknowledging at the same time his amenability to the tribunals of the land and to the interdiction of the public will. Hence, no sooner did Governor Mathews issue his proclamation against him, than he reappeared in Wilkes county and surrendered himself to the judicial authorities for trial upon the Governor's charges.* Being pronounced guiltless of any offence, and no grounds being found for his further detention, he recrossed the Oconee to his posts and preparations. No other prosecution was ever started, no other judicial action of any kind was ever taken or attempted against him. He consequently felt warranted by the people and State in what he was doing, and at liberty to proceed in it,—although condemned by the Governor

* *American State Papers, Indian Affairs, Vol.* 1, *p.* 495, 6, 7, 8, 9, 500.

and Judge Walton. When, however, upon the militia being called out, he was awakened, by their obedience and alacrity, to a knowledge of his mistake and of the popular aversion to his enterprise, he made upon the spot the best amends in his power by bowing to the now unquestionable public will and desisting from his ill starred work, ere it had culminated in aught of calamity.

To a Georgian there are no sadder pages in those huge folios, the American State Papers, than those containing the imperfect, disjointed, scattered details, concerning General Clark's conduct in the two matters we have now so fully sifted; sad, less because they tell of what was wrong in his conduct, than because they tell it (to borrow a phrase from the elder law books) *without more*, without completeness, without connection, without all the facts that throw light upon it,—without the explanations and mitigations that belong to it, and which make in his favor, and which are now consequently become less obvious and known, than the things which make against him. Few will ever be at the pains of such investigation as justice to him requires. Already has the professional historian failed in that duty and done him great wrong which there is danger will be copied and re-copied without scrutiny, as is too much the wont among book-makers, until at last the error will become ineradicable in history and go down to posterity as undoubted truth. It concerns the people of Georgia that such wrong to General Clark should be rectified. His character and career, his deeds and services, his fightings and sufferings, his wounds and sacrifices, are part of the treasured pride and glory of the State; of the divine pabulum derived to her from a suffering heroic past, whereon, to the end that her children may never become recreant, they should feed now and through all time, and grow strong in undegenerate patriotism and manhood, and in all the sturdy virtues of their strong-principled, strong-charactered ancestors,—like them ever prompt at the call of duty and honor, to discard ease and court danger and hardships. His character was a mixed one, it is true, as strong, commanding characters often are. But we cannot submit, because he had faults, and fell into errors, that his merits should be unduly shaded and almost shut out from view, and his character transmitted to the future aspersed with epithets of obloquy and disparagement. He deserves better than that his name should suffer by careless or prejudiced historic handling. He died ranking to his last hours among Georgia's most cherished heroes and benefactors, and Georgians cannot but recoil from whatever has the look of lowering him from that proud pedestal on which he had placed himself with hard, and hard-working hands, and by life-long patriotic devotion and self-imperiling. Our fathers, before we were born, had grown to him in a close, living embrace of love, gratitude and honor. His services to Georgia were such as it happens to but few men ever to have the combined opportunity and ability of rendering to their country. He was emphatically the Ajax Talamon of the State in her days of greatest trial. The British, the Indians and the Tories, were ever swarming around him or fleeing from him, or plotting, working, fighting against him. For seven long years his warlike tramp was almost everywhere heard, especially from Augusta to our Northern and Western border, and frequently also across the Savannah; wherever, indeed, danger was the greatest or the enemy strongest. He was made acquainted, too, with agonies, such as the body knows not. Whilst with that boy son, the future Governor of Georgia, at his side, he was in the field fighting and often bleeding, his British and Tory foes fearing to meet him, yet seeking to paralize him there, plundered and burnt his house, drove away his wife and younger children, and ordered them out of the State. No wonder that with such a man such treatment had the reverse of the effect intended. No wonder that from thenceforth he breathed and spread a more rapid falling vengeance than ever, if that were possible. No wonder that he lost no chance to strike a blow, and that in every blow, he made good McDuff's terrible prayer:

"Gentle Heavens!
Cut short all intermission; front to front,
Bring thou these fiends of Georgia and myself;
Within my sword's length set them; if they 'scape,
Heaven forgive them too!"

When weighing such a man, such a doer and sufferer for his country as this, indictments that might crush meaner personages, are but as dust in the balance against the rich, ponderous golden ore of his services and merits, and we hasten to shed a tear on whatever may tend to soil his memory and to pronounce it washed out forever.

His active career closed with the termination of the two untoward passages in it, which I have narrated, nor did his life last much longer. He died in 1799, at his home in Wilkes county, where he had settled in 1774, and was with his laborious hands among those, who struck the first blow in reclaiming from the forest that garden spot of the world, that earliest installment of Middle Georgia, which stretched out in richness and beauty from the Savannah river to the Ogeechee. He was the gift to Georgia of our good elder sister, North Carolina. Many, very many, have been her precious gifts to us both of men and women from the colonial times down to the present day. Many, very many priceless human gifts has Georgia been likewise ever receiving from other older quarters of our own country and from the old world—gifts which she has taken to her bosom and generously cherished along with her dear, home born children. But never has it fallen to her to have a son, native or adopted, whom she could more proudly boast and justly honor, or who has more deeply imprinted himself on her heart and memory than Elijah Clark.

CHAPTER V.

COLONEL HAWKINS.

One morning in the month of June, 1816, during the summer vacation of Mt. Zion Academy, being on a visit to my venerated grandfather, I was sitting listless and musing alone with him in his front porch, gazing through the sycamores that surrounded the house across the broad, cleanly cultivated fields of cotton and corn that sloped away to the south; their long, gentle slant terminated by the "verdrous wall" of towering primeval trees that had been left to stand, gorgeously fringing all that side of the plantation for a mile or more up and down Fort creek. The sun was nearing the meridian. It was the day, and a little after the hour, for the mail rider to pass on his weekly trip from Milledgeville to Greensboro, and my grandfather having already sent and gotten his newspaper from the tree box on the roadside, was engaged in reading it,—the great old Georgia Journal, founded by the Grantland brothers, which he enjoyed the more because they were Virginians, from Richmond to boot, editorial *eleves* of the renowned Thos. Ritchie. He had not read long before he suddenly stopped, and, letting down the paper from his eyes said, "Col. Hawkins is dead." The tone was not as if the words were meant for me or for anybody. They sounded rather like the unconscious, involuntary utterance of the soul to the conscious heavens and earth. All nature seemed to lend her voice to his words and to speak out in unison: "Col. Hawkins is dead." Letting his newspaper drop to his lap and resting his elbow on the arm of his chair, he bowed his head upon his half open palm and sat in silence, neither reading any more then nor speaking another word. I had all my life been hearing of Col. Hawkins, and had become familiar with his name as important in some way in connection with the Indians, but in what way I had never well understood. But it was now evident to me that he who was then resting in his fresh grave in the midst of the Indian wilderness on that little knoll by Flint river, was a greater and more valuable man than I had dreamed; that my grandfather certainly thought greatly and highly of him,—and to me what my grandfather thought was a measure and standard both of men and things. So God ordains to him who is early left to grow up an orphan boy. Seeing how much he was affected,—naturally a strong impression was made on me. From that moment the germ of a deep, undying interest in relation to Col. Hawkins was implanted in my mind, an interest more than justified by subsequent life long gleanings of information in regard to him, and which is still strong enough to make it impossible for me to pass finally away from the commingled affairs of Georgia and the Creek nation without commemorating him and doing him homage.

Large indeed were the claims of Col. Hawkins to be loved and honored all over Georgia, and especially along the Oconee river on both sides, and between the Oconee and the Ocmulgee. His services to our people had run through a long period and were of the most signal character. At the time of his death, it was for some twenty years that he had been occupying officially between Georgia and the Indians what may almost be called a heavenly, mediatorial relation, faithfully devoting himself as peace-maker, peace-preserver, and peace-restorer, all that time between the two mutually distrustful and bitterly divided races. Of this most arduous, delicate and sometimes dangerous duty, he had acquitted himself with an assiduity and sagacity, with an integrity, ability and success that had obtained for him boundless confidence and respect from both sides and rendered him dear and illustrious alike to civilized men and savages from the Savannah river to the Ohio and the Mississippi. For although he was the special resident Agent for the Creek tribe only, yet such was Washington's estimate of him that he made him General Superintendent also of all the tribes south of the Ohio; hence he became a well known and exceedingly important man to them all.

It was a noble expansive humanity that first planted him among the Indians and kept him there all his life. He went and he remained among them an angel of kindness,—an apostle of conciliation, friendship and good will. Unlike McGillivray, who belonged solely and intensely to the Indians in his feelings and actions, and with whom enmity to Georgia was a capital virtue,—unlike Elijah Clark, who was wholly Georgian, and was to Georgia, against the Indians, very much what McGillivray was to the Indians against Georgia,—their bitter, most dreaded, effective foe,—Benj. Hawkins' career was on and along a middle line, as it were, his part that of at once a parental guardian and protector of the Indians and a common friend and conscientious arbiter between them and their civilized neighbors. It is a fact most honorable to him, that in allowing himself to be appointed to this rather unique and very trying and difficult station, Col. Hawkins was actuated in no degree by the meaner motives by which men are too apt to be governed. Nothing of a money-loving, mercernary sort entered into his reasons. It was neither penury or embarrassment in his affairs, or thirst for wealth, or a chain of fortuitous circumstances, or the loss or want of prospects satisfactory to his ambition elsewhere, that operated upon him. It was his own large, man-embracing nature, and a generous passion to be useful, aye, beneficient to his kind, that impelled him. And he rises inestimably in our view, when we consider how much he gave up, what sacrifices he made to this feeling:—Sacrifices requisite in no branch of the public service so much as in that of Indian Agency, and which in Col. Hawkin's particular case, imparted to his conduct not a little the character of a romantic, sublimated benevolence and martyrlike self-devotion,—nothing short of which could have moved him in his actual circumstances to quit civilized habitation and society, and to bury himself for life in remote savage woods, and among still more savage people, from whose midst he never again emerged.

For he was born to wealth and experienced from the beginning of his life all its advantages in one of the best sections of North Carolina, in what was then Bute, now Warren county, on the confines of the most enlightened and refined part of Virginia. Throughout his youth his good opportunities were well improved. After proper preparation in schools near home, his father sent him, along with his younger brother Joseph, to Princeton College, for the completion of their education. The Revolutionary war interrupted the Institution and his studies, when he was in the Senior Class and almost at the end of his course. So he may be pronounced to have entered on life a young man of accomplished education, in addition to all the other felicities of his lot. Among other things, it merits to be particularly mentioned, that he became an excellent master of the French language. This acquirement it was that led to Washington's taking him into his military family to be his medium of correspondence and conversation with the French officers and others with whom he had to have intercourse in that tongue. But his duties on the staff were not merely of this light and literary kind. He braved the campaigns, encountering hardships and participating in battles, showing himself, though very young, on all occasions worthy of his epaulets and of his honorable relation to his illustrious commander-in-chief.

Judging from his career, he must have been precociously distinguished for talents, address and aptitude for affairs. As early as 1780, when he was but twenty-six years old, North Carolina made him her general agent for obtaining both at home and abroad, all kinds of supplies for her troops. In discharge of which office he made a voyage to St. Eustatia, in the West Indies, a small neutral Island, that seems to have served the same ends for our ancestors during the Revolutionary war as did Nassau for the Confederate States during the late war of Secession. He was entirely successful in *his* part of the business, but the merchant ship in which he embarked his purchases, chiefly munitions of war, was captured by the enemy and the supplies lost to the State. Returning home we see him soon representing North Carolina in the Continental Congress, his name first appearing on the Journal of that body the 4th of October, 1781. He was continued in this eminent position, by successive re-elections, until the 20th of December, 1786. On the accession of North Carolina to the new Federal Constitution, he was chosen one of her first Senators in the Congress of the United States, where a full term of six years fell to him in the allotment of seats*

It is proper to mention here, that before the new Government was organized, and whilst he was yet a member of the old Continental Congress, he was detailed, without interference, however, with his Congressional duties, into another public service of the highest importance, though of a very different nature. It was this: On the close of the Revolutionary war, the forming of amicable relations with the various Indian tribes in every direction around the United States, became a matter of the greatest and most pressing interest. Congress, taking to itself a concurrent jurisdiction with the States in all Indian matters, appointed Col. Hawkins as one of its Commissioners plenipotentiary, to be sent for the purpose of opening friendly negotiation with the four great Southern tribes, the Creeks, the Cherokees, the Choctaws and the Chickasaws. With the three last named tribes the commissioners succeeded in negotiating satisfactory treaties whereby they entered into peace and friendship with the United States, and placed themselves under their protection to the exclusion of every other nation or sovereign, and gave to Congress the sole power of regulating trade with them

*Spark's *Life and Writings of Washington*, *Vol.* 12, *p.* 424, 431.

and managing their affairs generally.* The attempt to negotiate a treaty with the Creeks proved abortive from many causes, at the bottom of which lay their entanglement with Spain by the treaty of Pensacola, and their difficulties with Georgia, which had the effect of keeping them aloof in a hostile mood, until that master stroke of Washington in 1790, which eventuated in the treaty of New York, by which the Creeks placed themselves in like relations to us with the other three tribes.

Col. Hawkins' senatorial term ended on the 4th of March, 1795. Before its expiration Washington, who had witnessed with regret, that the treaty of New York had only partially produced the fruits of peace expected from it, but who now saw his anxious policy of thorough Indian pacification verging towards full triumph, fixed his eyes on the long known, well tried North Carolina Senator, as the fittest man to take charge of the well-advanced work of conciliation, and then, also, after it should be wound up auspiciously, to crown and secure it by becoming the permanent agent for Indian affairs among the Creeks.

Col. Hawkins' family, one of the most numerous, influential and ambitious in his State, was very averse to his embracing such views. Wheeler, in his history of North Carolina, to whom I am indebted for many interesting things in this sketch, is emphatic upon their opposition,† for which several good reasons are given, such as his wealth, his high education and culture, his great advantages of family and social and political position, the strong hold he already possessed in North Carolina, his flattering future there, &c., &c. The historian, however, does not even attempt any reasons why all these considerations failed to prevent him from yielding to Washington's wishes. And yet, these reasons, at even this distant day, may be easily divined. Col. Hawkins, as we have seen, had been much among the Indians

See these Treaties in the Appendix to Watkin's Digest and Marbury & Crawford's Digest of the Laws of Georgia.

†*See Title "Warren County."*

officially ; he had penetrated the mighty forests which hid them, and seen and observed them amid their vast uncultivated woods ; he had been brought in close contact and converse with them under circumstances which presented them in their most impressive points of view. He had thus gotten to feel deeply interested in them and to be strongly affected by *that Indian fascination* which thousands, both before and after him, have experienced, without being able to understand and interpret it. Whatever it may be, or however it may be explained, it is certainly something so powerful and touching, as hardly ever to die away wholly from minds upon which it has once laid its spell :—And particularly in the case of such noble savage races as the Creeks and Cherokees, it always generated a feeling of the most lively sort in all who happened to become well acquainted with them in a kindly way in their own beautiful country. Behold here the true, though subtle cause of those feelings and that bias of mind which mainly actuated Col. Hawkins in accepting the Creek Agency, and not only in accepting it, but in making its life-long duties a labor of love to him and a source of high moral and intellectual occupation and enjoyment. It was this generous, intense fitness of the soul to the task on which he entered which, added to his other happy qualifications, made him such a wonderful exemplar of what an United States Agent and proconsul should be, for the greatest, proudest, most warlike and jealous of all our Indian tribes.

His *coup de 'essai* in this new service was the treaty of Colraine, negotiated in 1796, and which, also, as we have seen, was a *coup de maitre.* It was a much needed supplement to the treaty of New York, curing entirely all the wounds which, notwithstanding that treaty, had continued, more or less, to bleed and fester. At this point then began, and thus propitiously opened, Col. Hawkins' long, benign and exceedingly responsible official career, in connection with that formidable, but at length conciliated Indian people, with whose history his name was about to become identified in a manner so honorable to himself and to human nature.

He had a jurisdiction which, in the extent of territory it embraced, was scarcely less than imperial. Starting from the St. Mary's, far down towards the sea, the line ran directly across to the Altamaha, dividing the Tallassee country from the seaboard counties of Georgia. On striking the Altamaha, it turned up and along the western bank of that river and the Oconee, to the High Shoals of the Apallachy, where it intersected the Cherokee line; then turning westwardly, it followed that line through Georgia and Alabama till the Choctaw line was reached in Mississippi; then southerly, down that line to the 31st parallel; then along that parallel to the Chattahoochee; thence to that river's junction with the Flint, thence to the head of the St. Marys, and thence along that stream to the point of beginning. An immense region than which, as a whole, there is none finer under the sun, stretching more than four hundred miles from East to West and two hundred from North to South. This wide and greatly favored region became thence forward the scene of his labors, and to it and nature's unsophisticated children who roamed over it, and to all his duties to them and to the neighboring civilized people, he at once applied himself with that high moral sense and generous solicitude which noble minds always feel for great interests committed to their charge. From the outset he studied the people and their country, and accomplished himself in all knowledge appertaining to the one and the other. And here the advantages, growing out of his fine early education and out of the intellectual tastes, quickness and inquisitivenesss which were its fruits, stood out to view and served him in double stead, prompting and enabling him to become at once more thoroughly and variously qualified for the multiform duties of his station, and availing him also as a source of private enjoyment and mental support and comfort in his self-decreed official exile. Nor was it with the mind only that he labored, but with the pen also, and so perseveringly as to leave behind him a great amount of manuscripts concerning he Cr eeks and the Creek country. Of these manuscripts, to which the public of that day attached great importance, and not without cause, judging from such small published parts as have fallen under my eye,—a large portion perished in the burning of his house soon after his death. Another large portion escaped the flames and were afterwards confided to the Georgia Historical Society. But the great interest they once excited has long since become extinct, having gradually sunk along with the melancholy fortunes of the rude and remarkable people to whom and to whose country those writings relate. Yet may it not be, that ransacked and studied hereafter in distant future times, they will furnish to some child of genius, yet to be born, much of material and inspiration for an immortal Indian epic of which the world will never tire.

Under the faithful proconsular sway of Col. Hawkins, the Creek Indians enjoyed, for sixteen years, unbroken peace among themselves and with their neighbors, and also whatsoever other blessings were possible to the savage state, which it was his study gradually to ameliorate. To this end he spared no pains. Much was done to initiate, instruct and encourage them in the lower and most indispensable parts of civilization. Pasturage was brought into use, agriculture also, to some extent, both together supplanting considerably among them their previous entire reliance for food on hunting, fishing and wild fruits. To the better and more secure modes of obtaining a livelihood which civilization offers, he sought to win them by example as well as by precept. He brought his slaves from North Carolina, and under the right conceded to his office, he opened and cultivated a large plantation at the Agency on Flint river, making immense crops of corn and other provisions. He also reared great herds of cattle and swine, and having thus always abundance of meat and bread, he was enabled to practice habitually towards the Indians, a profuse, though coarse, hospitality and benevolence, which gained their hearts and bound them to him by ties as loyal and touching as those of old feudal allegiance and devotion. There was something in the vast scale and simple, primitive management of these, his farming and stock-raising interests, that carries the mind back to the grand, princely, pastoral patriarchs of the Old Testament—to Abraham, and Isaac, and Jacob, and Job. For food his herds roamed the boundless forests and grew fat upon the caney bottoms and grass-bearing uplands, and the mast that fell from the trees, costing him nothing, save their marking, branding, salting and minding, services well performed by his faithful negroes and their Indian assistants. The sanctity with which the Indians, throughout the nation, regarded his cattle, was a beautiful trait in their relations to him. Whatever bore his mark or brand, was everywhere absolutely safe. He often had as many as five hundred calves at a time, to separate which from their dams, Flint river was used as a dividing fence, across which, that it might be used in this manner, he built a bridge, with a gate at each end. There of evenings at that bridge's western end, hundreds of lowing cows, returned from their day's wild pasturing, moaned wistfully to as many answering calves bleating from its eastern extremity. For he repudiated the lazy policy which to this day marks herdsmen as a class, who with great droves of cattle and calves, are strangers to the luxuries of butter and milk. His milk was measured by barrels and churned by machinery, and great were the outcomes,—yet not more than enough for his vast hospitality to the Indians and white folks, and his regal munificence to his negroes. Had the great pastoral bards of antiquity not sung and died before his day, elated, they would have seized upon these scenes and celebrated them in their finest strains as more wonderous, grandly rural and baronial, than aught in all the charming bucolics they have left us.

But at length adverse circumstances and influences arose so powerful that it was impossible for Col. Hawkins with all his address and weight of authority among the Indians to maintain peace in the nation. The war of 1812, between this country and England, had been portentously brewing for a long time before it actually broke out. Seeing its approach,

Great Britain, through her numerous agents and emissaries among the Indians, by liberal largesses and supplies of arms to them, and by whatever other means were at her command in her neighboring Canadian provinces, had been for several years tampering with the North Western tribes, and fomenting among them a hostile feeling towards the United States. As soon as the requisite success had been attained on this border, she directed her attention to the Southern and Western tribes, and began her machinations among them also. The great argument by which she sought to delude and incite them was, that by uniting their own arms with the British, the tide of American aggression, which was rapidly dispossessing them of their lands and driving them further and further to the West, might be stayed and even made to recoil on the aggressors. Her real object, however, was to get well within her grasp and to brandish over us the thunderbolts of a terrific Indian war, held in hand and ready to be hurled upon our whole thousand miles of exposed frontier from the lakes to Florida, in the hope on her part that we thereby might be deterred from declaring war against her at a time when she was already so sorely pressed by Bonaparte and the French. Such was the view with which she conceived and prompted the famous incendiary mission of the celebrated Shawnee Chief, Tecumseh, and his brother, the Prophet, to the Southern tribes in 1811.* They had little or no success, however, with the Cherokees, Choctaws and Chickasaws. But better omens awaited them among the Creeks,—a thing partly owing to the greater residuum of suppressed enmity towards us that still rankled in that tribe, as also to their naturally more warlike and ferocious character; partly, likewise, because Tecumseh and the Prophet were of Creek blood and extraction, their father and mother having with their little children migrated in 1767 from the heart of the Creek country† to the Northwest,

*American State Papers, Indian Affairs, Vol. 1, p. 800; Pickett's History of Alabama, Vol. 2, p. 242.

†Pickett's History, Vol. 2, p. 241.

where Tecumseh himself was soon after born, who, however, when he grew up made a visit of two years to his ancestral land and people. The consequence was that when he arrived among them on his mission of mischief in 1811, he became quickly master of their sympathies as he already was of their language. He reached Tuckabatchee, the Creek capital and the seat of the Big Warrior, whilst Col. Hawkins was there holding a grand council of the nation. Keeping dark as to the object of his coming until Col. Hawkins had departed, he then disclosed his errand with that fierce Indian eloquence for which he was famous, and with all the most impressive collateral solemnities of savage superstition and patriotism. By these means and the powerful aid of that most extraordinary Indian religionist and fanatic, his brother, the Prophet, who accompanied him with an imposing retinue, it is not wonderful that he succeeded in kindling a flame among the Creeks which was to be nursed and kept smouldering until after the happening of war between the United States and Great Britain, when at some proper moment and given signal, that flame was to burst forth into one vast conflagration along our whole frontier.

It is a proof both of the powerful ascendant Col. Hawkins had acquired over the wild people among whom he dwelt, and with whom he had to deal, and of his great ability and fitness for the position he had so long filled among them, that although the anticipated war between England and the United States broke out and involved the Indians the very next year ; yet a large portion of the Creek territory, (all that part bordering on Georgia and extending west from the Ocmulgee to the Chattahoochee,) never became its actual seat, and consequently that our long line of frontier settlements never suffered a whit more than the interior parts of the State from the war's perils and alarms. This happy exemption was due almost wholly to the fact that Col. Hawkins' official seat and residence having been first on the Ocmulgee at the beautiful site opposite to Macon which still bears his name, and afterwards on the Flint river at the place still called the Old Agency, his personal influence, intercourse and acquaintance with the Indians on the Georgia side of their country was much greater and impressed its effects more strongly than farther to the West. Hence the Indians on the eastern side remained pacific, and not only so, but they became our actual friends and allies. For the purpose of protecting and keeping them secure and steady in this adherence, the friendly warriors were, on the advice of Col. Hawkins, organized into a regiment of which he became the titular Colonel, although he never took the field, deeming it better to devolve the actual command upon the noble and some years afterwards ill-fated Chief, William McIntosh,* who, like the great McGillivray, was only of the half blood in the civilization of lineage, but more than the whole blood in the better and loftier traits that do honor to man's nature.

The result of all these things was that the few hostile Indians who were scattered through this friendly eastern section of their country, disappeared and merged themselves with the more congenial belligerent elements in the middle and western parts of the nation,—on the waters of the Coosa, Tallapoosa and Alabama. There concentrated and fierce they stood at bay and fought and fell in many a battle under the heavy, rapid blows of that predestined conqueror of their race, Gen. Jackson, the second of that great heroic name in Southern history, where he stands and will ever stand towering and resplendent in the midst with him of Georgia and him of Virginia close touching and illustrious on either side.

Gen. Jackson having brought this great Southern Indian war to a close early in 1814, was not allowed to pause in his career. The Government wanted his genius, his energy and his indomitable will on another and a much grander and more important theatre near the mouth of the Mississippi. He went, and in the short, glorious campaign of New Orleans, gave the finishing stroke to the war with

* *Wheeler's North Carolina, title, Warren County.*

Great Britain, as he had already just done to that with her deluded savage allies. But before going to gather these brighter laurels, he received at Fort Jackson, near the confluence of the Coosa and Tallapoosa, the absolute surrender and submission of the crushed and starving Creek nation. There with his victor's sword, and in conformity with commands from Washington city, he dictated the terms of a treaty of peace and marked out narrower bounds to the vanquished and all their tribe. How much was taken from them and how little was left to them constitutes one of the most striking and consequential events in our Indian and Anglo-American annals. From that time the prowess, the spirits and the prospects of the long redoubtable Creek nation were broken forever. The capitulation of Fort Jackson was its death-knell and tomb. Even the three great friendly Chiefs, the Big Warrior, the Little Prince, and McIntosh were cut to the heart by this deep incision of a sword whose every gleam they had been wont to watch with loyal gaze and honor with soldierly obedience, though marshalling them into the jaws of danger and death. Col. Hawkins was profoundly saddened at the hard, wretched fate of those whom he had long cherished as if they were his children. A cruel dart too entered his bosom from the lips of the Big Warrior,* whom the Colonel was well known to have regarded as one of nature's great men and the ablest of Indian statesmen. The stern, long confiding chief mournfully upbraided him for having persuaded himself and so

*The name of Big Warrior was given him on account of his great size. He was the only corpulent full blooded Indian I ever saw, yet he was not so corpulent as to be either unweildly or ungainly. In fact his corpulency added to the magnificence of his appearance. His person and looks were in a high degree grand and imposing. *Tustenuggee Thlucco*, was his Indian name. He and Col. Hawkins first met at the treaty of Colraine in 1796, and were great friends down to the time of the treaty of Fort Jackson. He was probably the most enlightened and civilized man of the full Indian blood the Creek nation ever produced. He was wealthy and a lover of wealth. He cultivated a fine plantation with his seventy or eighty negroes, near Tuckabatchee, where he lived in a good house, furnished in a plain, civilized style.

many of his chiefs and people to stand neutral in the war or take part in it against their country. For years afterwards the story used to be told how the big tears stood in the aged Agent's eyes as he listened in silence to a reproach which he felt was at once undeserved and unanswerable.

Judging from Wheeler's history, it would seem that North Carolina was disposed to claim Col. Hawkins as not only peculiarly but exclusively her own. But his career, his labors and his merits are too broad, diverse and manifold and illustrate too many scenes and subjects of national importance with which he was connected, to admit of such appropriation. His fame is as well the property of Georgia, of the Creek nation and of the United States at large as of North Carolina. They all rush to compete with his motherland and to insist on having along with her a share in such a man, to whom they each owe so much of gratitude. In fact the more he is contemplated, the larger and more catholic becomes his hold on the heart, and we end by feeling that all mankind, civilized and savage, have a right to rise up and exclaim :—*He is ours also.*

PART II.

CHAPTER I.

MIDDLE GEORGIA.

We have seen in treating of the Oconee war how the Indians gave the name of Virginians to the hosts of unwelcome strangers that began to pour into their immemorial hunting grounds soon after the Revolutionary war, and continued to come in unceasing swarms until at length they filled up the whole country to the east of the Oconee river. Nor was the appellation wrongly given. For it is a fact that this country was mainly settled up in the first instance by direct colonization from Virginia and, in some parts, from North Carolina, and not by the old population of Georgia spreading out over it. We find evidence in our statute book of the early attraction of the Virginians thither. As far back as 1783, a petition came from Virginia and was granted by our Legislature, asking that two hundred thousand acres of land might be reserved in this region of the State for such emigrants from Virginia as should wish to settle down in one solid, homogeneous neighborhood; which reservation is noticed and ratified in the Act of 1784, organizing the counties of Washington and Franklin. This fact, though now long buried, possesses some historical interest still, as bearing on the important point that the great mass of the first settlers, who replaced the Indians in this part of Georgia, came from Virginia, particularly those who established themselves on the best lands. And they came not scatteringly and wide apart, but in quick succeeding throngs, bringing along with them their wives, children and servants, and their household goods and gods,—allured by the cheapness and fertility of the lands, the pleasantness and salubrity of the climate, the felicity of the seasons, the happy lying and commodiousness of the country, well wooded, well watered, with easy wagoning access to the flourishing commercial mart of Augusta and with, from thence, a fine navigation by the Savannah river down to the excellent seaport of Savannah, close upon the ocean; to all which was superadded the known aptitude of the country for the peculiar agriculture to which the Virginians were accustomed. For Whitney, young, poor, but restless with inborn-ingenuity, hospitably domesticated in the house of Gen. Greene's widow, near Savannah, had not yet invented that most wonderful and beneficent machine, the cotton gin, and the cultivation of cotton as a commercial commodity was unknown among us, and tobacco was still the master staple in upper Georgia as well as in Virginia. There are probably some very ancient people yet living who remember those tobacco-growing times and the queer custom of rolling tobacco hogsheads to Augusta and the great rigor of the tobacco inspection in that market.

Of the immense preponderance of the immigration from Virginia over that from all other quarters, some idea may be formed from the fact that in my native section when I was a boy, there were scarcely any but very young people who could claim Georgia or any other part of the world than Virginia as their birth place. Scattered here and there a few only were to be found who were born elsewhere out of Georgia than in Virginia. Washington county, however, in the limits which it still possessed up to the time of the present generation, must be set down as being an exception to this remark. For within those limits that fine old county was mainly colonized from North Carolina as I have had the best means of knowing, and my heart will forever attest what an amiable and generous people they and their descendants were fifty years ago, for a little earlier than then I made my debut in life among them and lived among them long enough to know and love them well and to be loved by them in return—so at least it has always been a satisfaction to me to feel. Maryland, too, sent a little aid, just enough to enable it to be said that she bore a part in conquering these distant wilds. Within my puerile range of knowing, it was but a single family she sent, poor when they came but destined to great opulence drawn by toil from the liberal earth. Often were they called Chesapikers and often in boyish ignorance, I wondered why. With such exceptions as these, all the rest, the great mass of the people, the elderly, the middle aged, the fully grown and not a few of the very young, were Virginians born.

And not only had they come from Virginia themselves, but as the Trojans carried Illium unto Italy, so did they bring Virginia into Georgia with all her divinities both of the field and fireside, and they filially preserved and perpetuated her here,—her ideas and opinions, her feelings and principles; her manners, her customs, her tone and character as well as her agriculture, her system of labor and her whole rural economy. Nor was it a small district only or a few isolated spots that the Virginians thus overspread and impressed with their own very superior type of society and civilization, but nearly all the best of the fair and extensive region lying between the Ogeechee and the Oconee, and that large part besides of the country between the Savannah and the Ogeechee which was originally comprised in the glorious old pre-revolutionary county of Wilkes, which having been acquired from the Indians under the Colonial regime only a very short time before the outbreak of the Revolutionary war, was still very thinly peopled at its close, and presented consequently very strong attractions for the best class of emigrants, who came in troops to those parts of the State where the lands, freed from the Indian occupancy, were yet wild and unappropriated and, under the old Head Right system, open to the first comers.

And now here and heretofore (in the course of my writing

about the Oconee war) I have developed the beginnings of that famed part of the State, known as Middle Georgia, and have found and traced its germ, showing whence that germ came and when, where and how it was first planted here, and have also shown what hard and perilous fortunes it had for a long time to encounter from Indian hostilities and incursions, whilst striving to maintain itself and get root and thrive in its new soil. But triumphing by degrees over all dangers and drawbacks, and blest at length with favorable auspices and a long spell of prosperity, it struck wide and deep into the generous land into which it had been transplanted, and flourished apace not only within its early cis-Oconee limits, but rapidly spread and propagated far beyond those limits as new opening was from time to time made by fresh acquisitions of Indian territory: First, from the Oconee to the Ocmulgee in 1802 and 1805; then from the Ocmulgee to Flint river in 1821; and finally from Flint river to the Chattahoochee and our present western boundary in 1825,—full forty-nine years ago, when at length the celebrated Black Belt across the center of the State was complete and Middle Georgia finished.

Already, too, some eleven years earlier, the sword of Gen. Jackson had achieved a great territorial enlargement for Georgia on her southern side. For, as we have already had occasion to tell, by the capitulation at Fort Jackson in 1814, the Indians were entirely swept off by the besom of conquest from the whole Tallassee country, beginning far down on the St. Mary's in the East and stretching all along the line of the then Spanish province of East Florida clean to the Chattahoochee in the West,—being that very Tallassee country for the more easterly portion of which Gen. Clark and Gen. Twiggs, as we have heretofore seen, had at Galphinton in 1785, concluded a treaty with the Indians; a treaty, however, which was not allowed to stand, having been, as heretofore shown, overslaughed by the treaty of New York in 1790.

How important an extension of her jurisdictional limits

the State was thus laid under obligations to Gen. Jackson and his treaty of Fort Jackson for, those who are curious to know may learn by consulting Early's map of Georgia published in 1818, where the whole of this new extension on our South is represented by one great blank space, not having been at that date yet surveyed by the State and laid off into counties or demarcations of any kind.

Georgia, by the above mentioned events, seeing herself finally rid everywhere of the Creek Indians, began to turn eager, impatient thoughts to her upper or Northern side where the Cherokees inhabited, a people who had far outstripped all our other aboriginal tribes in the progress towards civilization, and whose extreme, immovable attachment to their ancestral land seemed to place an insuperable obstacle in the way of our ever acquiring it by peaceful or humane means. But here again the powerful aid of Gen. Jackson was exerted in our favor, being rendered this time in his character and functions as President of the United States. Before his iron will and inflexible policy, backed by his despotic influence over Congress and the country, all opposition had to give way alike among the Indians and that great mass of the Northern people by whom their cause was espoused. It is now nearly forty years since, by the consummation of his measures, the Cherokees were removed to new homes beyond the Mississippi, and Georgia placed in undisturbed possession of the fine country they left behind, with all its mountains and vallies, its rich lands and mines, its health-giving climate and waters, its charming diversified scenery and those great commanding advantages of geographical formation and position which make it the eternal doorway and key between the Southern Atlantic and the immense transmontane valley of the Mississippi.

SECTION II.

I have often thought, in these sad latter days, that it was something to be thankful for to have lived in this period of interesting progress and development of Georgia, and to have grown up witnessing, from childhood to manly age, this inspiring expansion of my native land, of which one effect surely was to impregn my young mind with a rich, varied store of dearly cherished, ever-living memories concerning the State and what I have seen and known of her, the value whereof, as a resource of mental comfort and luxury, I have begun to feel more sensibly as I grow older and become more dependent for my enjoyments on the laid up treasures and recollections of the past. The past is peculiarly the domain of old age, in which it loves to roam at large, mustering up the dead whom it has known, reviving bygone scenes and sights, thoughts and feelings, living over again its departed manhood, youth and even childhood. Alas! to how few is such a second, retrospective life ever accorded! And how obvious, too, that whether any and what sort of enjoyment is to be derived therefrom, must depend, in the case of every individual, upon the nature and character of that past through which he has traveled and by which his mind has been, as it were, formed, peopled and furnished. Happy is he who has a past on which he can strongly draw and find amends for the sorrows and adversities of the present! To the young, ardent, hopeful; to the active, sanguine seekers after pleasure, riches, honor; to the favorites of fortune, who already rejoice in the possession or assured attainment of their respective objects of desire, this resource cannot be expected to appear in a very striking light. But to the aged, whose active career is closed, whose earthly hopes are ended, and who, moreover, lie prostrate and helpless under the blows of fortune, it is a resource second only to the consolations of religion and the conciousness of an upright life.

Among all the retrospects on which my mind has long loved to dwell, retrospects, I mean, having relation to those successive expansions and that progressive improvement of my native State, which have, to a great extent, taken place under my own eyes, as it were, there have been none so dear and interesting as those which carry me back to the earlier and better days of Middle Georgia—that Middle Georgia that was my birth place and has been my life-long abode, and that, for long, long years, was ever to me as a large earthly paradise in which I always felt myself everywhere at home and in warm sympathy with every thing around me. And it is still dear and precious to recall her as she was in her primal period and high meridian, although now her glory is gone and she scarce knows her former self amidst the staring ruin and mournful depression which have become her fate.

Striking indeed was the spectacle as her fair, ample spaces presented themselves to view in the several installments of their acquisition and settlement:—At the first, spreading out in all their unmarred primeval grandeur and beauty, a vast and towering woodland scene, nature's ancient, yet ever young, blooming work—then, passing in turn one after another, from the deep night of barbarism in which they had lain for unknown ages into the sudden light and life of high civilization. Elating to witness at the time, grateful to remember ever since, the successive expandings, the triumphal unfoldings of Georgia in this, her rich middle belt, her very zone of charms, as exulting she advanced by bound after bound from East to West, high-strung, hardy, laborious, "disdaining little delicacies," trampling down obstacles, disregarding hardships; subduing and transforming rude nature, forests falling before her, the wilderness budding and blossoming as the rose at her touch, rich crops springing up all around her, called forth by her industry from the willing earth. It was the white man with the axe and the plow, the hammer and the saw, and in all the array and habiliments of civilization, superseding the Indian in his hunting shirt and moccasins, with his tomahawk and scalping knife and his bow and arrows. It was Ceres, with her garland of golden sheaves, her basket and hoe and her divine gait and air, putting an end to the reign of Pan and the Satyrs. And no metamorphosis the world ever saw, or fiction ever forged, was more beautiful, picturesque and lovely than the change that was wrought, and wrought, too, with a magical ease and suddenness and on a largeness of scale that made the wonderful blend with the beautiful in the successive panoramas that were presented.

It was a spectacle which will not occur again; it is one of those things that has been seen for the last time; it will never more be repeated. Nature exhausted and insolvent, as it were, in this regard, has no more Middle Georgias, no more beautiful, healthful, fertile, well wooded, well watered Southern uplands to offer wild and inviolate as future conquests to Southern industry and civilization; nor even if she had, could the other requisite conditions ever be hoped for again. A mighty, though unavowed revolution, settling down firmly into permanent bad government, has rendered them impossible. The maxims and polity of our fathers have been discarded and in their stead a senseless, vindictive, prostitute Federal despotism now reigns. Rioting and rotting in low-minded splendor and profligacy, paralytic and shrunken on its Southern side, plethoric and bloated on its Northern, festering with corruption all over, it waves its baleful sceptre over us inflicting on these "delightful provinces of the Sun" a worse than Oriental fate. Already has it succeeded in making us from the richest and most prosperous people in the world, the poorest and most helpless. Already are its accursed effects widely seen and felt upon the very soil and face of nature, which we behold rapidly relapsing into uncultivated wastes and dwarf woods of second growth, requiring a second clearing and reclamation from hard-working human hands. And how different a work it will be whenever it shall come, from that which in bygone days animated the hearts and hands of the sturdy pioneers of this land in their original reclaiming of it from the wilderness. How little hopeful, how little elevating and stimulating will it be in comparison! How slow and thankless, how dragging and unrewarding! And then besides, whence shall come the hands to do it? We have them not amongst us. Our whole system of agricultural labor is disorganized and our laborers are not only demoralized but they hug their demoralization to their bosoms as the chiefest boon of their new found freedom. Nor is it strange to those who know human nature, especially negro nature, that it should be so. Is there, then, any relief which may be expected from abroad? Is there any outer quarter to which we may reasonably look for the help and reinforcement we need? None whatever. And most especially never shall we again see such another migration, such another transplanted civilization, as that which of yore poured from the bosom of the mother of heroes and statesmen at a most critical period into the lap of young Georgia and grew with her growth and spread with her expanding boundaries.

This train of thought brings the mind with force to what is now and must long be to us the greatest and most momentous of questions. The question, namely, of the *renaissance* of Georgia. And first of all, is she to have a *renaissance?* Is the Phœnix ever to rise from its ashes? Shall Georgia ever emerge from her ruins? or is it to be her destiny and that of her sisters of the South, to swell the long dismal catalogue of conquered States of ancient and modern times, that have never risen from the blow that felled them, but continued to go down, down, till at length they reached a depth where, hopeless of recovery, they have ever since lain and seemingly will forever lie, wretched, submissive, debased, under the horse's hoof, the despot's heel and the brigand's knife? If such shall not be our lot, it will not be because fortune is our friend or all history is not against us, but it will be because we shall work out our salvation from it by mighty and persevering effort and self-denial. For it will take both in full measure to rescue and save us. Yes, if such is not to be our and our children's lot, it will be because deeply sensible of the dreadful, impending future, we shall gird ourselves up like men to war against it at every point and by every means and with all our strength of body, soul and mind, resolved to know no rest, no ease, till fate shall be fairly conquered and chained to our car, and Georgia restored to honor, prosperity and greatness.

But let me not run before my work. In due time, if strength hold out equal to my task, this great question, which constantly looms up to view, will be reached and here and there handled as I may best be able. It is, indeed, a question of appalling magnitude and difficulty, but one, nevertheless, from which we may not shrink, one towards the auspicious solution of which, every son of Georgia, however humble, is bound to bring his mite of aid.

CHAPTER II.

MIDDLE GEORGIA (continued) AND THE NEGRO.

Besides the very superior character of the country and the first colonists and their descendants, there were other causes that lent their aid to the rapid peopling and improvement of the several successive new Purchases, as they were called, that from time to time accrued to Middle Georgia—from its beginning at the acquisition of the original county of Wilkes, down to its finishing enlargement by the second treaty of the Indian Springs in 1825. Noticeable among these causes was the lucky length of the intervals of time that elapsed between the different Purchases, sufficient to enable each new Purchase to become well peopled, prosperous and solidified before it had to encounter competition for settlers with other subsequently acquired Indian lands. To which add the advantages each new Purchase enjoyed in its turn from its immediate contiguity along its whole eastern side to older, well advanced settlements ;—also that each new acquisition as it came in its order, although not very small, was yet not larger than was wanted for the fresh tide of immigration that was waiting to flow into it, and did flow into it at once and fill it up with an excellent population from the very outset.

Furthermore, whilst adverting to these favoring causes, let us not forget that capital one—the humble, laborious, unpaid hands by which most of the harsh, heavy work was done, and without which such celerity of reclamation and improvement would have been impossible. Let not the poor negro and the important part performed by him, be left without special and in the phrase of the schools—honorable mention. Indeed not only in Middle Georgia in the several installments of its early settlement, but everywhere and at all times in the South, he was most useful and assistant, and justly acquired a hold more lasting than the relations out of which it grew, on the kindly feelings of those whom he served so long, so loyally and so well. How it is going to be with Southern men and women a generation or two hence and afterwards, cannot now be foreseen. It may be that they will get to be quite as dead and unsympathetic towards the negro as the negroes themselves were wont of old to feel that Northern men and women were in comparison with those of the South. This undesirable result is certainly that to which the new order of things seems to tend. But as for us, who were born and bred in a better day and under more propitious relations and influences than now prevail, such deadness and want of sympathy may be pronounced impossible so long as the negro continues to deport himself in his new state of freedom no worse than he has thus far done, in Georgia at least. We would be narrow, nay! even little in soul, if we did not look with large charity on the demoralization which the great shock and change through which he has passed, have undoubtedly wrought in him. For alas! are not the evidences thick around us of our having also undergone a demoralization not less great and signal, from the mighty shock and change, to which we likewise, have been subjected. Verily, kindness for the negro, a humane and friendly feeling towards him, a true indescribable sympathy with him, began with the lives, imbued the infancy and childhood, ran on with the growing years of the present generation of Southern men and women, and became so intimately entwined with their very natures as to be ineradicable except by his own egregious and incorrigible delinquency and worthlessness. It is our true interest that he should do well, and attain to a higher level in morals, merit and intelligence. Never shall we be disposed to underrate him, or to withhold from him a generous credit for all that he shall deserve in the future, any more than a just remembrance of all he has done in the past.

He is emphatically the child of the Sun, born of his most burning rays, and happily framed to live and labor, strengthen and exult under his fiercest glare, in the most firery climes. He is also eminently submissive, cheerfully servile in his nature, and apt and docile in a high degree in things that hold rather of the hand than of the mind. In all respects he met our Southern agricultural and domestic needs most admirably; and certainly among the great services he rendered us, that in which he was most important, was the conquest of the forest and the subjugation of rude nature to the axe, the plow or the hoe. It is impossible to look back on the immense amount of hard, heavy, valuable work done by him in first opening the country for culture, and afterwards as a life-long laborer in the very fields cleared by him, and then reverse the picture and gaze upon the widespread ruin he was subsequently made the involuntary, unwitting cause, (for he was the cause of the war and all its consequences) of bringing upon the scenes of his previous useful industry, without being painfully impressed in relation to him. How strikingly has it been his lot to be forced to be in the beginning, a blessing, in the end a curse to us and our land! Yes! forced both in the one case and the other. And now he has become a sore problem indeed; a warring, unnatural, morbific element in society, incapable of assimilation with the body politic, upon which he has been hitched, as it were, by sheer extraneous violence, and by a tie quite as baleful and criminal as that by which the fabled tyrant Mezentius, chained the bodies of the dead to the living. Can the living ever impart life and health to the dead through a bond so revolting? Will not the dead rather impart their own death and putrifaction to the living? And do they who, on the horrid maxim that there can be nothing wrong towards the vanquished, have inflicted this monstrous wrong on us and on human nature itself, and who are still exulting over their helpless victims,—do they cheat themselves with the idea that God is no longer just, and that the terrible curse of bad, wicked Government which they have vindictively fastened on us and our posterity, will not react in some way on themselves and make them and theirs writhe in long retributive agony under the eventual consequences of their unprecedented crime? For how can that great mass of ignorance, depravity and shameless unfitness, which they have clothed with the awful power of Government throughout the South, be prevented from working its deadly effects in National as well as in State affairs; from sending corruption and ruin through the body politic of the Union, as well as through those of its oppressed and outraged Southern members?

Such is the appalling problem now before the whole country, and that must needs be worked out for everlasting weal or woe in reference to the negro; whose mission upon earth, whether viewed as he is and always has been in Africa, or as he was and is in America, is truly one of the dreariest and most impenetrable of the mysteries of God. Nor is it rendered the less dreary and impenetrable by recent events in this great nation. In no age of the world has he ever emerged from barbarism and slavery on his own continent. Hideous land! where children are the slaves of their parents, and daily sold by them into slavery to others, without a pang! where every subject is the slave of his Prince or Chief, legally saleable by him to any purchaser that comes or can be found, just like an ox or an elephant's tooth! Where every man, woman and child is liable at any moment to be seized and sold into slavery, singly or in droves, by any horde of robbers that can succeed in catching them by night or by day, and where life is as little respected as liberty!

Such is the negro's immemorial normal condition in Africa. And who shall say that Heaven in revealing the American continent, did not design it as an asylum for him, too, as well as for the European? But what sort of asylum, and an asylum for him in what character? Not certainly in that of a freeman, a citizen, a voter, an office-holder or legislator, for all which he was wretchedly unfit, but as an asylum for him in the character or *status*, which attached to him in his own country, and in which alone he could be anything but a nuisance in ours. And if he did not escape entirely from the miseries and debasement of his African condition by being brought to these Southern States and planted here in his African *status*, he at least escaped from them in large part and as far as he was worthy of escaping, or as it was for his good to escape. He exchanged a worse and a barbarous for a better a civilized form of slavery, an exchange which was at once a blessing to him, to us, and to mankind, and to which he was not only indebted for a striking betterment of his condition, physical, moral, religious, but for all of civilization and christianity he has ever attained. It is undeniable, that instead of being worsted and debased by falling into our hands, his condition has been ameliorated and his nature elevated. Under our beneficent despotism, he was reclaimed from the grossest barbarism and superstition and trained up to a degree of civilization and religious culture from which it is yet uncertain whether the gift of freedom will carry him up higher or drag him down lower. Behold then what the Southern system of slavery has done for the negro! And yet christendom has permitted itself to be shocked and stultified in regard to it and to be kindled into an insane rage against us because of our supposed inhuman and unchristian wrongs towards him. Strange inhumanity, which betters the condition of its victims! Strange unchristianess which christianizes those on whom it is practiced!

The South has a stake incomparably greater than all the world besides in the tremendous experiment that has been, by mere force of hostile arms, set on foot on her soil and is now proceeding in her midst and at her sole cost, yet under a vindictive, unenlightened exterior guidance and direction. It will be the miracle of miracles if it succeeds. If by the blessing of Heaven, overruling the crimes and folly of men, such miracle should happen, our dear Southern land may hope eventually to rise from her ruin, a new creation, a veritable reconstruction, a true re-growth of order, strength, virtue and prosperity. But should the experiment fail, St. Domingo, Jamaica and sundry miserable, mestizo, anarchic Republics of Spanish America have already supplied examples of what is to be our lasting doom. Moreover, if it fails, the world will soon witness the beginning of a mighty reaction on the whole subject of negro slavery. The demonstration will then be deemed perfect of the negro's congenital and hopeless unsuitableness for freedom, and men will relapse everywhere into the old and for ages uncontroverted opinion that slavery is the *best* and therefore a *just* condition for him, and that is by far the most useful disposition that can be made of him in reference to the general interests of mankind. Again, over-crowded Europe and North America will be compelled, a century or two hence, by that necessity which is its own and only law, to turn wistful eyes towards the vast tropical and semi-tropical wilds of this continent, and to ponder the question how they may best be made available for the habitation and sustenance of their redundant millions. And then in case the grand trial now proceeding here of the fitness of the negro for freedom, shall result against him in the judgment of an enlightened, catholic public opinion, negro slavery will rise up stronger than ever in men's minds, and the negro aid will be once more invoked to solve the distressing problem of American and European wants by a life of compulsory labor. Compulsory, but not incompensated or unregulated, it is to be hoped. For there is no condition in society more admitting of regulation and modification than slavery. And surely an intelligent and healthy philanthrophy, aided by the growing wisdom and experience of christendom, will be able to find means of reconciling humanity and justice to the negro with his enforced civilization and usefulness in the world.

Why should nations have more bowels for the negro than for their own people? Is tenderness for their own citizens or subjects a characteristic of Governments when it conflicts with their policy, passions or ambition? Do they not at their pleasure tear their own men of youthful and middle age away from poor old parents, from dependant wives and children, and drive them at the point of the bayonet, into a military slavery, compared with which, that of our by-gone cotton and tobacco fields and rice and sugar plantations might well be hailed as an Elysium? And do they not pitilessly force them into the front ranks of battle as "food for gun powder," whilst the magnates and leaders for whom they are mangled and butchered, and to whom all the fruits of their immolation are to enure, skulk at home or far in the rear, safe contemplators of the scene? And if from actual war and its perils they chance to come out with their lives, what is then their fate? They are either kept under arms still as engines of tyranny over their own countrymen in times of peace, or they are sent back to their homes and beggared firesides to encounter squalid poverty and grinding taxation. Such is the treatment by all nations of their own people when they chose to call for their service as soldiers. With this more than analogous case, so unanswerable and so suggestive, constantly before our eyes, it is certainly not very illogical to suppose that the time will return when the negro will be forced to work as well as the soldier to fight, if he will not work otherwise, particularly in climes under whose fervid suns, he and he alone has been constituted by the Almighty capable of the perennial labor which a state of civilization and civilized agriculture alike require. How monstrous, that cultivated and christian men throughout all christian nations should be continually subjected, by millions on millions, to be sacrificed, brutalized and demonized by a horrid sevitude in the bloody trade of war, and that at the same time and in the same nations, the slaves and savages of Africa should be the pets of a fatuous philanthrophy which cries out against their being made to submit to a system of labor and discipline humane and beneficent, civilizing and christianizing in its character and effects?

For the present, however, and for a long time to come, if ever, it is quite impossible to hope that the negro's usefulness among us, as compared with former times, can be restored. His future, as well as our own, is involved in darkness and anxiety. Fortunate will it be for his posterity and ours, if any length of years shall ever bring about mutual relations as favorable for both sides as those which war has destroyed. The same state of relations can never, should never be attempted to be established again. Their attempted re-establishment would lead to a shock and ruin even worse than that which has been the result of their sudden and forcible destruction. All we can do is to wait for time and circumstances, to enable us from the present ruin to work out the best possible reconstruction for the remote future. In the meantime, the mind cannot help recurring often, especially when in its mournful moods, to our never-to-be-repeated Past, a Past that was in its day grievously misunderstood by the outside world, and which abounded in many things that will long be cherished as pleasant remembrances, as well by the negro as by the white man, among which there will be none more pleasant than those connected with their commingled life and labors in the several new settlements, by which from time to time Middle Georgia was by successive leaps expanded and developed into her full richness and beauty.

CHAPTER III.

MIDDLE GEORGIA (continued) AND THE LAND LOTTERY SYSTEM.

But not only was it the negro and the other causes I have noticed that imparted extraordinary animation and impulse to the new settlements in Middle Georgia in their infancy. Nay, say not in their infancy, for infancy except in its better and lovelier sense, they never had. They burst forth full grown, panoplied and almost perfect from their very birth. This interesting truth I had long and large opportunities of personally observing and knowing. From the time I was a small boy, I was much in Putnam county on visits to relations, who had moved thither from Hancock. Putnam was then but a few years old and I continued to be a frequent visitor there throughout my boyhood, youth and early manhood, enjoying all the time the best means of seeing and observing. Indeed, the last half of the year 1818, I lived in Eatonton, then one of the most beautiful, flourishing and refined up-country towns the State ever boasted, with a classical Academy of the highest order and an overwhelming patronage, at the head of which was Dr. Alonzo Church, subsequently for many years President of Franklin College. At the same time there was a Young Ladies Academy of not less repute and merit. As a seat of education Eatonton was at that date second only to Mt. Zion in Hancock, the renowned Seminary of that extraordinary man, the Elder Beman—Franklin College, which had gone down during the war of 1812, under the Presidency of Dr. Brown, being now again in a state of utter collapse, which lasted some two years, consequent upon the death, in 1817, of the new President, the long and deeply lamented Dr. Finley. In my after years I have often thoughtfully recalled all I ever saw or knew of Putnam county, from my earliest to my latest acquaintance and observation there, and compared the county and people as known to me from first to last with what I have seen and known of the best agricultural districts and populations in and out of Georgia, and I can aver that if in all the characteristics of a sterling civilization, Putnam county ever had a novitiate or minority, it had passed away and all traces of it had vanished before my knowledge of her commenced. And what was true of Putnam was equally so of much the larger portions of Baldwin, Jones, Jasper and Morgan, for they had like advantages of soil, climate, &c., with Putnam and a like superior population of first settlers. Again, the settlement of Monroe county and the country between the Ocmulgee and Flint rivers, began in 1822, having been acquired from the Indians the year before by the first treaty at the Indian Springs. In the beginning of 1827, I transferred my residence to Monroe, as a centre for the practice of my profession, and soon became well acquainted with the people, the county and all pertaining to them. I was greatly struck. I had seen by this time a good deal of the world, both in the North and the South, and was qualified to make comparisons and I could not get over my admiration of the growth and advancement of Monroe county. Such, indeed, was already her advancment that there was no room left for further progress except in clearing more land and gradually substituting fine framed and painted houses for the not less commodious log structures, which are necessarily the earliest style of building in all new countries. She had already a very dense population of the very best character, with the smallest possible admixture of bad or inferior elements. She had, too, plenty of well built churches of ample size, at convenient points throughout the county, and a stated ministry and regular services and a full attendance of worshipers in every church. Good schools, likewise, she had in every neighborhood, and he who attended the gatherings of her people at churches, military reviews, elections and other public occasions, or saw them as a friend, visitor or stranger, in the sacred precincts of their homes, could not help being impressed with their moral worth and tone, their manifest respectability and intelligence, as well as their obvious worldly thrift, industry and prosperity. What is thus said of Monroe was applicable also to the surrounding new counties though not in altogether so strong a degree. For Monroe was considered the crack county of that Purchase. And now lastly, 1827 was the first year of the settlement of the then new territory between the Flint and Chattahoochee, and from that time I took my semi-annual rounds for several years in the practice of law through a number of new counties and I can affirm from thorough personal observation that Troup, Meriwether, Coweta, Harris, Talbot and Muscogee never knew a low, coarse, or rude state of society. They stood from the very outset fully abreast with the best portions of the State in all those things which constitute the pride and glory, the lovliness and charm of virtuous and flourishing agricultural communities. How could it have been otherwise? Their immigration was mainly from the finest parts of the State, homogeneous, and composed of people equal in wealth, culture and all other advantages to the best whom they left behind, just as had been the case with the first settlers of the several preceding new Purchases further East. Families of substance and even of affluence, of the highest standing, accustomed to all that is desirable in life, to all that wealth, education and their adjuncts could bring, sold out and quit their old homes and hied to the new virgin wilds with absolute alacrity and enjoyment. And why? Because they knew beforehand amongst what sort and how superior a sort of people they would at once find themselves in their new locations, and that all the advantages and blessings of the older settlements they were leaving would be without delay transplanted along with them. Moreover, and it was an important item in the case, they went attended by their happy gangs of hardy negroes, their faithful, trained servants of the field and fireside, who quite unconscious themselves of the much exaggerated hardships and discomforts of a new country, were certainly a means of making them unfelt by their masters and mistresses and by those whom they were apt to love still more, their young masters and young mistresses.

But I must bid adieu to this seductive digression into which I have rather abruptly fallen at the moment when I was approaching another topic of a very different nature and which I must not allow myself to neglect. I allude to the Land Lottery System, a device for converting public lands into private ownership, so novel, peculiar and curious and so full, besides, of practical consequences, that it would be a capital omission not to notice it treating of the original peopling of the trans-Oconee country. For it was there the system had its origin early in the present century, being first applied by an Act of the Legislature in the year 1803 to the then new Purchase, being the first beyond the Oconee, from whence it was afterwards extended to all our subsequent territorial acquisitions wherever situated, as they from time to time came to hand. And, as it so happened that none of them were East of the Oconee, that river thus became, in addition to its other historical pretensions, the dividing line forever along its whole length between the portions of the State organized and settled under this new system and those peopled under the old Head Right mode. All East of the Oconee is Head Right, all West Land Lottery. Why the old mode so long in use in Georgia and everywhere else in Anglo-America, was abandoned by our fathers and the plan of the Land Lottery adopted in its stead, is certainly an interesting question, and one the answer to which will, in all likelihood, be wholly lost in a few generations more. For contemporaneous history has, I believe, overlooked the matter as beneath its dignity, nor do I know that there is any account of the reasons to be found any where on record or in print. Yet tradition has preserved them thus far, and those who will search among the peculiar circumstances which occurred in Georgia during the last years of the last century, will find in them also a clear solution of the novelty—for novelty our Land Lottery system undoubtedly was. None greater and more striking has ever occurred in the polity of any country, in regard to its public lands. It was a thing wholly new under the sun. No precedent for it existed on all the files of the past. There was not any where the shadow of a likeness to it, nothing analagous even. Georgia originated and contrived it out of whole cloth, and at once it acquired a strong popularity here which it never lost. And yet no favor or following out of Georgia did it ever find. It was never copied or imitated anywhere else, consequently as soon as the State's public domain was exhausted and no more lands remained to be distributed, the invention died out at once right here on the spot of its birth, and is now laid away forever among the innumerable bygone things interesting and important in their day, but which are never more to be repeated or seen.

In some respects the two systems of Head Rights and the Land Lottery, were not unlike. In both the aim was not the enrichment of the treasury so much as the rapid settling and development of the country. Having this main object in view, they both regarded the public domain in the light of a great fund to be distributed in free gifts or allotments of land among the people. It was in the mode of effecting this distribution that their difference consisted. The manner under the Head Right System was, to treat the whole country as one great blank, open to free competition, under the rule that the first comers should be first served and all served in the order of their coming. The process accordingly was to issue to individual applicants, upon their paying certain office fees and also sometimes an almost nominal price for the lands, certain authentic documents variously entitled Head Rights, Land Warrants or Warrants of Survey, by locating which on any particular lands, such individual applicants become the owners of those lands and entitled to have a grant issued by the State therefor, provided no body else had already taken up and appropriated the same land. This mode, however, though so universal, was always liable to considerable objections. Under it land titles were much exposed to difficulties and litigation by reason of the same surface being often covered and always being more or less in danger of being covered by conflicting Warrants or Head Rights in favor of divers persons. And this danger was everywhere greater in proportion as the lands were more desirable and more sought after. Also the poorer and less attractive lands would be neglected and very slowly taken up, so that from both causes combined, the country was very apt to become in the richer localities, a hot bed of law suits and conflicting claims, and, in the poorer, a confused patchwork of appropriated and unappropriated or vacant lands, which would eventuate in making it difficult to know and pick out what was vacant from what was not vacant. Moreover, to the great majority of people, especially widows, orphans, unmarried women and to the very poor generally, it was not only onerous but next to impossible to make the personal explorations, without which the right to take out and locate Head Rights was almost worthless. To all which if we add the frequent errors, inaccuracies and abuses growing out of an ill-contrived, incompetent and untrustworthy official machinery, we behold a formidable mass of evils the tendency of which was to obstruct settlement and throw the best lands into the hands of speculators and the rich and crafty, to the exclusion of a class who were by far the most proper objects of public bounty.

It was, however, much less as an escape from these long familiar and therefore not much regarded evils, than as a violent, virtuous, indignant reaction against two huge, new fangled villainies, which were still recent and in their intensest odium, that the Land Lottery system first suggested itself in Georgia, and found universal favor, and was adopted, and permanently pursued by the State in preference to all other modes of disposing of her public lands. These two great villainies were the Pine Barren Speculation of 1794-5, and the Yazoo Fraud of the same era. Incensed to the highest degree by these two monstrous iniquities practised upon the honor and property of the State, whereby organized bands of corrupt and corrupting speculators were enabled to cheat, swindle and make profit to the tune of millions,—the honest, outraged people of Georgia resolved that in all subsequent dispositions of their public lands they would sacrifice all other objects to the paramount one of closing every door and providing every security against the future perpetration of such like, or any other land frauds or villainies. Out of this feeling so honorable and redeeming to the State, was born the Land Lottery System. Under it the public lands, as they were from time to time freed from Indian occupancy, were at public cost surveyed into small lots of uniform size, and marked, numbered and mapped, and the whole returned to the Surveyor General's Office, from whence by commissioners chosen by the Legislature for the purpose, the State caused all the lots to be thrown into the Lottery wheel, and to become fortune's gifts as well as her own to her people.

By this course it is obvious, every temptation and means for the practice of fraud and corruption was taken away. For who was going to bribe the members of the Legislature or other public functionaries, high or low, when it was rendered utterly impossible by the very system adopted, for the corruptor to make or secure anything by means of the bribery? Who would ever think of bribing surveyors to measure or mark lots falsely or make forged or fictitious returns of surveys, when nobody could possibly know or foresee to whom any particular lots would be drawn, in the coming lottery? And how could speculators, single or combined, practice frauds upon the State, in regard to the lands, where every lot of land had already passed out of the State into private ownership, before it could become an object of speculation?

In addition to all which it was a high recommendation of the system that it gave to all, the poor as well as the rich, to the feeble as well as the strong, to women as well as to men, and to widows and to orphans, an equal and fair chance. It also gave instantly to every lot of land, an owner with an unquestionable title, and by this means, and by preventing the accumulation of large bodies of land in the hands of speculative individuals and companies, it promoted greatly the rapid settlement and improvement of the new regions, beyond any other system that could have been devised.

CHAPTER IV.

THE PINE MOUNTAIN.

Nature, when she drew near the completion of Middle Georgia, ere she put her finishing hand to the work, paused and said: What, shall be the last touch? What crowning gift shall I bestow? What impress set that shall never become commonplace? What proud, striking feature call forth on this Westernmost expanse that shall make it unique among the Midlands of the South, a charm and a glory to all beholders and through all time?

And she said I will give it a mountain, a mountain where mountains are not wont to be; a mountain, too, rich in precious inner treasures as well as in charms attractive to the eye. And as she spake, Behold! Earth heaved and the Pine Mountain uprose in modest grandeur and beauty, adorned as to its umbrageous sides and fertile, close clinging valleys and breezy cerulean summits, not only with pines, but with other trees also unnumerable. Far down to the South, it uprose in lonely loveliness and isolation, further down, and nearer to the sea, by more than one hundred miles, than any other mountain, or mountain knob, or outlier. And at its Eastern end, nature allowed a little river, the first that turned away from the Atlantic slope and went to woo the blue waters of the Gulf, to pierce its yet unhardened mass, and to seek the sea in a straight, onward course through its disrupted sides. But as the young mountain grew towards the West, it grew also compact and rock-ribbed. It swelled out larger and towered up higher, and at length after stretching away for some fifty miles, became too strong for even the mighty Chattahoochee, child of the eternal Alleghanies, forcing the impetuous river to bend conquered around its Western base, and to go fretting, foaming, writhing, tumbling over many a mile of rocky, unrelenting rapids down to where Columbus sits in long waiting at the foot of those first falls and all their vast water power. But mourn not, fair Coweta,* daughter of the ever-roaring, soul-attuning waters! Nor let thy firm heart fail thee under the trying fortunes that have been thy lot! How often does time justify bright dreams whose fulfillment has been long deferred! And may it not be in coming years when haply redundant capital flowing thither from afar shall become wedded by ties tight and strong to hungry labor in our new-ordered South as already in other lands, that those who shall then roam the green earth shall see thy long river staircase, from Columbus to West Point, one climbing street of pallatian mills, from whose lofty windows toward that street's upper end, the caged operatives will often look out and regale their eyes and hearts with the ever fresh aerial beauty of the Pine Mountain. Most probably, however, ere that great spectacle shall present itself, it will have for its forerunner, another hardly less inspiring, though of a very different sort. Around that mountain with its naturally fine circumjacent lands, its gushing wealth of pure healthful waters, and its delicious, salubrious climate, it has occurred to me that earlier perhaps than any where else in the old cotton belt proper of the State, there will be more and more seen a white population in full, manly, working harmony with the new condition of things with which the Southern people have to grapple; a white population that will know no

*Indian name of the site of Columbus and the Falls of the Chattahoochee.

shrinking from rough, hard, rural toil, from daily labor in the field throughout the day, throughout the year, under summer and autumnal, as well as under wintry and vernal suns; a population, consequently, which will be freed from dependence on the negro; and under whose superior industry and management, that fair region will be made to respond fully to its great natural advantages and to become a fit ornate setting to the central mountain gem which it encircles.

Of the various routes, two on the Eastern side of Flint river and five between the Flint and Chattahoochee, by which I had occasion to cross the Pine Mountain in old times when it was yet an interesting novelty, most of them being at points of great depression, such as the roads usually seek, presented no very striking views or other interesting features of scenery; and indeed the very sight of the mountain itself was hidden from the approaching traveler in those days, by the thick tall forests which everywhere environed it, so that the first notice of being near it was the actual climbing of its sides. I must, however, make an exception, here, of the direct route between Hamilton and LaGrange, which was first opened some forty-five or six years ago, to supersede the old roundabout way by King's Gap. This new road struck the mountain some few miles north-west from Hamilton, and by a gentle sidling ascent, rose gradually above the continually expanding campaign below, of which the rider on horseback caught glimpses larger and larger through the surrounding trees, which grew thinner and freer from undergrowth as he ascended. Thus he was well prepared, by the time he reached the crest of the mountain, to turn his horse's head to the South and stand at gaze. It was but for a few moments, however, that he would thus stand, for quickly he saw that he was at the most depressed point of that narrow crest and that it stretched away westwardly by a rapid, smooth ascent over a bare, gravelly surface, with a thin growth of mountain oaks inviting the horseman by its openness. After following this ascent for a few hundred yards, again he stood at gaze, and was satisfied not to stir another step. A fair, vast, uniform scene, which the axe had not yet perceptibly marred, was embraced at once by the eye, above all blue, below all green, the intermediate ether filled from Heaven to Earth with a profusion of intense summer sunlight, one single ray of which would suffice to illuminate the World.* Away beyond Flint river on the East and beyond the Chattahoochee on the West, the hills rose to meet the kiss of the bending skies. Not so toward the South, not so towards the fierce clime beneath which the great American Mediterranean rolls. There the green earth declined lower and lower in the distance and sank away more and more in lovely maiden withdrawal from the stooping Heavens, which at length when the strained eye could reach no further, descended curtain-like to the low-lying emerald expanse, shutting out from view all beyond.

On turning to the North, the contrast was very striking. Whereas to the South the country sloped away in a long, interminable, inclined plain till it reached the sea, on the Northern side it rose rapidly as it receded, the rivers and all their tributary streams running downward toward the mountain. Hence the prospect in that direction was soon shut in and bore no comparison with the view on the Southern side.

* I should not have thought of using this very strong expression, but for my vivid recollection of the total eclipse of the sun in November, 1834. I stood watching for the instant of entire obscuration. It lasted but for a moment. The very next moment a single ray shot from the sun to the earth through the darkness, fine as the finest thread, intensely luminous and visible throughout the whole ninety-five millions of miles of length. It literally illuminated the world, for it fell on every eye and alighted on every object. The next instant a pencil of rays shot out, but it only created a greater not a more positive or striking illumination. To not more than one in many millions of men, is it given ever to see a total eclipse of the sun; partly because it is a thing that so rarely occurs, partly because when it does occur, it is visible on so small a portion of the earth's surface. Well is the Astronomical Author of the American Almanac for the year 1834, justified in pronouncing it "the most magnificent and sublime of the phenomena of nature, compared with which Niagara sinks into mediocrity."

But what was done by nature for the Pine Mountain was not all external. Deep within its bowels she is and ever has been busy in mysterious workings. There she has established her wonderful hidden laboratories: At the chiefest of which no chymic hand save her own mixes and medicates the inimitable waters of the Meriwether Warm Springs, bursting in a lavish, chrystal sluice from the Mountain's Northern side. No fires but of her kindling have kept them through ages at the same exact happy temperature, delicious and healthful for bathing, and it is said, too, medicinal for drinking. Had such waters been found in any of the mountains around ancient Rome, marble acqueducts would have conveyed them to imperial palaces, marble bathing apartments would have welcomed them as they came gushing. There is nothing elsewhere, I have often heard it said, comparable to the delicate, exquisite luxury they afford. Certainly my own experience tallies with this belief, nor can I conceive of anything superior. But then they are the only Warm Springs that I have ever visited. The climate is worthy of the waters and the site and scenery worthy of both. In *Ante Bellum* times it was a place of great resort, thronged by the best company, and so it will be again if ever there shall be again money and means at the South for pleasuring, and if our people shall be wise and Southern enough to spend their means within their own borders, and thus help towards adding the adornments and attractions of art to the beauties and blessings by which nature appeals to us to stay at home and cherish our own household gods. How much better would this be on the part of the fortunate, prosperous few among us than gadding abroad to empty their pockets and air themselves, their silks and felts at the North to the annual contemptious admiration of our conquerors, robbers, oppressors there *"that some of the rebels should have some money left yet for summer flaunting and show after all."* To your tents, oh! Israel! To your own summer resorts if a summering you go, even though you should have nothing there better than tents or log cabins to shelter you! The matrons and maidens of the South whom the war left poor but heroines and patriots forever, stand ready to settle this point aright for you. To their husbands, fathers, brothers they exclaim, if we have money to spend, let it be spent here at home where it will help to sustain and cheer our own stricken Southern land.

But hereabouts and not far off are to be seen other kindred displays of nature's liberality to the Pine Mountain. Mindful of the Southern liver, often a prey to malaria, she has considerately imbedded some where in the mountain somewhat or muchwhat of brimstone and taught her purest waters to percolate there and to tarry long enough to become impregned with its virtues and then a little way off to the North to bubble up in the White Sulphur Spring—a resort dear in former times to the hepatic and to staid, quiet people.

Nor was she unthoughtful of those who, victims of no malady, might merely wish to spend a summer vacation in relaxation and gaiety, and laying up a stock of fine health for the future. Behold for these, in a sweet valley to the South, the famed Chalybeate Spring renowned for its tonic properties. Where lie the great subterranean iron ore beds from which the generous fountain distills and draws its strength, none can tell, save that they are deep hidden in the mountain's hard bosom, safe there from the miner's pick and the vagrant enterprise of searchers after "Mineral Riches." And none need fear as long as that mountain shall stand, that these its happily ferruginated waters will ever fail, or lose aught of their health giving efficacy.

Nature's rich dowry to the Pine Mountain is yet further augmented by another mineral spring which it has never been my fortune to visit, but which from all I have ever heard, ought not to be forgotten in an inventory of its wealth. It is the Oak Mountain Spring, so called from a neighboring spur or projection of that name from the main mountain range. Owing, it is said, to the neglect of the owner of the land to make or promote the making of provision for the entertainment and accomodation of visitors, this spring has hitherto been little known, being frequented only by those who are willing and able to erect accommodations and provide in all respects for themselves. And yet in spite of this drawback, its waters have acquired a high reputation with the few that know them, foreshadowing a wide celebrity and a thronged patronage whenever they shall fall under a propitious management. They have never been analyzed, and consequently their qualitics are vouched for by no chemical tests, and the warm praises and satisfactory experience of all who have ever given them a trial must be accepted for the presentas the only certificates of their merit.

Cross we now Flint river from the West, and two or three miles from its Eastern bank, in what was forty years ago a wild sequestered glen of the mountain, close by the side of a little rivulet, we encounter the greatest natural curiosity of all, the greatest not only in this region, but the greatest and most interesting it has ever happened to me to see in Georgia or anywhere else. It is the Thundering Spring, a boiling, uprushing column, six feet in diameter, of purest water and finest sand intermixed. The column on reaching the top of its deep cylindrical well overflows in a ceaseless flood on the side next to the rivulet and runs into it. So forceful is its upward rush that no dead or living thing, animal or vegetable, nothing lighter than stone or metal, can conquer it and go down. It is a wondrous Nature's bath, the bather being doubly laved, water-washed and sand-washed at the same time, treated over his whole body to an exquisite, healthful cutaneous friction far surpassing all the appliances of hygene or "adulteries of art;" —bobbing perpendicularly up and down in the water meanwhile, incapable and fearless of sinking. Upon first leaping into it, a man goes straight down under the water for an instant, and then pops straight back up to the surface again, like a submerged cork, and there floats at ease breast high out of the water, gamboling mermaid-like as long as he pleases. No bottom up to the time of my visit had ever been found to this unparagoned well, nor had it ever been at all ascertained that it had any other or more solid bottom than the seemingly inexhaustible and consequently interminably deep, loose, quicksands which it was forever bringing to the top and discharging along with its waters into the adjoining rivulet.

Of course, the hydrostatic principle which caused and perpetuates this spring in all its up-shooting vehemence is simple and obvious. But where shall we look for such another exemplification of that principle? Not certainly on the Atlantic side of North America. Nor have I ever heard of its match anywhere in the great trans-montane "unknown" of the Pacific slope. I can recall nothing of which I ever heard or read that is a match for it except the Geysers of Iceland, and they are beyond doubt an over match.

It is a thing that strikes the contemplative mind at once curiously and pleasantly that Nature should have passed by all the greater mountains and reserved this wonder of hers for one so petty and unimportant in comparison as the Pine Mountain. Some where in its upper strata she saw fit to construct in preference to all other places, her mighty reservoirs and to keep them perpetually filled with that ponderous mass of waters whose downward pressure forcing them along through some narrow, strong-walled subterranean passage, they came at last against the quicksands of this spot, where their further underground course being arrested by unknown obstacles, they burst their way suddenly and violently through the loose, overlying sands up to the Earth's surface and to the light of the sun and the wondering eyes of men.

The name of Thundering Spring is supposed to have been bestowed by the Indians whose exquisite sense of hearing doubtless caught sometimes the sound of the surging waters as they raved and boiled in their sandy depths. But its thunders have now long been silent or at least unheard, unable to penetrate and awaken the dull ear of Civilization.

CHAPTER V.

KING'S GAP—KING'S TRAILS.

King's Gap in the Pine Mountain, a few miles above Hamilton in Harris county, on the road to Greenville, is the last memento now remaining of a set of Indian Trails of that name that in Indian times perforated in various directions the upper part of the region between the Flint and Chattahoochee and, I feel certain, also of a much larger scope of the Creek Territory to the East, South and West. I first visited the country North of the Pine Mountain, in the Spring of 1827, when the Indians had just left and civilized settlement was just beginning. Carried by business, I crossed Flint river at Gray's ferry not much above the Mountain and took what had been King's Trail, but which by that time had been widened into a rude wagon road by the new settlers having chopped away a few bushes along its sides. It conducted me to a place called Weavers, the temporary seat of Justice for Troup county, which originally extended from river to river. Having delivered to the newly elected but yet uncommissioned Clerk of the Superior Court, my client's Informations against sundry lots of land charged to have been fraudulently drawn in the then recent Land Lottery, I enquired how I could get to Bullsboro, the just chosen judicial site of Coweta county, where I had similar business. Nobody could tell. Luckily the newly elected sheriff arrived at this juncture to learn whether his commission had yet come from Milledgeville. He told me there was no road to Bullsboro and that my best way would be to go home with him, on the Western side of the county, and to take a trail the next morning that ran up the Chattahoochee. I thanked him and went with him, resuming the same King's Trail by which I had come from Flint river and which struck the Chattahoochee at what is now West Point. Nor did it stop there, for seven years afterwards, in 1834, when the Indians were yet in the Alabama part of their country, I traveled along the continuation of this same trail, a lone horseman, from West Point to Tallasee at the foot of the first falls of the Tallapossa river, from whence the trail still continued, passing through Tuckabatchee, the Creek Capital and famed seat of the Big Warrior, and extending from thence to the old French Fort Toulouse, afterwards Fort Jackson, and also to Little Talasee, the still more famous seat of the renowned McGillivray.

The next morning my Sheriff-Host refusing everything but my thanks for his hospitality, told me I had nothing to do but to take another King's trail which he directed me how to find at no great distance from his house, and to follow it up the river some twenty or twenty-five miles, when I must begin to look out for some route striking into the interior of the county of Coweta. He knew there was such a route, but not how far off it was. I soon found myself in this second King's Trail ascending the country, and as I jogged along in the little, narrow, well defined path, just wide enough for a single footman or horseman, and along which no bush had ever been cut away, no wheel had ever rolled, King's Trail began to be a study to me, and I began to wonder what great Indian trader, of whom I had never heard, was great enough to have given his name not to one Indian trail only, but to two.

At first I could not help feeling some misgiving as to the persistent continuity of my little path, and dreaded lest it might give out or in the phrase of the new settlers "take a sapling" and leave me alone in the trackless woods; and once indeed, when the day was pretty far advanced, it seemed to divide, and both tracks were so dim that I was in doubt which to take. But clinging almost instinctively to the Western or river side, I soon found myself riding along the bank of a considerable water course which I felt no pleasure at the prospect of having to ford. While this anxiety was yet strong upon me, suddenly the trail plunged into a piece of rich bottom land, evidently an old Indian clearing, now, however, grown up into a very dense thicket of young trees and clustering vines which overarched and darkened the narrow way. But still the little path continued distinct and unobstructed, and when I was expecting every moment to come where I should be obliged to risk fording the stream, behold! I began to ascend a hill, and it grew lighter and lighter and soon I was on a clear open hill-top with the shining waters of the Chattahoochee, flashing in the sunlight before me and a plain open road inviting me, leading eastwardly from the river. Few contrasts have I ever encountered in my life more thrilling and joyous than the almost instantaneous transition from that dark thicket to this bright scene. It was Grayson's Landing, on which I stood, as I not long afterwards learned—a place much noted in old times as a crossing in the Indian trade.* It took its name from Grayson, a Scotchman, who was a great Indian trader eighty or ninety years ago, and whose name sometimes occurs in the American State papers on Indian Affairs. He trafficked and traveled and lived among the Indians until becoming rich and attached to them, he ended by taking an Indian wife and settling down permanently in the Indian country at the Hillabee towns, some distance to the West or South-west from this point on the Chattahoochee. At these towns it was, if I remember aright, that Col. Willet unexpectedly first met McGillivray in his great Mission as Washington's confidential agent in 1790. It

*Grayson's Landing is now, I have heard, not quite so noted a crossing as in old Indian times, though it is still a crossing, under the name of Philpot's Ferry, in Heard County, just below the mouth of New River, which is the identical river, then certainly entirely new to me, that I so much dreaded to ford in the spring of 1827,

was also through these same towns and along the trading route that led from them to the river at Grayson's Landing, and from thence onward by the way of the Stone Mountain to the Savannah river, keeping all the while within the Indian Territory, (for Georgia and the Creeks were then at war) that Col. Willet soon after escorted the great ambassadorial cavalcade of Creek Chiefs to New York, headed by McGillivray himself, the Sovereign Chief.

As I paused for a while on the beautiful overlooking hill that sloped down to the river bank, gazing around and breathing freer, I little thought on what historic ground I was standing, or that the Eastwardly road, the sight of which was still making my heart leap, was only a very modern widening of still another King's Trail—a fact I learned subsequently. It had been wrought into a wagon road during the previous winter by the hauling of corn and provisions from the not very remote old settlements to be floated down the Chattahoochee from this point for the supply of the new settlers on both sides of the river.

My faithful steed felt not less than myself the inspiring change from the petty trail he had been threading all the day through the woods to the bright open track that now solicited him, and he sprang forward with rapid, elastic steps that brought me a little after nightfall to my destination, rude but hospitable Bullboro, some two or three miles North of the beaten road along which I had been pushing hard during the afternoon. My business was quickly despatched the next morning, and again in the saddle, two more days of lonely, meditative travel found me at my new home at Forsyth and at the end of my tour, but not at the end of its fascinating effect. My mind still remained under a charm, as it were, and most especially did that ubiquitous King's Trail pursue and haunt me, demanding solution of the name it bore, demanding to whom, great among the Indians in trade or in any other way, that name had ever belonged that it should have become the favorite designation of so many of their important trails. But nobody did I ever encounter who was able to enlighten my ignorance or aid my enquiries or in the slightest degree appease my curiosity. To all which add, that soon afterwards I had occasion to make another trip to the new country, which revealed to me still another, a fourth King's Trail, the one deflecting from the Gray's ferry route, through the Pine Mountain at King's Gap, and passing from thence down to where Columbus now stands. And thus the interest of the curious question which had beset me was intensated and increased. It persued me more and more and wrought itself finally into my sleeping as well as my waking hours.

I dreamed that I was in the saddle again, and that I had already been there a long time, wending along yet another King's Trail, one tending downward in its course towards the Atlantic wave and Orient Sun. Already I was far gone on my journey, far down on the ridge which divides the waters which prefer the Gulf from those which go into the Ocean. The pine forests were already thickening with their gloom the dim dubious twilight that enveloped me, sacred ever to dreams. Methought I was drawing near the land of Tallassee so dear of old to the Indian heart, and remembered not that neither there, nor where I actually was, nor along the Atlantic Coast nor in the high uplands through which my long darksome ride had stretched, were the Indians any longer to be found. It was not night, it was not day. No stars were out, there was no sun, no moon, and yet the sky looked blue through the sombre air. The greater beasts were all in their lairs and no large living thing was astir save me and my horse. But the owl's hootings and the whippoorwill's night-long, monotonous lament serenaded me on my way, and ever and anon the leather-winged bat flitted before me, saluting, whilst the tall, heavy topt trees glowred solemnly over the sleeping, semi-nocturnal scene. The further I went the more I fell in love with my dear, unfailing little path, it was so single, so unerringly true and right and safe. Calm was my faith that it would not desert me nor lead me into evil or peril, though I was without any distinct thought whither it was carrying me save only that it was tending seaward. And to the sea at length it came, and with lovely, modest assuredness and directness, crossed the shelving, sandy beach and kissed the vast Ocean's briny lip. My horse planted his fore-feet fetlock deep in the edge of the sea in sign of ready obedience and stood awaiting my intimations. He gazed with me on that great convex liquid world, and with me vainly strained his vision to descry its invisible bounds. But this unavailing strain of the eye continued not long. Old Neptune, proud of his Trident and wantoning in his sea-controlling power, kind also to the uneasy, perplexed surveyor of his tossing domain, struck a divine blow on the topmost billow of the remote outline, and quickly the ever-bending, never-ending convexity of the dread waste of waters subsided and became a vast, level, aqueous plain, on which a slight mist rested low, and I beheld the Halcyon brooding and hatching her young on the still wave. No upswelling watry sphere intercepted now my vision which lengthened immeasurably, adequate to the broad, flat, ocean floor that spread out before me, beyond which I caught a view of the old World and of Georgia's parent land, and saw, too, wonderful to tell, my tiny little King's Trail recommencing plain on the British shore at the very water's edge and inviting me over. The dim trans-Atlantic East was beginning by this time, however, to redden under the rays of the yet unseen Sun, when Lo! on a sudden, all my dream vanished, for dreams cannot stand the sun, and left me and my true steed standing where we were statue-like and aghast forever.

And now for days and weeks this dream haunted and harrassed me more than King's Trails had ever done—so importunate was it to be interpreted. How stolid I was! How slowly penetrable my mind to the light! But the dream pursued me none the less for my dullness, and I had no option but to work and worry, as best I could, at its solution. At last in a happy moment, light began to break in by piecemeal upon me; and first, it occured to me how devotedly loyal to the British Crown, all the Indian Traders, great and small, of the Colonial Era were—the McGillivrays, the McIntoshes, the McQueens, the Barnards, the Galphins, the Graysons, the Pantons and others. Then it slowly came up to my mind what mighty influence these shrewd, enterprising traders acquired among the simple savages, and how they employed that influence and their utmost art besides in making them, too, loyal and devoted to the mighty Trans-Atlantic King, whom they were taught not only to reverence as their Great Father, but almost to worship as their more than human Earthly Sovereign. And then next, who does not know that all over Great Britain, the Public Roads are and ever have been called the King's Highways as well in common as in legal parlance? And now putting all these things together, I knew (for indeed it was very plain) whence King's Trails came and how they got their name; for that the Indian traders who had been accustomed across the ocean in their old country to hear the broad public roads *there* called by the King's Title, had naturally as well as interestedly bestowed the same title on the narrower trading and traveling routes through the Indian country *here*, practicable only for pedestrians and ponies and pack-horses. The Indians themselves easily accepted the designation, partly through mere indifference, partly from real homage for the great King and their estimation of his trading and official subjects who came among them, as they were taught to believe, not to make war upon them, or to wrong them out of their lands, but for better and more agreeable objects. Thus King's Trails in Georgia were legitimately descended and named from the King's highways in Great Britain. Behold! then here, how clear the evidence and argument (though suggested by a dream) that these King's Trails not only had their derivation from England, but were of no mean lineage there, but of undoubted right royal genealogy.

Nor is this although a curious, by any means a singular case of high loyalty in colonial times delighting to express itself by the bestowment of the regal name. The State of New York has to this day, a King's county and a Queen's. Others of the Old Thirteen the same or similar. Maryland, for instance, has her Queen Ann and Prince George, Virginia her King and Queen, a King William, a King George, to say nothing of her Princes and Princesses of counties. South Carolina cherishes her King's Mountain, glorious by Revolutionary battle and blood and victory. And her Charleston, Queen City once, sitting lowly and beautiful, Venice-like, in the lap of the sea, radiant with pearls, yet richer far in wealth of the soul than of the mines! She, although stricken and in sackcloth now, cannot but take pride still in that King Street of hers, Royalty's namesake and remembrancer, felicitous beyond compare in its superb sweep of slowbending, graceful curvature and in the stirring scene of cultured life and animated traffic that used to pervade its farstretching, crescent-like length; narrow, but the more beautiful because narrow, darkened and adorned at once by its tall rows of imposing houses on either side, softly illumed at the same time by Heaven's overarching azure as its mild-beaming, eternal sky-light. In like manner, as long as King's Gap shall remain or as the tradition of King's Trails shall last, Georgia may lay a true, an ancient, and though a modest, yet not an unromatic claim to somewhat of her own, reminding of Kingly State and times, and of the sceptered hand and gemmed brow our Ancestors loved and honored once, but which, in their greater love for freedom, they hastened to renounce and abjure for a Republic under which the hapless people of the South now lie prostrate, victims of a system of mis-government, oppression, wrong and corruption hideous to contemplate, diabolical to inflict, terrible and debasing to endure, and which is assuredly destined in its miserable effects, to be not much worse felt in the long run by its victims than by its perpetrators, who in their insane, vindictive blundering to enslave and ruin us, are forging chains for themselves likewise, and are even now blindly pulling down the temple of American liberty in ruins on their own heads.

CHAPTER VI.

THE PINE BARREN SPECULATION OF 1794-5.

Having been led in speaking of the causes of the Land Lottery System, a couple of chapters back, to mention the infamous Pine Barren Speculation of now some eighty years ago, it is not inopportune to pause here for the purpose of branding a little more memorably that very extraordinary and nefarious piece of money seeking greed and criminality. Indeed, the fact that its revolting effect on the popular mind, combined with the still greater shock of the Yazoo Fraud, conduced largely to the subsequent abandonment by the State of the old Head Right mode of disposing of the public Territory and the adoption of the Land Lottery System in its stead, imparts to it no small historic interest and gives it a valid claim to be noticed and rescued from oblivion. To this end we now shift the scene, and quitting the rich, variagated, oak and hickory lands of the Upcountry, changeful with the seasons from grave to gay, from green to sere, content ourselves a while with gazing on the dreary platitude and unchangingness of regions nearer the sea, sad with perpetual verdure, with streaming, ever-gray long moss and the aerial moaning of the lordly pines over those vast and lonely wilds. Here the sandy barrens salute us—the land of the gopher and salamander, of fish and game, of wiregrass and wild cattle and of herdsmen and hunters almost as wild, who love their rough lives of desultory labor and leisure, never fearful of want, however scanty their store in hand, for the woods and streams hold always stores for them, which their pleasure in capturing is scarcely less than their zest in enjoying. How beneficent is God! Who conciliates to the denizens of every land the homes he has given them, and has rendered even these uninviting and never to be cultivated realms of nature dear to the hearts and sufficient for the wants of the unsophisticated dwellers there. Nor dear to *their* hearts only, but to those likewise of all the truly filial children of Georgia wherever they inhabit, from the mountains to the sea. To all these her broad maternal bosom has everywhere a touching fascination and charm. They love every inch of her soil, broken or level, sterile or fertile, all her upcountry and lowcountry, her oaky woods and piny woods, her hills and dales, her mountains and valleys, her forests and fields, her rivers and streams, her towns, her cities and her rural scenes. For all, all is Georgia!

Montgomery county, created in 1793, by cutting off the lower end of Washington, originally comprised all the country, now embraced in several counties, beginning from the upper line of Emanuel as first formed, and extending from the Ogechee on one side and the Oconee and Altamaha on the other as far down as the upper edge of Liberty county. The whole was one immense, sterile pine forest, the same that so much impressed the celebrated English traveler, Captain Basil Hall, forty-six years ago, whose interesting and graphic account of it* is now and will for centuries to come still be as true and applicable as it was when written. Here flow the Ohoopies the Canoochies, the Yam-Grandy and other streams notorious for barren lands, the haunt of deer, and for limped waters rich with fish. Here nature reigns and will continue to reign supreme as she has done for ages past, secure in vast barrens not less mighty than mountains and marshes and deadly climes under equatorial suns, in giving perpetuity to her throne against man's invasions. Here, too, as in other similar pine regions of the South, even war and a dire peace prolific of curses everywhere else, have alike swept over innocuous, inflicting no change. It is grateful to feel that there are some things of earth, not amenable to change at man's hands; some things

*See his Travels in North America in 1827-1828. Vol. 2. Chapters 19-20.

sacred, stable, ineffaceable in this fickle, fleeting, ever-perishing world, the prey of crime, revolution, ruin and decay. How this feeling deepens by time and thought and renders the eternal monuments of nature of whatever sort dearer and dearer to the soul of him who has always loved her in all her diversities and who has grown old and sad, contemplating the frailty of men and the vanity and transientness as well of their proudest as of their poorest works.

It was in this wide extended, sterile solitude that the scene of the Pine Barren Speculation was laid by its authors and projectors. Here they found fitting soil for sowing their crop of villainy, fitting ground whereon to plant the lever of their scheme of fraud. Here they beheld outspread and neglected millions of barren acres—so barren as not only to have attracted no immigration but no attention. No settlers were drawn thither even by the gratuitous terms of the Head Right system of that period, requiring the payment of nothing but office fees. Whilst the counties of Green and Hancock, which had been carved out of the upper end of Washington, had already become populous and flourishing communities, the huge lower section now converted into Montgomery county, remained a desolate waste. But these lands, though they had no attractions for honest, industrious settlers, presented a temptation at once, novel and powerful to unprincipled speculators, who did not suffer them to remain long unnoticed after they were set off into a separate county. Lynx-eyed fraud quickly saw its opportunity in the very neglect to which they were abandoned, and pounced upon them for its own vile enrichment soon after the new county was formed. It conceived the bold, cunning idea of coining their very barrenness into an infamous value never before imagined, and to this end it devised and worked out that monstrous scheme of villainy which was still the subject of loathing rememberance and mention in my early boyhood. Its originators and managers had made up their minds from the outset to shrink from no exorbitance of iniquity that might be deemed conducive to their ends ; and they played accordingly an intrepid and magnificent game of felonious knavery.—Fraud, forgery, bribery, perjury—such were the crimes that stood in their way, but at which they balked not. The incorrupt mind recoils from the horrid catalogue and would fain regard the story of so much diabolism as a distempered fable. But, alas! the daily experience which surrounds and shocks us, or rather has ceased to shock us in these our own times, forbids such a solace. In the presence of the stupendous pecuniary atrocities which are now of familiar occurrence, practiced alike by men in private and public life, the grossest villainies of the past are dwarfed and vindicate themselves as at once entitled to a stronger belief and a mitigated infamy.

The plans of the miscreants were well laid and unflinchingly followed out. In the vast uninhabited woods they planted or found at wide distances the necessary accomplices and tools: First, men who were to act as magistrates and form one of those peculiar legal devices of that day called Land Courts; of which the function was to issue or rather to profess to issue the land warrants which were the initial step under the Head Right system. Next, other men were planted or found, who as county surveyors, were to make or rather to profess to make and return the locations and surveys contemplated by these Warrants. And the pains were also taken to have all these official accomplices regularly elected and commissioned to the offices they were intended to abuse; their election to which was a thing not difficult to effect among the ignorant, unsuspecting settlers scattered thinly over the immense wilderness. And it was this obvious facility of electing men that could be used as tools, that undoubtedly stimulated and encouraged, if it did not originally suggest, the idea of the great Pine Barren Speculation, the whole machinery of which stood on these basely designed elections. Here, too, moreover, we see the reason why this fraud followed so quickly after the formation of Montgomery county and had not been attempted or ever conceived sooner. For as long as the Territory remained a part of Washington county, the voters entitled to a voice in these elections were altogether too numerous, intelligent and vigilant to have permitted any hope of success in such a conspiracy.

Organized now and ready to enter on their flagitious work, these vile persons had every thing entirely to themselves and in their own hands. There were none to interfere with them, or embarrass, or deter, and they carried out their projects without fear and with gratuitous boldness and extravagance. Not satisfied with seizing on the two or three millions of acres that really existed in the new county and casting them into their mint of fraud, they trebled the number and went to the length of issuing and returning into the Surveyor General's office, Land Forgeries to the amount of six or seven millions of acres. This fact appears by two printed Reports, now before me, made by the Surveyor General in 1839 to a special Finance Commission, composed of Judge Berrien, Judge Wm. W. Holt and myself. One of these Reports presents the *actual* number of acres in each county of the State ; the other, the number in each county *as shown by the maps and Records of the Surveyor General's office.** Upon comparing the two, it will be seen that the number appearing by the official maps and records as lying in the original county of Montgomery, exceeds the true number, by several millions. How did such a monstrous excess get into the Surveyor General's office and upon the maps and records there?

There never has been, there never can be but one answer to this question. Fraud and forgery aided by official connivance and corruption, afford the only solution. There is no other possible way of accounting for the phenomenon. Had the lands been but moderately fertile or had they possessed any other qualities or accidents of a nature to confer value and make them the object of desire and competition, it would not have been strange for the same thing to have happened to them from these causes as from like reasons has often happened elsewhere in rich new countries under the Head Right system : namely, that after all the *veritable* land should have been actually and in good faith first

*See copies of these statements at the end of this chapter.

taken up and covered once with warrants and surveys, the avidity of acquisition might have been so great as to lead to the same identical lands being afterwards again and again taken up by other persons, thus covering or, in the expressive phrase coined specially for the case, *shingling* the country with layer after layer of successive competing Head Right warrants and claims, all which being returned to the Surveyor General's office, necessarily occasioned a great excess of land on the maps and records there beyond what existed in nature. But it would be glaringly absurd to account in this way for the redundant millions in the Surveyor General's office of the utterly worthless lands of which we are now speaking; lands, which nobody wanted or would have even as a gift, and for which there never has been the least competition. Why, as late as 1839, not more than half the land in that region was (judging by the Comptroller General's report, made to the above mentioned Finance Commission*) deemed worth owning and paying taxes for; although the lumber trade had by that time given some value to portions of it lying near the rivers, that had previously been valueless.

Thus the spuriousness of an immense proportion of the surveys and returns in question is manifest. But though the most of them were undoubtedly the progeny of fraud and forgery, yet not all were so. A good many genuine ones were with covinous shrewdness and design intermixed, and this intermixture of *somewhat* that was genuine was an important, well considered point in the scheme of fraud, in as much as it tended to give color and unsuspectedness to the *muchwhat* that was false, fraudulent and fictitious.

But not only was it a part of the scheme that genuine surveys should be thus intermingled with the spurious in the returns made to the Surveyor General's office, but it was also requisite that good lands should be lyingly intermingled with the barren on the maps and records there. For all the vast quantity of land real and fictitious that was

*See Comptroller General's report at the end.

returned into the Surveyor General's office as having been duly surveyed and taken up, could have been turned to no profit by the conspirators but for another adroit stroke of villainy to which they had recourse and without which their whole plan would have broken down. I allude to the *false land-marks* put on the maps and plats of the surveys. Something base and fraudulent in this way had to be done to enable them to palm off any large amount of these pine barrens as rich lands. This was, indeed, the vital point in their nefarious strategy, and in order to make sure of it, they caused the different kinds of trees indicative of a rich soil, such as the oak, the hickory, the walnut, dogwood, buckeye, etc., to be entered as corner and station trees on the maps of the surveys :—Not however on the maps of all the immense number of surveys which they had caused to be fabricated and returned, but on enough of them to answer their purposes, a judicious, deceptive interspersing of lands marked as rich among the barrens which notoriously formed most of the county. Suspicion was thus kept down and an imposing verisimilitude attained, and along with it as much land feigned to be rich as they could expect to be able to work off on ignorant second purchasers or as they would be willing to pay Grant Fees for.

For there was no evading the payment of the Grant Fees, which, though little in each case, would in the aggregate have amounted to a great sum. Up to this point, fraud and forgery had cut off costs and labor making both very light, but for which, the outlay in office fees requisite for their vast operations would alone have been an insuperable impediment in their way. But now fraud and forgery could no longer be made to serve any purpose. Their turn was at an end as soon as the forged documents of survey were accepted and registered in the Surveyor General's office. Thenceforward what had to be done was simply to get from that office certified copies of these maps and surveys, upon which being presented and passed at the rest of the State House offices; (among others, at the Treasury, where the Grant Fees were paid and a receipt countersigned therefor,) genuine Grants under the Great Seal and the Governor's signature were issued as a matter of course, except in cases where a caveat had been interposed, a thing which never happened in relation to these lands, there being no competition for them.

The actors in this huge, concatenated fraud had now accomplished so much of their programme as was to be carried out in Georgia. They had sowed the seed here, but they had to go elsewhere to reap their villainous harvest. Had they dared to offer their fraudulent and fictitious lands for sale here where their worthlessness and nothingness were so well known, it would have led to the public explosion of their whole plot and to their own no small endangerment besides, for those were times in which such caitiffs felt all the while in Georgia no little dread of a certain Judge Lynch who not unfrequently, disgusted with the too slow footsteps, or too dim vision, or too feeble or too uncertain arm of the more regularly constituted powers, came to their relief by a prompt assumption of their difficult duties. These speculators therefore in barren lands, at once daring and cautious, betook themselves (as was indeed their plan from the outset) to other localities, to the distant places where their unavowed and unsuspected copartners and confederates lived and whence they themselves had come with evil, vile intent among us. And there they and their coadjutors failed not to find those who fell victims to their swindling arts. To what extent they succeeded in effecting sales, in turning the barrens of Montgomery into gold in their own pockets and involving innocent, deceived people in loss for their own base emolument, is of course unascertainable now, and has long since ceased to be a matter of interest or curiosity. That their success was not small, however, is probable from all the circumstances of the case and from the general rumor and belief which descended from those times down to a later period.

For to those remote parts whither they hied to enact the crowning scene of their villainy, to find the bag of gold at the end of their tortuous drama of iniquity, fame had carried exciting accounts of the fertility and advantages of the Oconee country. Nor was she careful in her loud, undiscriminating praises, to make due distinction between the richness of the upper portion and the sterility of the lower. People afar off were thus greatly misled and prepared to be easily practised upon and cheated, and were, moreover, carried away by the cheap rates at which these supposed fertile lands were offered for sale by men whom they cost very little more than the crimes they had committed in connection with them. And when in addition, the solemn grants of the State of Georgia were paraded under the autographic signatures of her Governor and great State House officers, with her huge, dangling, waxen Great Seal appended and with also certified plats of survey attached to each grant under her Surveyor General's official hand, richly marked besides with natural growth indicative of a fertile soil, it is by no means surprising that thousands should have been befooled and swindled. And that such was the case contemporaneous story indignantly told and was not unsupported by after-occurring facts. For many a bootless pilgrimage from distant States and sections was made years afterwards by the sufferers and their agents in search of those fabled lands. In vain, however, did they thread the woods and interrogate the trees. No land marks, no corners or stations could they ever find responsive to the well drawn, false speaking charts they brought along with them. No oaks, and hickories, no walnut, dogwood or buckeye, nor any kindly soil did they ever encounter to cheer their wearisome explorings or raise their sunken spirits. But barren wastes spread out sad and interminable before their eyes, and the tall sighing pines sounded a lugubrious sympathy in their ears. The golden dreams they had been made to cherish were dispelled for ever. Reluctantly they awoke to the bitter reality of being the victims of a great concocted turpitude, and with heavy hearts wended their way back to their far off homes, full of indignation, and cursing and hating more than ever before the villains and villainies of the world.

The following statement was furnished from the Surveyor General's office, June 17th, 1839, to the Finance Commission, showing the ACTUAL *number of acres in each county.*

Appling	680,426
Baker	899,297
Baldwin	156,160
Bibb	152,563
Bryan	276,480
Bulloch	605,440
Burke	665,600
Butts	113,030
Camden	720,000
Campbell	147,963
Carroll	482,180
Cass	439,130
Chatham	268,800
Chattooga	223,986
Cherokee	467,780
Clark	179,200
Cobb	406,961
Columbia	320,000
Coweta	282,881
Crawford	250,319
Decatur	707,609
DeKalb	281,253
Dade	112,235
Dooly	650,693
Early	602,549
Effingham	310,400
Elbert	327,680
Emanuel	753,920
Fayette	218,801
Floyd	317,343
Forsyth	183,515
Franklin	499,200
Gilmer	530,572
Glynn	253,440
Greene	268,800
Gwinnett	347,083
Habersham	403,476
Hall	258,277
Hancock	288,640
Harris	297,680
Heard	165,763
Henry	333,540
Houston	392,884
Irwin	1,269,426
Jackson	337,920
Jasper	245,760
Jefferson	376,320
Jones	241,920
Laurens	450,560
Lee	340,203
Liberty	393,600
Lowndes	1,238,203
Lincoln	126,720
Lumpkin	396,025
Macon	240,308
Madison	124,800
Marion	350,562
McIntosh	422,200
Meriwether	335,885
Monroe	302,623
Montgomery	407,680
Morgan	228,480
Murray	407,740
Muscogee	291,903
Newton	256,299
Oglethorpe	286,720
Paulding	423,617
Pike	266,962
Pulaski	515,355
Putnam	236,800
Rabun	249,515
Randolph	519,968
Richmond	201,600
Scriven	345,600
Stewart	482,170
Sumpter	369,857
Talbot	331,468
Taliaferro	86,400
Tatnall	761,600
Telfair	264,960
Thomas	900,720
Troup	280,100
Twiggs	231,680
Union	419,168
Upson	184,580
Walker	399,663
Walton	164,015
Ware	879,360
Warren	274,560
Washington	416,720
Wayne	380,160
Wilkes	323,840
Wilkinson	288,000
Total	35,515,526

Statement furnished June 17th, 1839, to the Finance Commission by the Surveyor General of the number of acres of land in each county of the State agreeably to the MAPS *and* RECORDS *of his office.*

Appling	684,426
Baker	899,297
Baldwin	159,982
Bibb	152,563
Bryan	111,091
Bulloch	358,217
Burke	619,006
Butts	113,030
Camden	1,928,688
Campbell	147,963
Carroll	482,180
Cass	439,130
Chatham	55,619
Chattooga	223,986
Cherokee	467,780
Clark	22,136
Cobb	406,961
Columbia	145,055
Coweta	282,881
Crawford	250,319
Decatur	707,609
DeKalb	281,253
Dade	112,235
Dooly	650,693
Early	602,549
Effingham	1,149,791
Elbert	121,870
Emanuel	356,869
Fayette	218,804
Floyd	317,343
Forsyth	183,515
Franklin	5,126,548
Gilmer	530,572
Glynn	1,785,375
Greene	324,278
Gwinnett	347,083
Habersham	408,476
Hall	258,277
Hancock	56,727
Harris	297,680
Heard	165,763
Henry	333,540
Houston	392,884
Irwin	1,269,426
Jackson	175,120
Jasper	245,760
Jefferson	71,593
Jones	241,920
Laurens	450,560
Lee	340,203
Liberty	870,680
Lincoln	14,624
Lowndes	1,238,203
Lumpkin	396,025
Macon	240,308
Madison	39,518
Marion	350,562
McIntosh	667,251
Meriwether	335,885
Monroe	302,623
Montgomery	7,436,995
Morgan	228,480
Murray	407,740
Muscogee	291,903
Newton	256,299
Oglethorpe	55,018
Paulding	428,617
Pike	266,962
Pulaski	515,355
Putnam	236,800
Rabun	248,515
Randolph	519,968
Richmond	443,457
Scriven	242,656
Stewart	482,170
Sumpter	369,857
Talbot	331,468
Taliaferro	564
Tatnall	395,840
Telfair	364,960
Thomas	900,720
Troup	280,100
Twiggs	231,680
Union	419,168
Upson	184,580
Walker	399,663
Walton	164,015
Ware	879,360
Warren	95,239
Washington	5,018,048
Wayne	380,360
Wilkes	2,224,920
Wilkinson	288,000
Total	54,816,782

A TABLE—*Exhibiting the quantity of acres of* 1st, 2d *and* 3d *qualities and PineLand—The number of Slaves—Amount of Stock in Trade, and value of Town Property—The aggregate number of acres of Land—The Tax on each quality, and the aggregate amount of Tax paid on the whole, in the State of Georgia, agreeably to the Tax Returns of the several Counties, filed in the Comptroller General's Office for the year* 1838.

Counties.	1st quality	2d.	3d.	Pine.	Stock in Trade.	Town Property.	Slaves
Appling,....	393	8,336	5,204	81,000	3,700		205
Baker,.......	3,977	33 716	13,347	72,143	74,750	8,900	708
Baldwin,.....	5,252	82,740	57,871	129,204	182.900	254.075	4,125
Bibb,.......	11,996	86,529	78,113	159.423	732,447	1,345,105	4,498
Bryan,.......	3,123	16,761	10,993	130,556	1,800	3,856	1,847
Bulloch......	1,810	11,229	12,080	416,725		7,900	847
Burke,.......	1,935	47,754	288,483	352,824	18,602	27.100	6,417
Butts,.......	2,253	54,396	99,542	28,924	19,450	30,337	1,819
Camden,.....	12,591	39,902	26,950	304,643	• 96,436	117,592	3,256
Campbell,...	4,339	43,222	88,583	27,333	17,080	8,031	875
Carroll,......	890	43,121	69,019	24,642	10,905	8,759	280
Cass,........	18,220	76,184	64,645	10,279	44,250	35,218	1,137
Chatham,....					667,589	2,648,792	11.136
Cherokee,...	4,276	38,897	42,706	9,676	20,194	12,290	321
Chattooga,..	0,000	0,000	0,000	0,000	000	000	000
Clark,.......	5,033	96,532	250.792	102,592	108,312	300,995	4,895
Cobb,........	2,425	55,932	52,313	5,152	19,505	36,425	381
Columbia,...	1,779	87,875	145,075	184,684	19,076	16,582	6,832
Coweta,. ..	3,437	126.412	124,476	102,134	52,305	38,135	2,683
Crawford,...	2,116	69,789	50,669	525,150	65,529	15,385	2,462
Dade,.......	580	5,315	5,246	882	800		36
Decatur,....	4,990	50,756	22,848	120,100	53,224	13,113	1,750
DeKalb,.....	4,784	83,723	216,871	31.784	90,965	66,625	1,622
Dooly,.......	3,208	26,207	5,157	136,094	30,846	14,708	781
Early,.......	4,580	45,953	14,687	96,632	40,550	64,225	1,580
Elbert,.......	4,056	52,191	222.363		80,465	49,970	3.166
Effingham,...	957	2,417	13,857	222,398	3,371		1,211
Emanuel,....	453	12,700	11,524	389,916	4,133	800	568
Fayette,.....	1,278	80,207	107,201	23,419	27,181	22,707	1,124
Floyd,.......	14,404	73,929	65,814	27,637	51,320	22,010	1,342
Franklin,....	3,554	55,045	357,270	56,062	18,562	17,390	2,159
Forsyth,.....	4,348	43,193	56,897	11,840	20,320	28,249	447
Gilmer,......	2,211	7,343	26,924	571	2,838	2,401	35
Glynn,.......	2,090	21,959	9,721	121,804	14,350	28,456	2,666
Greene,.....	5,408	76,746	179,327	53,750	118,487	37,837	5,595
Gwinnett,..	2,988	61,463	246,139	47,817	45,052	31,460	1,914
Habersham,..	7,074	31,987	95,953	213,688	36.713	26,718	843
Hall,........	4,708	48,268	232,738	17,882	30,665	14,290	957
Hancock,....	2,438	54,090	152,506	173,431	83,900	69,887	5,424
Harris,.......	7,061	183,002	110,129	27,325	60,452	104,331	4,311
Heard,.......	5,911	56,275	61,737	32,482	27,720	12,035	1,367
Henry,.......	1,790	119,231	220,633	42,204	59,838	35,023	2,925
Houston,.....	6,055	88,830	32,867	226,296	59,213	35,736	4,199
Irwin,.......		5,369	3,000	84,755	2,300	1,114	204
Jackson,.....	2,345	66,366	244,606	51,389	23,468	12,550	2,356
Jasper,......	2,270	113,997	168,661	40,349	101,441	78,125	5,244
Jefferson,....	1,602	45,952	91,062	278,584	46,600	21,096	4,327
Jones,.......	2,363	139,636	129,455	262,521	53,760	41,459	5,650
Laurens,.....	5,918	156,753	54,666	16,322	13,350	21,319	2,168
Lee,.........	9,124	38,668	23,271	95,282	15,000	15,000	1,263
Liberty,.....	4,104	43,754	23,696	193,626	8,650	22,248	5,326
Lincoln,.....	4,526	50,939	135,708	62,286	24,603	10,340	3,253
Lowndes,....	1,330	79,094	12,508	265,334	3,534	3,443	678
Lumpkin,....	3,658	21,984	21,057	13,816	58,665	58,920	354
Macon,......	1,856	26,015	16,631	141,773	2,350		1,159
Madison,....	526	12,070	191,517	26,670	8,950	5,929	1,336
Monroe,.....	4,777	180,742	231,870	105,192	106,826	106,590	9,361
McIntosh,....	38,700	46,868	31,871	188,015	87,466	111,932	3,798
Meriwether,..	5,255	158,705	132,492	60,185	77,850	37,713	4,384
Marion,......	1,132	41,019	14,957	93,418	11,600	8,551	734
Montgomery,	1,660	13,150	3,387	74,404	2,200	255	357

Counties.	1st quality	2d.	3rd.	Pine.	Stock Trade.	Town Property.	Slaves
Morgan,	5,082	186,609	117,275	15,097	114,882	64,050	5,367
Murray..,	7,291	30,103	23,424	11,999	14,110	18,950	123
Muscogee,	9,604	102,668	82,340	246,954	537,675	1,183,080	4,322
Newton,	887	113,490	177,884	113,387	64,602	68,830	2,008
Oglethorpe,	4,479	91,214	183,595	46,548	54,700	13,200	6,229
Paulding,	1,666	20,507	11,893	1,838	2,800		261
Pike,	20,315	79,665	158,449	86,218	33,900	22,744	2,190
Pulaski,	5,756	46,024	46,847	160,512	16,900	6,023	2,805
Putnam,	3,208	112,413	159,495	45,500	87,100	82,[illegible]19	6,653
Rabun,	2,091	11,260	73,620		2,160	6,634	78
Randolph,	3,601	118,365	38,264	114,129	16,760	21,380	1,557
Richmond,	9,968	61,225	79,963	258,459	1,555,155	2,171,170	5,438
Scriven,	6,129	27,912	36,073	285,025	13,980	3,155	2,477
Stewart,	1,920	164,163	29,454	174,027	121,225	88,694	3,452
Sumter,	5,822	83,286	10,915	76,545	29,258	23,798	970
Talbot,	8,290	195,385	74,997	78,711	94,162	50,440	5,511
Taliaferro,	4,913	25,805	117,731	25,275	70,018	50,375	2,461
Tattnall,	380	14,619	19,349	487,162	2,000	1,000	654
Telfair,	510	13,876	14,611	313,612	9,700	1,100	661
Thomas,	2,639	64,749	11,714	232,005	53,650	29,580	2,384
Troup,	11,183	110,177	124,849	61,226	212,124	71,467	6,956
Twiggs,	6,436	94,425	55,281	146,244	51,619	13,950	4,074
Union,	1,910	13,588	11,762	30,193	4,441	1,000	62
Upson,	3,008	84,722	100,457	61,038	47,736	35,520	3,437
Walker,	7,936	65,463	61,509	10,368	30,010	34,403	708
Warren,	882	39,756	167,212	64,406	60,310	35,771	4,155
Walton,	3,095	102,073	200,328	36,930	33,700	12,943	2,943
Washington,	4,634	51,610	119,158	377,312	38,350	48,875	3,444
Wayne,	440	1,843	2,358	67,710	6,300		466
Ware,	1,002	10,293	5,488	41,271	1,300	200	81
Wilkes,	2,889	72,981	248,497	79,540	73,400	117,688	6,681
Wilkinson,	1,472	36,833	15,809	259,830	26,509	9,772	1,695
	410,415	16,604,331	8,057,293	10,494,297	7,244,994	11,059,144	242,923

LAND.

1st quality	410,415
2d "	16,604,331
3rd "	8,057,293
Pine Land	10,794,297
Total number of acres	35,366,336
Stock in Trade	7,244,994
Town Property	11,059,154
Slaves	242,923

AMOUNT OF TAX PAID ON EACH.

AVERAGE TAX.

9 5-8 mills per acre	3,954 74
5 6-8 " "	8,571 73
2 1-2 " "	1,712 17
1 6-8 " "	1,259 35
At 15 5-8 cts. per $100	11,320 30
" 15 5-8 " "	17,279 92
" 15 5-8 per Slave	37,956 71
Total Tax	$82,052 92

The whole amount of taxes paid, agreeably to the returns made, is $111,338 44

CHATHAM COUNTY.—The quantity and quality of Land returned in this county cannot be ascertained from the Tax Book returned, and not included in the foregoing additions.

CHATTOOGA COUNTY.—No returns have been received from this county.

COMPTROLLER GENERAL'S OFFICE, Milledgeville, 21st June, 1839.

GENTLEMEN:—In compliance with your letter of the 2d April last, the foregoing Tabular Statement is furnished, as containing the information requested. The statement required would have been prepared at an earlier period, but for the great labor necessary in obtaining from the books in this Department, correct information as to the several classifications of Land, &c. desired, and the difficulty of procuring competent assistance to perform the work.

I am, very respectfully your obedient servant,

JOHN G. PARK, Comptroller General, Georgia.

To Messrs. A. H. Chappell, J. M. Berrien, and W. W. Holt, Commissioners, &c.

CHAPTER VII.

THF YAZOO FRAUD—SECTION I.

The great Yazoo Fraud was conceived earlier than the Pine Barren Speculation, but as it had a much longer gestation, it turned out that the two reached their birth about the same time, and were consequently contemporaneous though not twin villainies; for there never was any actual connection between them either as to facts or persons. It would be impossible for people nowadays to form an adequate idea of the immense and almost wild stir and excitement caused by the Yazoo Fraud in its day; and it was by no means a short any more than a commonplace day that it had. Not only was it radicated far back in the then Past, but curious explorers will detect its roots and ramifications interwoven with national matters of that period important enough to claim a place in history. And when we come down later and take a view of the great cancerous abomination in its several vicissitudes and more advanced stages, how complicated it is seen to become alike in its facts and in the questions and principles it involves! How the huge villainy stands out and strikes us, distent with odious interest and energy at every turn, making its way over all obstacles, discouragements and delays, first through the State Legislature, next through the Cabinet, Courts and Congress of the United States, and in the end, after near twenty years of unholy striving and perseverance, triumphing at last and plunging its felonious hands deep into the National Treasury.

That memorable crime which was consummated in the Legislature of Georgia on the 7th of January, 1795, is the one to which I am now referring. The intelligence of it no sooner reached Washington than it caused him great concern, for he instantly saw its enormity and dangerousness, having already a few years previously had to deal (and stern and decisive was that dealing) with its comparatively innocent and less formidable and now almost forgotten predecessor, the much smaller Yazoo Sale of 1789. Upon obtaining from Augusta, then the seat of Government of Georgia, the authentic documents on the subject, he hastened on the 19th of February, 1796, to lay them before Congress with a message in which he characterised the matter as one "of exceeding magnitude, that might in its consequences affect the peace and welfare of the United States." But Georgia on this occasion saved trouble to the National Authorities, or rather she staved it off to a remoter day. For, as if seeking to make amends for her apathy in regard to the Yazoo Sale of 1789, she was now fierce and rapid in her action, and stepping forward at once she of her own mere motion and with her sole arm struck down this new and more monstrous Yazoo crime to which corruption had just given birth on her soil, leaving to the Federal Administration at that time no other task to perform in relation to it than mere arraignment and some steps of precaution and inquiry. It was only a temporary respite, however, that resulted to the United States from the indignant, patriotic promptitude of the State. For it turned out that the Hydra was only "scotched, not killed" by Georgia. In a few years it came to life again, developing a new head not vulnerable to the blows of the State and only amenable to the National arm, and from thenceforward it unceasingly harassed the United States and exhibited such pernicious and deathless faculties for mischief and annoyance that, finally in 1814, Congress was glad to give up the warfare and compromise with the great iniquity by passing a Bill appropriating five millions of dollars to the appeasing of its claims.

Into the politics of Georgia it continued to be ever and anon dragged for years afterwards laden with unforgiven guilt and intense public odium. At length in the year 1825, in the first popular election for Governor we ever had, and by far the hottest and fiercest known to our annals, a fiery farewell eruption of this old political Vesuvius of the State was provoked by some slight unfavorable reminiscences that were stirred up connected with the name of one the candidates for the office. For our people had not learned even down to that period to pardon to any man the smallest participation in that great parricidal crime. And if their vengeance has not been since inflamed in regard to it, it is only because time has both extinguished the causes and dimmed the recollections by which it could be kindled anew.

The wonderment, perplexity and curiosity which the very word Yazoo used to excite in juvenile minds in Georgia fifty and sixty years ago I have never been able to forget. Its strange exotic sound to the ear and look in print was the first and not a very small thing. Then, besides, it was a word which had evidently long been, as it still was, perfectly familiar in the mouths of all elderly and full grown people, so much so, that taking it to be universally understood they never bethought them that it needed explanation to anybody, no, not even to the listening boy whom they saw sitting silent and attentive. Most frequently it was of the Yazoo Fresh they spoke, yet often of the Yazoo Fraud. Sometimes it was the Yazoo Sale and the Yazoo Lands, and then again the Yazoo Script and Yazoo Shares. The Yazoo Legislature, the Yazoo Speculators and Yazoo Companies were likewise frequent topics, nor was the story of the burning of the Yazoo Act with fire drawn from heaven by Gen. Jackson with a sun-glass left untold. Thus numerous, various and unlike were the things called by name of Yazoo; and all of them too so much the theme of talk! And yet where was Yazoo, and what was it? It seemed to be all over Georgia and yet no mention was ever made of any place in or out of Georgia where it was to be found or seen. Was there, indeed, any such place, and if there was, why should it cause so much talk and give its name to so many and such different things? Or, perhaps it was not a place, but only a thing; and if so, why was it such a noted thing, and why were so many other things baptized with its name? And did it pertain to land or water, or was it amphibious and akin to both? All was vague, misty, mysterious, perplexed, yet pervaded not doubtfully with the general idea of somewhat that was sinister, abhorrent and damnable.

This uncertainty, however, which tormented young imaginations was more and more dispelled, so far at least as the question between land and water was concerned, by every spell of heavy, unrelenting rains, by every extraordinary and destructive inundation of the creeks and rivers. These occurrences never failed to renew and strengthen the association in youthful minds between Yazoo and water. For then the Yazoo Fresh was sure to be in the ascendant in people's mouths and thoughts. Another Yazoo Fresh was feared or threatened, or such another fall of rain and rise of the waters had never been seen since the great Yazoo Fresh when all the streams and rivers rose high above all former watermarks and the mountain torrents and windows of heaven were opened to swell the proud Savannah, and the glorious river vindicating the honor of its banks, swept in angered majesty over the scene so lately desecrated by a monstrous and unprecedented public villainy, and for the first time and the last too for more than forty years, made beauteous Augusta, Georgia's capital, a subaqueous and navigable city.

Terruit Urbem;
Terruit *cives*, grave ne rediret
Saeculum Pyrrhæ nova monstra questæ,
Omne cum Proteus pecus egit altos
Visere montes;

Piscium et summa genus hæsit ulmo
Nota quæ sedes fuerat columbis,
Et superjecto pavidæ natarunt
Aequore damæ.

Vidimus flavum Tiberim retortis
Littore Etrusco violenter undis
"Ire dejectum momementa Regis
Templaque Vestæ.*

But the watery visitation lasted not long. The whelming flood rushed quickly away, as if hastening in sorrow from the havoc it had done and left the broad riparian plain which Augusta adorns, bare to the genial sun once more and to the woful gaze of men. And also in years ensuing, when more time and knowledge had accrued to the younger folks, the idea of water associated with Yazoo gradually subsided from their minds and in its stead, land and fraud and many cognate abominations came up to view and grew to the name and asserted themselves the originals to which the alien word was first applied in Georgia. For it was a word not native here. It was outlandish in its origin, born in a distant savage nook and imported from thence across hundreds of miles of Indian wilderness and odiously denizened amongst us. Its birth place and long its only and sinless home, where its utterance called not up remembrances of turpitude, was far away on the confines of the Mississippi,

*As it may be interesting to the non-latinist to see in an English poetic dress these fine stanzas from Horace describing an inundation of the Tiber at Rome, I subjoin a translation by Covington, which may perhaps also have some interest for the classical scholar both on account of its own merits and as showing the unapproachableness of the original:

Appalled the city,
Appalled the cit'zens, lest Pyrrah's time
Return with all its monstrous sights,
When Proteus led his flocks to climb
The mountain heights;

When fish were in the elm tops caught
Where once the stock dove wont to bide,
And deer were floating, all distraught,
Adown the tide.

Old Tiber, hurled in tumult back
From mingling with the Etruscan main,
Has threatened Numa's Court with wreck
And Vesta's fane.

in the land of the Choctaws, a region as wild to the eye as its own sound to the ear. There it had been for unknown ages articulated by barbarian tongues as the name of a petty stream meandering sluggishly from the North to lose itself in the bosom of the Father of Floods. But what made that petty stream so important and how came it to supplant not only the Alabama, the Tuscaloosa, and the Tombigbee, but the great Tennessee and even the mighty Mississippi itself, and to impose its own ignoble name in preference to all theirs on the immense territory watered by them all, and also on the stupendous feat of villainy of which that territory was the subject matter and prize? These are points which used of yore to bother not a little the heads of both old and young in Georgia and which, I durst opine, may be still obscure to many at the present day. But even if it be so, there is little reason why I should hang back longer from my destined task in order now to lift the veil and clear up the mystery. For it is one of those curiosities of American territorial history and controversy the explication of which will assuredly come out in the course of that handling of the Yazoo Fraud upon which it is high time I should enter, if indeed I would redeem the promise held out in the heading of this chapter.

SECTION II.

Beyond doubt no greater or more consequential event of a mere worldly character has ever happened in the world than the discovery and settlement of America. What an infinite variety and multitude of things new and momentous under the sun have been owing directly and indirectly to that vast and pregnant occurrence! How it has teemed with results of all sorts and sizes, creating new, modifying or annihilating old interests, reaching all over the globe, and sure of pervading all futurity! Among the earliest and most striking of the novelties to which it gave birth, was the practice originated by Spain on this continent of what may be called conquest by contract; by the associated enterprise, capital, cupidity and ambition of bodies of private adventurers, acting at their own pecuniary cost, though under regal sanction and protection, and enjoying a meretricious partnership with royalty in the honor of ruling and the lucre of plundering the conquered countries. War and the acquirement by force of new dominions was by this cruel means rendered easy and unexpensive to a government sitting enthroned and unendangered across the Atlantic, ignorant or unthinking of the diabolical lawlessness and inhumanity which sprang from its policy and sullied its arms, and which have indelibly tarnished the Spanish name. It was thus that Mexico was subdued for Spain by Cortes, Peru by Pizzaro. Such too was the origin of the atrocious, warlike wanderings of Fernando deSoto* and his martial companions, over the immense regions stretching Northwardly from the Gulf of Mexico, which at that day and for a long while afterwards were massed by the Spaniards under the then comprehensive name of Florida† and which now form in addition to the present Florida, the great States of Georgia, Alabama, Mississippi, Tennessee, Arkansas and Louisiana. If what was first seen and known of the New World warranted its discoverers in calling its inhabitants barbarians, assuredly cause enough was soon given to those barbarians for regarding the civilized new-comers as demons, who had on a sudden preternaturally appeared among them to be the curse of their land and the destroyers of their race.

The course of Great Britain, however, towards the natives in those parts of America colonized or acquired by her was nobler and more humane. She sought not to enslave or oppress or plunder them, or to extort tribute from them like the Spaniards, nor did she imitate the bad Spanish example of sentencing them to be brought under her yoke by the agency of armed bodies of irresponsible free booters wearing their Monarch's livery and flaunting his license, and only

*Bancroft's History of the United States. Chapter 2d. Vol. 1. Pickett's History of Alabama. Chapter 1. Vol. 1.

†Bancroft's History of the United States. Vol. 1. Page 60.

the more licentious because so licensed, and who emulated the worst piratical hordes in their infamous disregard of the laws of nature and of nations. It was on the contrary the pervading principle of the policy of Great Britain, that war and peace, negotiations and treaties with the Indians and all territorial acquisitions from them, whether by conquest, purchase, or in any other way, should be strictly affairs of Government to be transacted only by and through its recognized officers and agents, civil or military, and never to be given up to private hands, or subordinated to private interests of any kind, or under any circumstances. Equally contrary was it to the British system for the Government to sell or convey to private persons or companies the right of soil in any lands before the aboriginal title therein had been first regularly extinguished by the Government itself, nor would the Government in any manner, direct or indirect, warrant or tolerate private individuals or companies in buying or conquering lands from the Indians. Such rights and all others affecting the control over Indian relations, it always retained to itself and vigilantly guarded as a high and incommunicable prerogative.

This bare statement of what the two systems were shows the ineffable superiority of the British over the Spanish in point of justice, good morals, wisdom, and humanity. And to the latest times, upright and enlightened natures among us will continue, when recalling the harrowing scenes through which even Anglo-America had to pass in her long process of colonization and settlement, to find an exalted satisfaction in remembering the correct and humane maxims towards the Indians practised by our great ancestral nation, and handed down by her to us as a part of that blessed national inheritance which war, revolution and the rending of all the ties of national unity were not able to cause us to surrender or lose. Nor let it be forgotten that the advantage of observing these maxims was always mutual and eminently reciprocal between us and the Indians. Whilst they were rendered thereby more secure against the intrusions and outrages of bad and lawless white people, our frontiers were at the same time more exempt from Indian incursions and depredations, and our whole country from the horrors and calamities of Indian wars.

Right here then at this point the first great damning feature of the Yazoo crime presents itself to view in its violations of these benign, long consecrated principles of our Indian policy—principles so dear to peace, righteousness and humanity in our relations with the Indians, of such pervading and perpetual importance, and so much demanding uniform and universal enforcement, that the makers of our new Federal Constitution deemed it their duty to incorporate them in that great instrument among the trusts exclusively assigned to the General Government. And there they have ever since been preserved, wrapped up in the great powers of war and peace, the treaty making power and the power to regulate commerce with the Indian tribes. Nor did the new Government after getting into operation long defer the necessary legislation for giving full effect to these inherent principles of the Constitution. And moreover such was the estimation in which Georgia herself soon came to hold these principles, that when Gen. Jackson and his compatriots in 1798 undertook the work of framing a new Constitution for the State, warned by the then recent Yazoo enormity and determined to take away the possibility of its repetition, they took care to insert in that Constitution a prohibition against the sale of any of the State's Indian territory to individuals or companies, unless after the Indian right thereto should have been extinguished and the territory formed into counties.

Grossly disregardful, however, of these great and sacred principles the Legislature of Georgia unhappily showed itself to be on two occasions during the period of the early immaturity of the State. Men not of us, men from abroad, many of them of fair, some of them of high name, had long had their avaricious gaze fixed on Georgia's vast and fertile

Indian domain (great speculations in wild lands were a fashion and a rage in those days) and they had conspired with self-seeking, influential persons among our own people to enrich themselves by despoiling the State of it on a huge scale. For years they had stood on the watch for a favorable moment for taking hold. The main cause which had kept them back was the unsettled state of the title, which was in strong dispute between South Carolina and Georgia, and they cared not to have to treat with two contending States, or to buy from either what was contested and claimed by the other. At length by the convention of Beaufort, in April, 1787, this dispute was settled in favor of Georgia, and its settlement would have been the signal for an open, energetic movement of the land-seekers on our very next Legislature but for the fact that an exceedingly formidable competitor appeared on the carpet, whom it was deemed best first to dispose of and get out of the way. This competitor was none other than the Continental Congress itself, which some years before had made earnest appeals to the States owning Indian lands to cede them to the United States as a fund for paying the Revolutionary debt. Georgia not having made any response to these appeals, Congress, in October, 1787, at its first session after the Beaufort Convention, urgently called upon her again to follow the magnanimous example of Virginia and other States and make the much desired cession. The Legislature in February ensuing, responded to the call, but how? Why, by offering to make a cession confined to the territory south of the Yazoo line, the part most compromised by the litigous pretentions of Spain, as we shall hereafter see, and that offer, too, clogged with conditions impossible to be accepted by Congress. Whereupon the offer being rejected and certain modifications proposed by that Body which would make it acceptable, those modifications were transmitted to the next Legislature, that of 1789, for its consideration and action. But no action whatever did it take in regard to them. There can be no doubt that the unworthy course pursued by the Legislature of 1788 in making an offer that was obliged to be rejected, and the equally unworthy conduct of the Legislature of 1789, in not considering and acceding to the modifications proposed by Congress, were the result of the bad inspiration and influence of the Yazoo speculators who, as yet, stood cloaked and in the dark as a secret organization. One thing is certain, that by some untold means, both the competition of Congress and its proposals were smothered and thrust out of the way, and the speculators succeeded in getting the field clear and wholly to themselves, free from all competition.

Of the advantages they thus had they made very successful use in dealing with the petty diminutive Legislature of that era, numbering only eleven Senators and thirty-four Representatives. History records not, that they had any difficulty in outdoing Congress in its suit for the lands, and in getting for themselves the first Yazoo sale, that of 1789, although their success being at the cost of gross incivism and supplanting of their country, brought them no small store of dishonor, and added new ingredients to the other elements of guilt to which we have adverted in their conduct.

By that piece of Legislation the State sold by metes and bounds and on a credit of two years, to the South Carolina Yazoo Company lands estimated at five millions of acres, for $66,964; to the Virginia Yazoo Company, lands estimated at seven millions of acres, for $93,741; to the Tennessee Company, lands estimated at three and a half millions of acres, for $46,785; amounting in all to fifteen and a half millions, though as now well known exceeding that quantity by many millions of acres. All these lands, (among the best and most desirable on the Continent) lay far to the West, on the waters of the Mississippi, the Great Tennessee, the Tombigby, and their tributaries, and had always been and were still Indian Territory in the undisputed possession of several powerful and by no means very friendly Indian tribes, to whom different portions of it belonged, the Creeks, Cherokees, Choctaws and Chickasaws. In addition to which Indian occupancy, Spain was disputing with the United States the title to the whole of these lands, and vastly more, and an intense territorial quarrel was then pending between the two countries as to the ownership and sovereignty of the same.

No sooner, nevertheless, had the bargain been made with the Legislature than the three Companies determined to proceed at once to selling and settling the lands they had respectively bought, regardless of Indian rights and of the effect on our relations and negotiations with Spain. To this course of conduct they were influenced as well by necessity as by choice. For except by immediate sales, they had no means of raising money wherewith to pay Georgia for the lands; which, if they failed to do, within the prescribed time of two years, the lands were to revert at once to the State, and their whole speculation would come to nothing.

It is remarkable that Georgia took no notice at all of these mischievous possessory movements of the Yazoo Companies. The sale to them had by some means, long sunk into oblivion, glided through the Legislature in silence, at least without making any noise or meeting with any opposition that has come down to us either by history or tradition. And now the seizure and disposal of the lands by the purchasing companies under that sale, was on the point of taking place just as silently and with quite as little opposition, so far at least as the State was concerned.

Washington, however, was on the alert and fully awake to the case and to the lawless, unconstitutional and dangerous character of all these doings: Lawless, because in violation of the aforementioned well settled maxims in our Indian policy: Unconstitutional, because at war with those wise provisions of the Federal compact, which confided the whole subject to Federal management: Dangerous also in a high degree, because big with four great Indian wars, or rather with one Indian war with four formidable tribes at one time, backed by Spain to boot: Dangerous again, because seriously embarrassing and imperiling our aforesaid already critical negotiations with Spain. Against the whole thing therefore Washington took a most decided stand. He issued his proclamation strongly denouncing and forbidding all intrusion on the Indian lands under any pretenses or claims whatever by the Yazoo purchasers, or any other persons. He brought the military as well as the civil arm to bear to defeat the contemplated settlements, and happily succeeded in breaking up and dissipating the whole project without tinging the drawn sword with a drop of blood. The result was that both our Indian and Spanish relations were kept in their same state and suffered no detriment.

The Companies, thus thwarted in seizing, selling and settling the Indian lands they had bought for less than a cent an acre, were at their wit's end. Their two years credit was rapidly expiring, and they knew not how or where to get the money to pay the State. Two hundred and odd thousand dollars was a large sum to raise in those days in coin or in any good money. They could not raise it. They were consequently driven to the shift of gathering up and tendering as payment the nearly worthless paper currency of the times, which being rejected and the issuance of titles refused, they sued the State in the Federal Court—which suits were soon brought to an abrupt close by an Amendment of the Federal Constitution, declaring that the Federal Judiciary had no jurisdiction to entertain suits against a State.

Thus ended the first Yazoo Sale, a glaring attempt on a large scale to introduce here by the action of Georgia and under her patronage, the vicious Spanish-American mode of private seizure and conquest of Indian countries. For the Legislative act of sale, when probed to the bottom and scanned through its thin translucent pretenses, amounted to nothing short of an intentional license granted for a price to the Companies to go and take at their own cost and charges, the lands they had bought. It even affects a dishonorable uncertainty of their being any Indians "on or near" those lands, and takes the hypocritical precaution of providing that if there should be any, the grantees should "forbear all hostile attacks on them" (not, be it noted, all intrusion on their territory) which the grantees would be very apt to interpret in their own favor as not depriving them of the right of repelling Indian attacks on their peaceably disposed new settlements. A war of defense against the Indians, being thus initiated, might of course be kept up and prosecuted, the grantees would argue, until peace and security were perfectly achieved, that is to say, until the Indians were well subdued and their lands vested in the conquerors.

Such was too much the logic and ethics toward the Indians of that period of mingled dread and exasperation in Georgia. But even if it had been otherwise, and the prohibitory words in the Legislative Act had been meant by the State in the largest imaginable good faith and kind sense towards the Indians and their rights, still they were unavoidably mere empty, ineffective words. For what chance was there for Georgia to make good her prohibition in those remote savage wilds over which she had never extended her Government, where she had not a man at her command, and where besides she could not go herself in any garb, civil or military, without instantly getting an Indian war upon her hands? For hard would it have been to make the Indians believe that a people who had sold their country to bands of speculators, had come thither as *their* friends to protect them against those speculators, and not as their enemies and the accomplices of their robbers. Thus there was no possibility whatever of the State enforcing her prohibition, even if she had meant it in ever so good faith. And as a right without a remedy is worthless, so this prohibition being without means or ability on the part of the State to enforce it, was a mere mockery, especially when, as here, an open door and strong temptation was offered for its violation. That the Companies regarded the matter in this light is clear enough from the fact already stated, that they began immediately taking steps for seizing, selling and settling the lands. Indeed the measures of two of them for this purpose, the Tennessee and South Carolina Yazoo, enlisting the hardy pioneers of Kentucky, Tennessee and the lower Mississippi in their enterprise, were openly military and warlike. And the fact that the Government of Georgia never in any way forbade, discountenanced or frowned upon their proceedings, is unanswerable proof that those proceedings were in unison with the secret spirit and intent of the Yazoo Sale, though feebly and insincerely disowned by its letter. The State being thus worse than delinquent, her own people and the whole country were left, as we have seen, to be indebted to the Federal Executive alone for the thwarting of the first Yazoo iniquity and the prevention of the chaos of crime, mischief and misery it carried in its bosom.

SECTION III.

All the imputations that have thus been seen to lie at the door of the Yazoo affair of 1789, apply more strongly and with a great addition of guilt to the much worse case of January, 1795, infamously distinguished as the Yazoo Fraud proper, and to which we are now coming—a case rendered worse not only by the crime being of more collossal proportions and accomplished by fouler means, but also by its having been perpetrated in the face of a solemn warning against it furnished by the history and fate of its less monstrous predecessor—perpetrated, moreover, in defiance of the august quarter from whence that warning had proceeded. But notwithstanding the intenser criminality with which this later Yazoo affair was thus chargeable, it had a bright side in one respect for the honor of Georgia. It brought out the strongest possible proof that her people would not endure turpitude in their public affairs. No sooner was the deed of shame consummated in their Legislature, than they rose up in their vengeance against both the deed and its doers, nor stayed their hand till the wicked work was undone and the character of the State vindicated. Assuredly, in the annals of no community, can be found a more striking and redeeming resentment and uprising of the people against a great political wickedness than our ancestors exhibited in this instance. And let it be borne in mind that it was an uprising not less against the iniquity of the thing itself, than against the bad means by which it was accomplished, which were unknown at first and only brought to light after the storm began to rage. Should it be asked what caused the conduct of Georgia on this occasion to be so different from what it had been in the similar case of 1789,—the clear answer is, that the difference was owing to the effect which Washington's stern course and true teaching in 1789 had produced on the minds of our people. That effect had been to correct whatever was wrong in their earlier ideas on the subject, and to awaken and educate them to right views and a just sense of their duty touching it,—thereby making it quite impossible that any such like villainy should again ever prosper in their midst for want of opposition, or find at any stage the slightest toleration at their hands.

The consequence was, that when the new cohorts of speculation rallied and took the field in 1793, full of confidence and sanguine of being able to seize and carry off the prize that had by that time fully dropped from the hands of the preceding band of land-jobbers, they were destined to a signal repulse. The Legislature of that year proved itself staunch and altogether impregnable to their designs.*

Of course, they fretted sorely under the unexpected disappointment, and it was whilst thus fretting and occupied in laying their plans for securing a better result whenever they should enter upon another attempt, that they were suddenly bestirred and hurried in the matter by certain very important confidential intimations from the National Capital. These came from General James Gunn, who was not only one of the chiefs of their enterprise, but was also their especial watchman and spy in the United States Senate of which he was an unworthy member from Georgia, and were to the effect that, through his opportunities as a Senator, he

American State Papers, Public Lands, Vol. 1, 147.—*Flournoy's Affidavit.*

knew beyond doubt that our territorial negotiations with Spain were drawing to a close, and would soon end by her fully surrendering to us her claims to all the so-called Yazoo country,—indeed, to all she had ever claimed against us East of the Mississippi: That therefore there was no time to be lost by the associated speculators, and that it was indispensable that their scheme of purchase should be pushed at all hazards, and by all expedients, fair or foul, through the next Legislature:—For that after this Spanish cloud, that had for more than a dozen years overhung and darkened the title of Georgia and given a handle for calumniating and cheapening her immense landed wealth, should be dissipated, as it now soon would be, all prospect would be gone of their ever being able to buy these immense regions from her for the trifling price on which they had fixed their expectations,—if, indeed, the purchase could be made on any terms, —a thing exceedingly doubtful, considering the great reaction of opinion as to the value of the lands that was sure to result from the Spanish riddance that was now imminent, combined with the permanent and general Indian pacification which would be its certain speedy consequence.

These revelations had a strong effect on the Yazooists, not unlike in one respect that produced on the Rothschilds by their twenty-four hours' soonest intelligence from the fatal field of Waterloo, in June, 1815. Activity was marvelously quickened in both cases. The great money-lenders and money-controllers of the world, the pecuniary patrons of kings and governments and ever vigilant speculators on the vastest scale in their debts and securities, astounded the London Exchange for one whole day by the magnitude and multiplicity of their operations, to which none could find the clue till the next morning. So not until the treaty of San Lorenzo was concluded in October, 1795, and made known to the country, was it fully understood what had impelled the Yazoo companies to press their nefarious project on the preceding Legislature with such desperate energy, and such costly, unstinted corruption. Then, indeed, the cause stood out in clear light and became obvious to every body—it being plainly seen what great and just reason they had for fearing that the last chance was in hand they were likely ever to have for cheaply getting hold of the priceless landed empire on which they were villainously intent, and which, whilst they saw the General Government on the point of freeing from its Spanish entanglement, they also saw it, at the same time, still suing for to Georgia on behalf of that noble national object,—the payment of the Revolutionary Debt.

Of the pestilent territorial claims of Spain that gave rise to this entanglement and which have so often started up in our path, complicated, first, with our Indian Affairs and the Oconee war, as we have heretofore shown at length, and then, also, with that monstrous Yazoo iniquity which we are now handling, furnishing to the banded speculators a reason of their own for being in such eager hurry to buy up the State's Western lands, and giving them at the same time a cherished pretext for decrying their title and value, it will be well here to take a rapid, comprehensive review, although at the cost of being carried far back into Revolutionary and pre-Revolutionary times. For such a review ample apology, it strikes me, will be found in its general affinity to the early history of Georgia as well as in the light it is calculated to shed on the Yazoo Fraud.

RETROSPECT OF THE SPANISH TITLE.

North America was long an arena of strife for dominion between France, Spain and England. France having at an early day seized upon the shores of the St. Lawrence, based thereupon a claim not only to the frozen realms adjacent and the immense icy regions further North, but also to those more genial climes spreading out behind the mountains from the margins of the Great Lakes to the heads of the tributaries of the Mississippi; along which great river she planted also that grandest of her colonies, Louisiana, under whose shadow she asserted herself sole sovereign of the mighty stream and all its sequacious waters and almost boundless dependant lands from its mouth to its source on both sides. Spain had posted herself along the Gulf of Mexico from the waters of the Mobile to the Southern Atlantic, and from thence shot up her claims perpendicularly and indefinitely to the North, interpenetrating those of France and England. The latter power stood thrust as it were between the two others, occupying the entire Ocean front from the Canadas to Florida. But westwardly she paid no respect at all to the exorbitant claims of her neighbors, coolly ignoring and overriding them with still more exorbitant claims of her own. Quite regardless of their airy conflicting pretensions, she boldly projected the long lines of colony after colony, among the rest of South Carolina and Georgia, across the Continent from the Atlantic to the South Sea, as the Pacific was then called.

This state of things was almost obliged to result sooner or later in war. For how else could these omniverous competitors for the mastery of the new world be quieted among themselves and have their litigious limits adjusted? It came at length, a tripartite struggle between the three Powers, memorable for its great territorial consequences, for the mournful defeat and fall of the proud Braddock in the depths of an Indian wilderness, and for its sadly glorious crowning scene—Wolfe's heroic death clasped in the arms of victory on the heights of Abraham. It was a great seven years war and gradually, after our own more famed war of the Revolution, came to be called by our ancestors the old French war. It lasted till 1763, when it was brought to a close by the treaty of Paris, concluded in February of that year. That treaty was France's death blow in North America. By it she lost to England the Canadas and the whole North, and also all of Lousiana on the eastern side of the Mississippi down to the 31st parallel of latitude. To Spain she lost all the rest of Louisiana on both sides of the Mississippi, and was thus literally expelled from the Continent. Then England yielded up in favor of Spain all her

Trans-Mississippi pretensions and accepted that river as her western boundary ; and Spain on her part transferred to England, Florida, embracing under that name all that she had previously to the war claimed East of the Mississippi.

And now we come to divers facts important in the territorial controversy that subsequently arose between the United States and Spain and having, through that controversy a bearing on the Yazoo Fraud. Among which facts it is first to be noted that under the Spanish rule, all Florida had been but one Province with large limits stretching up towards the North indefinitely, as has just been observed, and adverse both to England and France. Great Britain, upon Florida becoming hers, changed this thing. She divided the one province into two, East and West Florida, and fixed their northern boundary. That of East Florida she made to begin at the junction of the Flint and Chattahoochee, running from thence to the head of the St. Mary's, and following the course of that river to the sea. That of West Florida, with which alone we are now concerned, she made to begin on the Chattahoochee river where the 31st parallel of latitude strikes it, and to follow that parallel to the Mississippi.

Had Great Britain allowed this line to remain unaltered, had she thought proper, during her brief domination, to let alone this, her first fixation of the Northern boundary of West Florida, very different from what actually took place would have been many subsequent circumstances and events in relation to a vast and interesting region. In the first place, had this line of the thirty-first parallel remained undisturbed, that Spanish claim of title afterwards so earnestly urged against the United States for all the country between the Chattahoochee and the Mississippi lying above that parallel, would have lacked its only plausible foundation, and in all likelihood would never have been brought forward. Consequently, that Spanish Protectorate of the Indians and interference with them against us, which originated wholly out of this claim of title, would never have occurred. It is altogether probable likewise that the Yazoo Fraud itself might never have been hatched, and in case it had been, it is almost certain it would have failed of successful accomplishment. For the litigious state of the title between our country and Spain was the main root from which it sprang, inspiring, as we have seen, a hope of achieving the vast purchase, or champerty rather, at very little cost. How adroitly the Yazooists intermingled insinuations against the title of Georgia with the arts of bribery, corruption and influence with which they prosecuted their purchase before the Legislature, needs not to be told in detail here. Verily, it required the combined force of these and all other base means they could command, to effect the passage of their monstrous scheme.—And then, furthermore, had Great Britain never changed this line, the very word Yazoo would have remained in its original obscurity, nor would ever have been raised into notoriety, nor fastened as a name on a large and interesting portion of the earth's surface.

But Great Britain, in the course of a few years was led, by reasons not now worth emunerating, to make a great change of the line as at first established by her,—a change destined to be prolific of no little strife between her two conquering successors, Spain and the United States. Carrying the Northern boundary of West Florida much further up, she made it to start from the Mississippi at the mouth of the Yazoo and to run from thence due East to the Chattahoochee, striking the latter river not far from what is now West Point. Naturally, this line soon became famous as the new upper boundary of British West Florida, and it got to be familiarly known as the Yazoo line, and the country above and below it to an indefinite extent came to be called the Yazoo country. Wherefore, upon the subsequent reconquest of British West Florida by Spain, which took place in May, 1781, it is not strange that Spain should have claimed, as she did, to have become the owner, by virtue of that conquest, of all the country bearing the name of British West

Florida, that is, of all South of the Yazoo line. But not content with this, she went much further, and without either logic or justice on her side, extended her pretensions to all the territory on the North of the line to which the vague name of Florida had of old been applied by her, asserting that she was remitted to her ancient claims there also by her reconquest of West Florida, although British West Florida did not reach so far up. From the foregoing it is seen how it happened that the vast region of which we are discoursing acquired the name of Yazoo, and why in the first legislative sale, that of 1789, the two main purchasing companies took Yazoo (the word not having yet become obnoxious) as part of their name and were called the Virginia Yazoo and the South Carolina Yazoo Companies. Hence, also, in the act of 1795, although all four of its companies eschewed the now tainted name and it was not allowed to occur in the law from the beginning to the end, yet it continued to stick like the shirt of Nessus, and neither the lands, the law, the companies, the enacting Legislature; nor anything else connected with the transaction have ever been able to this day to get rid of the abhorred designation.

It was more than a dozen years after the establishment of this Yazoo line by Great Britain that the important event occurred to which we have just above adverted, namely, the Spanish reconquest of West Florida from that power in May, 1781, a date at which our Revolutionary war was yet in "mid volley,"—eighteen months before the provisional, and more than two years before the definitive treaty of Peace, Limits and Independence between the mother country and the United States. This reconquest was a long premeditated thing with Spain. All the while after the treaty of Paris, she had been ill at ease under the loss of Florida, for which she had never felt that Great Britain's relinquishment of her shadowy claims West of the Mississippi deserved to be called an indemnity, or was anything more than a mere empty salvo to Spanish pride. She had been constantly on the watch, therefore, for an opportunity of revenge and reseizure, and found it at last, so far as West Florida was concerned, by leaping on Great Britain while she was oppressed by a tripple war with her rebellious colonies, and their French allies and the unallied Dutch. Never was conquest more complete and unequivocal, the British Governor, Chester, making an absolute surrender of the province and retiring with the British Forces and functionaries, and leaving everything in the hands of the victorious Spaniards. Nor was there ever any attempt at recapture.

The effect was that, *as between Great Britain and Spain,* all British West Florida from the Gulf up to the Yazoo line became undoubtedly Spanish, nor was there aught left to England within that space capable of being conveyed by her in any way to the United States or any other power.

And yet what in fact did England do? Here is what she did: By both the aforementioned treaties, provisional and definitive, she ceded the whole country, as well below as above the Yazoo line, to the United States down to the 31st parallel, wholly disregarding the aforesaid Spanish reconquest. And what is stranger still, she did on the very day she made this definitive cession to the United States, to-wit, on the 3d day of September, 1783, enter into a conflicting treaty with Spain conveying in full right to her East and West Florida, without saying one word about their boundaries, leaving Spain consequently at liberty and in a position to contend for whatever boundaries she pleased against us.

Behold here what a wanton bequest of territorial dispute and quarrel our chagrined and vanquished Mother country threw at parting into the laps of the United States and Spain.:—A bequest, too, which, so far as related to the region South of the Yazoo line, seemed at first glance decidedly to throw the advantage on the side of Spain and against this country. But it was only at the first glance that it had that seeming. For upon close scrutiny it became clear that the United States were entitled to go *behind* these conflicting treaties into which Britian had entered with Spain and ourselves, and to treat the one made with us as being not so much a *cession or the source of our title* as an acknowledgement by the mother country of our pre-existing rights and boundaries acquired, sword in hand, by successful war and our Declaration of Independence. By this mode of viewing the subject (and it is certainly the true one), our territorial rights and limits recognized by the treaty of 1783 are made to relate back and take effect from a date anterior to the Spanish conquest of 1781, and to be superior consequently to the Spanish claim founded on that conquest, just as our Independence itself is to be regarded not as a grant or concession from Great Britain, but as a right acknowledged by her to be already ours, conquered by war and dating back to the 4th of July 1776. We see thus that revolution and the sword are the true fountain head from which we trace in this case our territorial title and boundaries as well as our blood-purchased right of self-government:—Of both which the above mentioned British treaties with us are to be considered but as a recognition and settlement.

Such is the principle, not the less sound because a little subtle, which comes to our rescue, supplanting in our favor the Spanish claim of title to all that part of the contested territory lying South of the Yazoo line. It is not surprising, however, that Spain should have been exceedingly averse to yielding up so fine and large a region on so fine a point as this. But when she went further, and upon the ground of having conquered British West Florida, overstepped the Yazoo line and advanced pretensions to an immense country which had never been embraced in that province, no wonder the American Continent grew impatient and almost lost respect for a power that juggled in this manner for more than it could with decency claim.

Thus, upon comparison of the two titles, Spanish and Georgian, as they stood previously to the treaty of San Lorenzo, that of Georgia on which alone the United States relied and triumphed in their negotiations with Spain, is found to be prior in time and consequently stronger in point of right (*prior tempore, ergo portior jure,*) than the Spanish title; both being founded on conquest from Great Britain and our conquest being the oldest of the two by nearly five years. But even supposing the title of Spain, though vanquished in her diplomatic strife with our country, to have been in reality better than that of Georgia by means of which the United States vanquished it, yet the United States would be precluded after the victory from assuming an altered language and denying the superiority and validity of the title of Georgia under which that victory had been won. For Governments no more than individuals, after conquering under a flag, whether of war or of words, have a right to turn upon it and rend it. The wise and beneficent principle of *estoppel* so well known in law and so sacred to peace, honor and the repose of rights and property, here comes into play, and not only forbade the United States from setting up the vanquished Spanish title in opposition to that of Georgia, but furthermore required that this vanquished title should not be allowed in the hands of the United States to have the effect of vesting any right whatever, against Georgia, but should be made to enure, for whatever it might be worth, to her benefit alone, and to the perfect clearing and firm establishment of her right and title.

SECTION IV.

Such is a condensed account of the Spanish title and of its eventual surrender to the United States who were contestants against it under the elder and better title of Georgia. The leagued speculators forewarned by Gen. Gunn, knew, as we have seen, as early as 1794, how certain and near at hand this surrender was, and by the many able and distinguished men whom they counted in their ranks, (among whom were prominent politicians, eminent jurists and learned judges;) they were all the while kept well enlightened as to the manner in which this surrender whenever it should happen, would work; that it would enure, as we have above stated, to the benefit of Georgia and to the disembarrassment of her right in and to the immense territory they were seeking to purchase from her. But whilst their confidence in the clear title of what they were aiming to buy from Georgia was thus perfect and free from doubt, they dreaded not a little the enhanced estimation of the lands and other difficulties which they foresaw rising up in their path in case they should fail to consummate their purchase in advance of the coming Spanish cession. Among those other difficulties was the ever haunting danger from the patriotic competition of the United States government. For though they had succeeded in triumphing over it in 1789, they saw it again starting up and all the while threatening them. To which when we add the vast unprincipled cupidity by which they were devoured and the mania then widely prevalent for speculating in wild lands, we behold the reasons which stimulated the Yazooists to the hurried and profligate efforts of which they were now guilty in order to grasp, while they might, an enormous prize which they apprehended would not remain long within their reach.

These efforts they consequently commenced making very soon, not waiting even for the meeting of the Legislature. For months beforehand, the ringleaders and their most wily, trusted accomplices were hard at work to secure success from that body when it should assemble. They kept, however, a thick veil over their machinations. It was quite unknown to the public how they were busied. Little was it supposed that they were industriously occupied in perfecting their schemes, in tampering with the elections to the Legislature, in enlisting men of influence far and wide, and in getting up funds for the purpose of corruption and paying for the lands. Even upon the assembling of the Legislature in November, no siege was at first laid; no lobby showed itself; no demonstration of any sort was for sometime made. Every thing was kept still, quiet, unsuspected, awaiting a very significant, pre-arranged, auxiliary event, namely, the re-election of Gen. Gunn for another six years to the United States Senate, which was no sooner accomplished than it was hailed everywhere by his associates as a great preliminary triumph, and an auspicious prelude to the grand Yazoo campaign, which was now at once boldly opened at Augusta under the leadership of Gunn himself, robed in all the bravery of his renewed Senatorial dignity—A dignity basely sought by him on this occasion with the direct intention of prostituting its great influence to the shame and betrayal of the people who honored him, and to the vile enrichment of himself and his confederates, who had not over estimated the importance of his election to their cause, rightly judging that a Legislature which should re-elect such a man to so noble a station would not be found proof against the augmented bad influence with which they had thereby armed him, nor be beyond the reach of those arts of corruption that were pre-determined to be exerted by himself and his co-workers, who took it for granted from their failure at the preceding session that such arts would have to be employed in order to success now.*

Quickly then upon Gunn's re-election the veil was entirely thrown off by the Yazooists and four great land companies developed themselves that had evidently been already organized and in waiting for that signal. These companies soon perceived that in playing the part of competitors against one another they would be greatly in each other's

*Extract from Mr. Randolph's speech on the Yazoo claims in the House of Representatives of the United States, January 31st, 1805: "There is another fact, too little known, but unquestionably true, in relation to this business. The scheme of buying up the Western territory of Georgia did not originate there. It was hatched in Philadelphia and New York (and I believe in Boston, of this, however, I am not certain), and the funds by which it was effected were principally furnished by monied capitalists in those towns. The direction of these resources devolved chiefly on the Senator (Gunn), who has been mentioned. Too wary to commit himself to writing, he and his associates agreed upon a countersign. His re-election was to be considered as evidence that the temper of the Legislature of Georgia was suited to their purpose and his Northern confederates were to take their measures accordingly. In proof of this fact, no sooner was the news of his re-appointment announced in New York than it was publicly said in a coffee house there, "Then the Western territory of Georgia is sold."—*Benton Ab. of Congressional Debates, Vol. III, p.* 331.

way and that by combining their resources and influence they would almost certainly be able to control the Legislature to their purposes. They hastened accordingly to enter into a coalition, the parties to which, more grasping than their predecessors of 1789, resolved on seizing and partitioning among themselves all the immense country from the Alabama and Coosa in the East and the Mississippi in the West, and from the Northern boundary of Georgia along the 35th parallel down nearly to her Southern limit on the 31st degree of latitude—a region of surpassing natural advantages and comprising some forty or fifty millions of acres of what was mostly very fertile land in a very fine climate, every where well watered and abounding in good navigable rivers.

Over the proposals and efforts of the combined speculators to buy this almost imperial expanse the State's unworthy representatives higgled and hesitated for some time, not, as the upshot showed, in order to obtain a better price for the State, but with a view only to bigger bribes for themselves. At length, paid to their own full satisfaction for their votes, they sold the whole coveted region at one "fell swoop" of legislation for the sum of $500,000 to the four leagued companies, the purchase money being apportioned among them as also were the lands, according to their own wishes and dictation; the State getting one-fifth of the money in hand and receiving mortgages on the lands themselves for the remainder, which was fully paid before the expiration of a stipulated credit of ten months. The Georgia Company was the leviathan of the coalition, paying just one-half of the gross amount of the purchase money, $250,000, the Georgia-Mississippi Company paying $155,000, the Upper Mississippi Company, $35,000, and the Tennessee Company, $60,000, each getting by metes and bounds lands proportioned to their respective payments.

In this gigantic transaction we behold shamelessness and audacity, falsity and artifice vying with the pecuniary corruption by which it was disgraced. For instance, the Legislature had the hardihood, as we are informed in the preamble to the Rescinding Act, to accept this price of $500,000 in the face of a proposition by other parties equally reliable to pay $800,000, which was refused for no better reason than the smaller bribes, or perhaps the no bribes, by which it was backed. How grateful the bare idea that the failure of these higher bidders was owing to their virtue! Moreover, also, during the time the measure was on hand the speculators grossly misrepresented the amount of the lands they were seeking to buy, pretending that they amounted to not more than 21,000,000 or 22,000,000 of acres.* After the bargain was clinched they quickly made the discovery that they had gotten at least 40,000,000 acres. And then the pretense set up in the Act of a necessity to sell these lands in order to raise funds to pay the State troops and to extinguish the Indian title to lands lying elsewhere, is transparently false and hypocritical on the very face of the law. Further still, among the numerous badges of fraud and villainy by which the case is deformed, not the least remarkable is that these great territories were clandestinely sold, as it were, by the Legislature without any notice whatever having been given to the public that they were for sale.

*In the debate on the Yazoo Claims in January, 1805, in the House of Representatives, Mr. Lucas, of Virginia, said:

"It ought to be observed that the four land companies, who are original purchasers under the Act of the Legislature of Georgia, passed on the 7th of January, 1795, stated in their petition containing their proposal to the Legislature to purchase certain lands belonging to the State of Georgia, that the lands contained within the bounds which were described in their petition amounted to 21,750,000 acres It was evidently upon the faith of this statement that the Legislature consented to sell that land for $500,000. However, it is now ascertained that the quantity of land thus described amounts to 35,000,000 acres and the companies themselves compute it to be near 40,000,000. From this it appears evidently that the companies have deceived the Legislature by stating what was not true. * * * * *

"The Legislature have consequently sold twice as much land as they intended to sell, or which is the same thing, they have sold it one-half cheaper than it was their intention, and all this loss is the result of the false statement given by the land companies."—*Benton's Ab. of Congressional Debates, Vol. III, p.* 323.

But in order to see this Yazoo affair in its full turpitude, it is necessary to advert to another law enacted at the same session. I mean the Act passed for the purpose of making provision for paying with Indian lands the State Troops for their services in defending the State in the Indian war which had been so long pending and which, indeed, was not yet perfectly terminated. This law authorizes Surveys and Head Rights in favor of the citizen soldiers to be located on lands yet in the occupancy of Indians lying in the Tallassee country and to the South of the Oconee. Such and so thorough, however, was the change of ideas that had been wrought among the people of Georgia by the policy and principles of Washington as displayed and enforced in his warfare against the Yazoo sale of 1789, that whatever they may have previously thought on the subject, they now certainly disclaimed all right of entering themselves or of authorizing by their laws and grants, others to enter on the Indian lands within the limits of the State until the Indian title should be first extinguished and the consent of the general Government given. Accordingly in this State Troops Act, care was taken to insert a clause declaring that the Act was not to go into operation until after the extinction of the Indian title, and in regard to the Tallassee country, not until after obtaining the consent of the General Government. Such were the restrictions the Legislature felt bound to put into a Law appropriating Indian lands for so favorite an object as that of compensating our citizen soldiers.

But when it came to the Yazoo Law and the selling of a realm of Indian territory to gangs of profligate speculators for almost nothing in comparison with its value, a mighty change comes over the Legislature. It now no longer gave heed to the principles and policy of Washington. There is now no waiting for the extinguishment of the Indian title, or the consent of the General Government; no postponement of the operation of the Law for these or any other events. On the contrary the sale is absolute, immediate, unconditional, trammeled with no delays, contingencies or restrictions. In a word the restrictions studiously inserted in the State Troops law are as studiously left out here, and the door is intentionally left open for the State's bribing grantees and whoever might become their sub-purchasers to possess themselves, so far as the terms of the Law are concerned, of the Indian lands at their own pleasure and by their own arts and means. And in order to add strength to such their claim under the law and place it beyond cavil, recourse is had to an extraordinary and most discreditable Legislature trick—*A lying Title is prefixed to the Law.* It is falsely christened an "Act supplementary" to the State Troops Act. Thus, by forging the relation of principal and supplement between the two laws and thereby making them for all purposes of judicial interpretation one and the same law,. the construction was the more strongly necessitated that the insertion of the restrictions in the State Troops Law and their omission in the Yazoo Law was tantamount to their express exclusion from the latter, according to the universally recognized legal maxim, *Inculsio unius est exclusio elterius.* Behold here by what unworthy parliamentary legerdemain the Yazooists contrived to strengthen the argument of *their* exemption from restrictions demanded at once by righteousnesss and good policy and by the laws and constitution and treaties of the Union; restrictions also to which our meritorious citizen soldiers were subjected by the very same Legislature that in the very same breath exempted the Yazooists therefrom. Certainly we see here a device altogether worthy of the law-learning and technical artifice and skill which abounded in the Yazoo ranks ; a device moreover, which nothing but Yazoo corruption could have carried in triumph through the two Houses of the General Assembly and then through the Executive Branch of the Government also. For corruption must have found its way there too, if not directly to the very breast and pocket of the Governor, which we would fain hope was not the case, yet undoubtedly to those by whom he was advised and influenced.

It was the ill fate of Col. George Matthews to fill the Executive Chair at this date and to affix the signature that at once made the monstrous iniquity a law and fastened forever upon himself the character of a great public criminal. Vain would be any attempt to palliate his conduct, although there have been writers who ventured upon such attempt. The best that can be said in mitigation for him is that his entire action in the matter seemed to be the result as much of weakness as of wickedness, and excites our sorrow along with our anger whilst we are sternly consigning his name to dishonor. The heart cannot but feel some generous relenting towards this heroic, hard-fighting and thorough-going, though uncouth and unscholarly Revolutionary patriot and warrior, when we behold him elevated, after the close of the war, to a great political post for which he was wholly unfit and where he was destined almost certainly to fall a victim to his own utter incompetency and the misleading arts and influence of those around him on whom he was obliged helplessly to lean. The wounds received and the laurels won by such a man in the terrible days of his country's dangers and trials, "plead like angels, trumpet-tongued," in his favor ever afterwards, and cause us to look upon his worst political misdeeds with a gentleness of reprobation which we extend not to mere civilians and men who can show no blood-earned title to the public gratitude. But, nevertheless, Governor Matthews, in spite of this kindly popular feeling towards him and although no direct charge of being personally bribed and corrupted, so far as I ever heard, was at any time alleged against him, was politically ruined in Georgia by the odium of his official complicity with the Yazoo Fraud. It was enough for the people that by his single dissent he might have defeated that stupendous villainy and that he did not do it, but on the contrary gave it his assent and vitalized it with his signing hand. And besides there were other strongly exasperating circumstances against him. The two bills, the State Troops Act and that for the Yazoo Sale, were both before him for his signature at the same time. The former he signed and returned on the 28th of December. The latter he refused to sign and sent back with his objections on the same day. How it happened that so soon afterwards as the 7th of January he was gotten to forego all his objections and to sign another bill substantially the same, only enough altered to give him a pretext for saying that it was not the same but another bill, was never explained and naturally gave rise to deeply damaging surmises against him. And assuredly, moreover, his case was not bettered by the unhappy fact of his total neglect in his list of objections of the 28th of December, to take any notice of a matter so capital and striking as the omission in the Yazoo Bill of the above mentioned restrictions contained in the State Troops Act, which he had just examined and signed. His failure to notice and brand this omission cannot be viewed otherwise than as a mark of his sanction given to it at that time by *implication*, as afterwards it was *expressly* given when on the 7th of January, he finally signed the bill and made it a law.

The clue to the excessive anxiety we have noticed on the part of the Yazooists to have on the very face of their Legislation clear, merchantable titles, free from all restrictions or contingencies, is to be found in the fact that their scheme was designed from the beginning to be one of rapid sales and conversion into money, not of protracted ownership awaiting the extinction of the Indian title by government and the subsequent gradual increase of the value of the lands. It was in order that they might successfully carry out this scheme that they wanted a law which they could parade and bepraise in the markets of the world as giving a present absolute estate, not merely future contingent rights and expectations. With such a law and titles under it good and specious on the surface though well known to themselves to be in reality unsound and vulnerable to attack by both the United States and Georgia, they hoped to be rapidly able to succeed in alluring into large purchasing strangers and uninformed, distant people, that class who are always predestined as their victims by wicked, shrewd-contriving speculators.

But not only did these shrewd, enterprising speculators want and resolve to get *per fas aut per nefas*, titles that should be in all respects current and alluring in the land market, but they wanted all the world as a market for their immense and unrighteous landed wares. To this end, however, it was necessary to contrive some way of evading the law of Georgia disabling aliens to hold land in this State. And here agian it was deemed expedient not to drive at their object openly but to seek it by legislative indirection and trickery. Their cunning plan was to have a clause inserted in the very Act of Sale affecting a patriotic hostility to foreigners becoming owners of real estate in Georgia. By this clause the Yazoo purchasers and their associates are prohibited from disposing of the lands in part or in the whole, in any way or manner, "*to any foreign king, prince, potentate or power whatever.*" The palpable, precogitated object of inserting this clause was that the Yazoo companies should by *clear implication* be entitled to sell and convey to all other foreigners than the very few who fall under the description of "kings, princes, potentates and powers." And not only is this almost boundless license of selling to foreigners thus surreptitiously incorporated in the law, but it is also required to be set forth in the very face of the grants that were to be issued under the law to the companies, in order that foreigners might thereby be the more strongly tempted to become buyers, seeing that their right to buy was doubly secured both by the law itself and then by the State's grants and conveyances founded upon it. Fit companion-piece this to the villainous "supplementary" device to which it is appended and which we have but a moment ago had occasion to reprobate and brand!

SECTION V.

Not for more than three score years and ten, not indeed until a new and monstrous race of political caitiffs, foul harpies of the North, the vile brood of a peace worse than war, of a reconstruction worse than ruin, swarmed down upon our fair and hapless South and made it one vast sickening scene of official atrocity and villainy, securely practised under a remorseless Federal patronage, had the people of Georgia ever gotton over their vivid, loathing remembrance of this old Yazoo crime. Now, however, that renowned turpitude of the last century has been unseated from its preeminence. Far outstripped by the teeming infamies, political and pecuniary, of these latter times, it is no longer capable of exciting amazement in the recollecting mind. Little wonder is now felt that in young, immature Georgia, some eighty years ago, a gigantic, corrupt speculation, as remarkable for the ability and standing of the men concerned in it as for the abundance and baseness of the means they employed, should have succeeded in debauching and triumphing over a poorly enlightened and very diminutive legislative body of those early times.

Yes! very diminutive that body still was. For, although, by the formation of new counties the Senate had grown larger, still it consisted of only twenty members, every man of whom, save one, was in his seat on the final passage of the bill, and all voted except the President, Benjamin Taliaferro, ten for the law, eight against it. Had it been necessary for the President to vote, it is well known that he would have cast his vote in the negative, so that the measure really had a majority of but one in the Senate. In the lower House the number of members still remained at thirty-four, there being a peculiar provision in the new constitution against the number being increased by the creation of new counties. There were but twenty-nine members present, including the Speaker, Thomas Napier, who did not vote. Nineteen votes were given in the affirmative and only nine in the negative. It effected this, its second passage, through this body on the second of January, through the Senate on the third, and on the seventh Governor Matthews affixed his hesitating signature, and the atrocious deed was complete that has ever since resounded as a great shame in our history, blurring its virgin page, blighting every name implicated in it, and leaving more or less of blemish wherever a shadow of imputation connected with it has ever fallen. It required a mighty and multifarious effort to accomplish it. Many men and every sort of men and means were subsidized and yet the change of a single vote in the Senate would have defeated it as we have just seen and said.

I will not undertake to reproduce in detail here the revolting scenes of which Augusta was the theatre during that infamous session, when everything was venal, when the Legislative Halls were converted into shambles, and the honor of the State and the grandest public interests were shamelessly put up to open sale for the vile lucre-sake of traitorous Representatives and their corruptors. Reason abundant is there forsooth to deter from attempting such portrayal. For I hold no graphic pen, and then what pen could impart to those scenes aught of horrific effect or pungent interest nowadays, when men's minds have become seared by spectacles of the grossest depravity in the high as well as low places of the government passing continually before their eyes and passing not only without punishment but without shame or rebuke? Suffice it to say that every vote given for the law save one, that of Robert Watkins, was undeniably a corrupt vote purchased either with money or the gift of subshares in the speculation, or both. In aid moreover, of the measure, the active exertions and influence of men of weight and character out of the Legislature was in very many instances secured by similar means, or by prevailing on them to become interested on like terms with the original members of the companies. It is due, however, to the memory of numerous persons who became connected in this latter way with the speculation, seduced by the great and distinguished names of some leading men in it, to say that they were alike unknowing and incapable of the turpitude involved in the project, and that not a few, on their eyes being opened, instead of making haste after the example of their chiefs, to sell out and pocket their gains, repudiated the whole thing, receiving back subsequently under the provisions of the Rescinding Act of Georgia, the portions of the purchase money they had respectively contributed, whilst there were others who simply abandoned the pittance of one-fifth of the purchase money which it had devolved on them to pay. The report made on the 16th day of February, 1803, by Messrs. Madison, Gallatin and Lincoln, commissioners* under an Act of Congress for investigating the Yazoo claims, is accompanied with a long catalogue of the names of persons, Georgians and others, secondary as well as original purchasers, who had thus withdrawn their payments from the State Treasury, amounting in the aggregate to $310,695 15. Thus it appears that in this as in most cases where a great multitude of people are implicated, not only were there many different degrees of guilt, but those also were to be found who by their conduct eventually saved themselves from the reproach of knowingly persevering in crime.

In this connection, the honored name of Patrick Henry† comes strikingly up and claims some mention. Yielding to that rather too great greed for money which is said to have characterized him and not duly reflecting, it may be hoped, on the objections to the speculation, he became a leading member of the Virginia Yazoo Company of 1789. When, however, the heavy frowns and antagonism of Washington aroused his attention to the demerits and criminality of the project, he seems to have stopped short; at all events he allowed not himself to be connected with the subsequent Yazoo scheme, and is no more to be seen taking any part or

*American State Papers, Public Lands. Vol. 1, p. 200.

†American State Papers, Public Lands. Vol. 1, p. 132, 150.

interest in the thing, sought for although his great name was to give it sanction and enhance its chances of success. Happy for his imperishable fame, this rather narrow escape,* and that in him a strong sense of character and an almost exorbitant love of shining repute among men were sufficient checks against that mean passion for riches which was the bane of not a few public and official men in that day as well as in our own more impure times.

In painful contrast with this conduct of the illustrious patriot orator stands that of a number of conspicuous, contemporary characters whom, although clothed with public honors, neither that or any other consideration availed to restrain or reclaim from a career of turpitude and incivism into which they were drawn by the accursed thirst of gold. Their names, consequently, have found an unenviable berth in history, forever associated with the stench and stigma of the Yazoo Fraud. Nor do they deserve a better fate than that the more important among them at least should be recalled and gibbeted in these evil days of expiring public virtue and growing national vice and degeneracy. So may bad men, filling and betraying high public trusts, be taught what awaits them at the bar of posterity, however much they may flourish and prosper during their own base lives.

Behold, then, occupying a place among the most exalted national dignitaries of his day, and at the same time figuring in the van of this corrupt and corrupting speculation, James Wilson, of Pensylvania, a signer of the Declaration of Independence, a member for years of the old Continental Congress, a member also of the Convention that framed the Constitution of the United States and at this very time one of the Judges of the Supreme Court of the United States, appointed at the first organization of that great tribunal, the very tribunal before which he well knew might come, and before which eventually did come, though after his

*Narrow, indeed, for some detriment he actually sustained in public estimation in Virginia from his connection with the Yazoo business, notwithstanding his early disappearance from it. Wirt's Life of Patrick Henry; near the end.

death, the question of the validity of the title acquired by himself and his companions in this vast and profligate transaction. Behold this man stooping from his proud official elevation, bringing disrepute on the sublimest judicial Bench in the world, and becoming an active, leading partner interested to the extent of three quarters of a million of acres* in a foul, lawless, unpatriotic speculation of gigantic magnitude and wickedness. Behold him there not only mightily interested, but by that interest so demoralized as to become an industrious, bare-faced worker in the vile cause ;† behold him and from him learn how little assurance of purity the highest public station gives, and how little any official atmosphere is worth either as a safeguard or antidote against that moral poison for which poor human nature has such a lamentable affinity. Judge Wilson, unhappily, had run a long debasing career as a speculator, especially in Indian lands, dating back before the Revolutionary War, the proofs of which are to be found in the American State Papers by the petitions and memorials with which he, although a Judge of the Supreme Court, was not ashamed to importune Congress in behalf of Companies of speculators to which he belonged and of which he was the organ‡ :—speculators, too, whose claims had a worse than Spanish character and stood upon a worse than the Spanish principle, because wholly unsupported by that precedent, governmental warrant and authority, which even the Spanish system imperatively required. These circumstances in regard to the Judge were doubtless well known to persons connected with the speculation residing in Philadelphia, the Judge's home, and became well known to Gen. Gunn also, whilst serving in Congress there. Hence the early and too well received overtures that were made to him. It was a great point to the Yazooists to have gained such a man as Judge Wilson to their ranks, though for his own fame and

*American State Papers, Public Lands. Vol. 1, p 141.

†White's Statistics. p 50.

‡American State Papers, Public Lands, Vol. 1. p, 27, 72, 73. Sanderson's Lives of the Signers; Title, James Wilson.

the honor of the great tribunal in which he sat, it is to be lamented that instead of listening to the overtures that were made to him, he did not like our more than Roman Senator, Gen. James Jackson, firmly and indignantly repel them.

Side by side, fit yoke fellow with this Judge of the highest Federal Court, stands Nathaniel Pendleton, District Judge of the United States for the District of Georgia, who to his services as a lobbyist for the concern added those of chairman of the meetings of the coalitionists, signing and issuing as such the certificates for shares donated to the bribed members of the Legislature and the hirelings employed to buy and influence their votes. Of the nature and amount of his reward no trace is to be found, but that it was great in proportion to the dignity and sanctity of the ermine he soiled and to the baseness and importance of the services he rendered there can be no doubt.†

See, also, in the train of these two Federal Judges, their bold Aid-de-Camp, Mathew McAlister, District Attorney of the United States for Georgia, a leading member of the Georgia Company, one of the original grantees, who unlike the culprit Judges and some others, shrank not from having his name emblazoned on the face of the Act, where it stands opprobriously eternized, little advantaged by Gen. Jackson's consuming fire. See, also, William Stith, Judge of the Superior Courts of Georgia, and at that time there were but two such Judges and but two Circuits, the Eastern and the Western, to which the two Judges were equally elected and in which they had to preside by turns, thus bringing each Judge into every county of the State once a year in his judicial ridings. Judge Stith sold his great influence growing out of his office and these, his annual visitations all over the State, for $13,000 in money and some delusive hopes of the Governorship that were held out to him. The money he actually pocketed and found himself reproached afterwards

†American State Papers, Public Lands, Vol. I, p. 145, 147. White's Statistics, p. 50.

for not being generous with it to his poor relations.* His colleague in the Judgeship, the pure and upright George Walton, one of Georgia's immortal Signers, was incorruptible, and his name is a pride to the State forever, free from spot or blemish.

Stepping across the Savannah river, Colonel, afterwards General, Wade Hampton claims our attention as one of the imposing figures in the Yazoo group. He was a member elect to Congress from South Caorlina, a man, moreover, of high prestige from having been a gallant officer of the Revolution, distinguished now for his great wealth, his commanding position in society, his extraordinary energy, enterprise and capacity in affairs, all which necessarily made him a power wherever he put his hands or set his head. Behold this man, destined in after years to immense riches and to become widely famous as the most princely planter of all the South, and whom in his vigorous old age Mr. Madison honored by reproducing him on the field, first as a Brigadier General, in anticipation of a war with England, and then upon the breaking out of the war, as a Major General. But he was not more successful in adorning his gray hairs with new laurels than were the other Revolutionary veterans whom the President unluckily called from retirement and clothed with high command. The only distinction he won of which I am aware was that of being the ill-starred Gen. Wilkinson's evil genius, superseding him by Presidential order at New Orleans, in 1810; quarreling instead of co-operating with him on the Canada line in 1813; and yet never called to any account or subjected to any Presidential censure therefor. But behold him now in his proud meridian of manhood, embarking in this vast speculation with his great means and influence, and a much more colossal interest than any other man. And further, behold him losing no time after the buying from the State, but with characteristic sagacity and celerity hastening to become a mighty seller of what he had bought, and in less than a year safely shifting

*American State Papers, Public Lands, Vol. I, p. 148.

off his enormous portion of the prey into other hands at a huge profit and putting the money in his pocket, eluding thus the annulling vengeance of Georgia, which he well knew would soon start up in pursuit, but which he also knew could not overtake and rend the great villainy until another Legislature should meet and have a chance to act upon it.*

Along with Col. Hampton, South Carolina sent to Augusta on the great felonious occasion another man of hardly less note and force, though noted in a different way, namely, Robert Goodloe Harper, also a member of Congress, destined to become distinguished on that theatre, great both as a lawyer and statesman, whose speeches, long ago collected and published in two goodly octavos, I read and even studied in my young days and thought they ranked him among the giants of those old times. What drove him or drew him from the political field and from South Carolina afterwards, and sent him to Baltimore to bury himself there for the remainder of his life in the practice of law, I have never known. It may have been a combination of causes. For in addition to his large interest of 131,000 acres, and consequent great activity in the Yazoo matter, he was one of those who persevered in 1801, through all the thirty-six ballotings, in casting the vote of South Carolina for Aaron Burr against Mr. Jefferson in that fearful conflict for the Presidency; and so persevered in the face of the unquestioned fact that Mr. Jefferson

*American State Papers, Public Lands, Vol. 1, 197, and elsewhere under the Yazoo head. Military Affairs, Vol. 1, page 462, 479.

Extract from White's Statistics, page 50:

"In the lobbies of the Senate and House alternately, were to be seen a Judge of the Supreme Court of the United States, from Pennsylvania, with $25,000 in his hands, it was said, for a cash payment; a Judge of the District Court of the United States, from Georgia, passing off shares of land to the members for their votes; and a Senator from Georgia, who had perfidiously neglected to proceed to Philadelphia to take his seat in Congress, and who was absent from his post until the three last days of the session, bullying with a loaded whip and by turns cajoling the numerous understrappers in speculation. There were to be seen also a Judge of our Superior Courts and other eminent Georgians, &c.

"Our sister State of South Carolina was also represented by one who was regarded as a prince of speculators, &c."

was alike the electoral and popular choice of the State. The odor of both which passages in his life became afterwards so intensely bad in South Carolina as to have probably rendered the atmosphere there decidedly unsuited to him, politically, professionally and socially.

Coming back to Georgia, we behold on the speculators' dark roll not a few names of that day highly respectable in all the walks of private life, from the shades of which, as they never emerged while living, it would be wrong to drag them from the repose of the grave now that they are dead. Among them there were not wanting gifted minds and aspiring spirits who yearned for a high and bright career, but their political star, quenched beneath the horizon by their Yazoo complicity, was never allowed to ascend and shine in our firmament. Such seems to have been generally the fate of those who had come within blighting contact of the great villainy. To the sons of ambition it was the deadly political sin of that era, and for it no length of time or depth of penitence or merit of subsequent demeanor could ever bring amnesty or oblivion.

The names we have recited and others of less celebrity, but of no mean pretensions in their time, show what an imposing array of talent, character and influence, and especially what a strong Law Staff the Yazooists boasted in their ranks, and account abundantly for the legal skill and subtlety and the remarkable technical artifice and ability apparent in the contriving and framing of the legislation procured from the State. And it is by no means surprising that by the combined efforts of so many such men, with abundant pecuniary means at their command and no scruples or restraints of principle in their way, surrounded and reinforced, as they were besides, by a numerous phalanx of active subalterns and colaborers, our raw, petty, unschooled Legislature should have been jostled from its propriety, started, as it were, from its perpendicularity, and made the more easy to give way before the grosser engines of bribery and corruption that were held in reserve and at length brought powerfully into play.

SECTION V (Continued.)

To quit the Yazoo Legislature with only the little notice that has yet been taken of

JAMES GUNN

would be unjust as well to him as to our theme, and would be pretty much such a slighting of him as it would be to snub Satan in giving an account of Pandemonium and its population, which, by the way, Dante came very nigh doing, for in all his long, downward journey under the escort of Virgil through the nine circles of his ever-narrowing, ever-intensating Hell, he fails to encounter or mention his Diabolic Majesty until having reached the nethermost depth where the reign of frost begins and never ends, he comes upon him at last writhing in lone, unsociable misery, wedged in eternal ice, with a hard, merciless chill upon him in the very neck of that inverted, infernal hollow cone.*

What made this very undeserving or rather ill-deserving man, Gunn, so unduly prominent and distinguished in Georgia for a number of years is a puzzling question, one which finds no sufficient solution in any *facts* of his history which have come down to us. He belonged not to Georgia but to Virginia during the Revolutionary war, and came to the South in the army of General Greene, when that illustrious commander was sent hither by Washington towards the close of the great struggle to retrieve the Carolinas and Georgia after that tremendous blow, the loss of the battle of Camden. The first trace of him I have succeeded in discovering presents him as a Captain of Dragoons in the Virginia line, above which rank he never rose, nor is there any evidence of his ever having won distinction in it. Indeed, nothing is particularly known of his military career except

*"*Lo 'mperador del doloroso regno*
Da mezzo 'l petto uscia fuor della ghiaccia."
Dell' Inferno, Canto 34.

"The emperor of the dolorous realm from mid breast stood forth out of the ice."

his wanton and even wicked impressment and bringing to Georgia for his own use of the celebrated stallion Romulus, about which the indefatigable widow, Amy Darden, never ceased to beset Congress, until finally she got her pay after nearly forty years of importunity; and then, secondly, he was afterwards guilty of another disreputable and improper piece of conduct about horses which brought upon him formal censure and reprimand from Gen. Greene; and lastly, it is recorded of him that he failed to arrive in time with his dragoons to take part in a difficult and hazardous affair near Savannah as late as 1782, in which Gen. Wayne had ordered him to co-operate. The success of that attempt was complete, however, without his presence or aid, and as it was the last blow of the war (for in a very short time Savannah was surrendered to Gen. Wayne by the British and the war ended in Georgia as it had already done substantially, at least, everywhere else,) no inquiry was ever instituted whether his non-arrival in time was his misfortune or his fault. Such, neither more or less, is the whole story of Gunn's Revolutionary services so far as it is known at this day.

Upon the close of the war, he took up his residence in Georgia, and seems to have thriven rapidly under the sunshine of peace. For soon we read of him under the title of Colonel heading a posse of militia and breaking up a gang of runaway negroes who, having become demoralized during the war, had quitted the plantations, some for the British camps, some for the swamps, in one of which on Bear Creek they, after the peace, fortified themselves in their rude way both for greater safety and with a view of living permanently by plunder, fish and game. This dispersing of the runaways was undoubtedly a very good thing done by Col. Gunn, but it was also the easiest and least perilous thing in the world, and any other Colonel or other commander of the posse could have done it as well, and the solemn pains with which it is circumstantially narrated in a stately history of the State savors a little of the ludicrous, and fails to help us to any solution of Gunn's subsequent rapid rise and distinction.

For even if this feat could be supposed (as it cannot be) of any worth towards such a solution, it was more than counterbalanced by the ruffianly, disgraceful conduct of which he was guilty towards Gen. Greene.* That pure and noble man, second only to Washington in Revolutionary merit and glory, and to whom Georgia and the Carolinas owed such an incalculable debt of gratitude for their final deliverance from the clutches of the enemy, a debt which Georgia rejoiced to acknowledge by bestowing upon him a fine estate and a beautiful homestead near Savannah, this man who had so well earned and was so worthily enjoying honor and homage from the whole country, had hardly set his foot on the soil of Georgia as a resident, invited citizen, when he was met by Gunn with what sort of welcome and hospitality? With pistol in hand, with challenge to mortal combat for alleged wrong done him by Gen. Greene as his commanding officer in the aforementioned matter about horses. Not the least strange thing in the case was that such a man as Colonel, afterwards General, James Jackson, should be Gunn's second and the bearer of his challenge. In apology for him, however, let it be remembered that he was then a very young man, not more than 27 or 28 years old, and that he was by temperament not only pugnacious and intrepid in the highest degree, but also impetuous and somewhat hasty. Moreover he was a strong believer in the Code to which all gentlemen bowed in those days, and which holds every one answerable by duel for whatever wrong he inflicts on another's honor; a code which allows not a man to decline serving his friend or even a stranger as a second in a proper case. To all which it must be added that he was fresh from association with Gunn as a brother officer in the field, and that he looked upon him as a gentleman and as his own peer; an opinion which must have subsequently undergone no small modification. Now all these things made it obligatory on Jack-

* Simms' Life of Gen. Greene, chapter 35.

son, according to his views, not to refuse to be Gunn's second in any proper case, and the only error committed by him was in too hastily consenting to be his second before looking well into the case, and being sure it was a proper one. I say this was his only error, because his subsequent conduct made it so and made abundant amends for it besides. For upon his calling upon Gen. Greene with the challenge, and the General's declining to accept it and stating to him at the same time the circumstances which had prompted it, and his reasons for not accepting it, Jackson saw at once that Gen. Greene was right and that a challenge was not proper in the case; and so seeing, he determined on the spot to withdraw from the matter and did withdraw, communicating to his principal this determination and his reasons. But these reasons, which were as imperative as honor itself with the noble Jackson, who ever felt bound to recede from what was wrong as well as to insist upon what was right, were thrown away upon Gunn's base, diabolic nature, and he renewed the challenge by another hand, which, upon Gen. Greene's again declining, the brute who sent it threatened to assault him on sight in the streets,—a threat, indeed, which he never attempted to execute, though from his character no man could have felt sure of his abstaining from this outrage. So much was Gen. Greene wounded by this treatment on his first reaching his new home in a land of strangers, that he laid the whole matter before Washington by letter and asked his opinion and advice. Washington's reply fully sustained and commended the course he had pursued. Indeed, what can be more preposterous or pernicious than that superior officers, even up to the very highest, should be held answerable to their subalterns by duel for their acts towards such subalterns in the administration of their commands?

It only remains to be remarked about this behavior of Gunn's, that if any thing could add to its enormity, it is the fact that he had pocketed the alleged wrong for so long a space, and reserved his call in regard to it for a time and circumstances which made that call an outrage, not only on

Gen. Greene, but one also on the pride, honor and hospitality of Georgia; a call, moreover, from which he refused to desist even after his second, and that second such a man as James Jackson, had so strongly advised against it and stamped it with his disapproval and withdrawal from it as a second.

Yet in spite of all his unworthiness and demerits, Gunn continued to mount up. He next became a Brigadier General of militia, an office bestowed then, and for half a century afterwards, by the direct votes of the Legislature. Nor did he stop there. When Georgia acceded to the new Federal Constitution, and the new Federal Government under it was about to go into operation in 1789, he was chosen along with William Few, as one of our first Senators in the National Congress, where his good fortune still pursued him, and, in the allotment of periods of service among the Senators, gave him a full term of six years, while only four years fell to his colleague, Few.

No particular causes have reached us for this, his great and undeserved political advancement. He had no popular hold, such as grows out of long residence among a people, and strong and widely ramified sympathies and attachments with them. Nor, as we have seen, was his brow wreathed with laurels, gathered on the battle fields of the Revolution, far and near, like those of Gen. Anthony Wayne and Col. George Matthews, our unhappy Yazoo-ruined Governor, causing our people to take them, new comers as they were, at once to their bosoms and to clothe them with their highest honors, and as they would still more have rejoiced to have done by Gen. Greene, had it pleased the Almighty to spare him to us. And, then, after Georgia, upon the close of the war, became Gunn's home, he did nothing of which we know to commend him to his new fellow citizens,—much certainly to discommend. There is but one way, and that not a very flattering one to him, of accounting for his extraordinary rise. It is simply that he was well gifted as a demagogue, as a shrewd, supple courtier of the people and their officials and representatives; altogether unscrupulous, now bold, bullying, overbearing, now cringing, caressing, insinuating, according as circumstances demanded; master alike of the arts of intimidation and cajolery; in fine, possessed of the talents and qualities by which in free elective countries bad and worthless men so often attain to influence and power; dexterous, unprincipled, invincible in seeking, incompetent and base in filling office. It is not hard to understand how such a man should have won the Senatorship the first time. The second time his success was undoubtedly in no small degree the work of his potent Yazoo friends and partners, and whom he repaid in the manner he had stipulated and to which we have adverted, namely, by the prostitution of his Senatorial influence and opportunities to their service. His energy, activity and conspicuousness in the scenes of the Yazoo Fraud stand in strong contrast to his insignificance, bordering on nothingness, in his Senatorial sphere, in which he was mainly distinguished for his tardiness of attendance and general indifference to duty. Some natures there are, which are aroused and find a congenial element only in plotting and doing things ignoble and bad, sinking into torpor and inanity in all the upper and purer atmospheres of life and action. Such a nature undoubtedly belonged to Gunn, who, with all his fair opportunities, both military and political, is destined, should he unhappily live in history, to be known there only as the chieftain of a great land robbing villainy and as the precursor and type in this country of a class of public men, now become shameless and common, pecuniary profligates and felons, disgracing the Congress of the United States and all the important places in the Government.

His life and his long and inglorious Senatorship ended very nearly together. The precise time of his death I do not know, though it must have been not long before the meeting of the Legislature in 1802, for we find that Body indulging in a singular eccentricity of legislation in regard to him, exempting his estate from escheat and vesting it in a nephew, a Virginian, bearing his name. His last term in the Senate expired on the 3d of March, 1801, and that striking contrast to him and proud exemplar of all patriotism and of all public and private honor and elevation of character, Gen. James Jackson, had already been chosen to replace him now, as some years previously, on the expiration of Mr. Few's time, he had been chosen to serve with him as a colleague.

SECTION VI.

The banded speculators had now gotten all they wanted from the Legislature: A law of sale making them unshackled owners of vast and invaluable tracts of Indian territory, free from any dependence on the extinction of the Indian title or the consent of the General Government; conditions designedly left out in their case and for their behoof, whilst they were rigorously required, as we have seen, as against our citizen soldiers. In all other respects, likewise, this Yazoo Law was moulded by the speculators to suit their own views and interests, and in so moulding it, they made it a Law, which even more strongly than the Yazoo Act of 1789, was calculated to interfere with Indian rights and Spanish pretensions, and with our Spanish negotiations, and to put the peace of the country with the Indians and with Spain at hazard and at the mercy of the Yazoo purchasers, and of whomsoever might become their sub-claimants.

Such being the manifest political tendency and danger of this second Yazoo sale in its aspect on national affairs, it could not but attract the attention of Washington, who, faithful to his policy of 1789, at once took his stand against this huge aggravation of the crime then so well thwarted by him. Accordingly, the first alarm on this new occasion was sounded by him; the first movement in opposition came from him. Upon receiving from Augusta a transcript of the nefarious Legislation, he lost no time in laying it before Congress, with the following Message:

"February 17th, 1795.

"*Gentlemen of the Senate and House of Representatives:*

"I have received copies of two Acts of the Legislature of Georgia, one passed on the 28th of December, the other on the 7th of January last, for the purpose of appropriating and selling the Indian lands within the territorial limits claimed by that State. These copies, although, not officially certified, have been transmitted to me in such a manner as to leave no doubt of their authenticity. These Acts embrace an object of such magnitude, and in their consequences may so deeply effect the peace and welfare of the United States, that I have thought it necessary to lay them before Congress. * * * * * * * * *

(signed) GEO. WASHINGTON.

It would be quite superfluous to enter upon any inquiry as to the grounds Washington had for the importance he attached to this subject, and for the great solicitude it occasioned him. Enough certainly is to be found in the foregoing pages to render that matter plain. As little difficult is it to see why in his message he coupled the State Troops Act of the 28th of December, with the Yazoo Act of the 7th of January, and communicated them together to Congress; although the former viewed merely by itself was an innocent thing, containing nothing that was wrong or alarming; a result that was prevented by the clause in it prohibiting any steps being taken under it until two months after the Indian title should be extinguished, and in regard to the Tallassee country, not until the consent of the General Government should be given. But although thus innocent in itself, it was perverted to iniquity by being tied to the Yazoo Act, the sinister aims of which it was made at once malignly to aid and elucidate.

It is note worthy that Washington, after simply submitting the matter and the two obnoxious Legislative acts of Georgia to Congress, stopped short with a very brief expression of his opinion about them. He recommends no Legislation nor suggests any measures whatever to the two

Houses. The reasons for this reticence in his message are obvious. *No new Legislation was wanted.* A law had been passed in 1793 regulating Indian affairs and intercourse, which was ample in its provisions for all emergencies that could arise. So Washington thought, and so the Committee to whom the subject was referred, and Congress itself thought; therefore no further Legislation was proposed from any quarter. The Committee contented themselves with a Report and Resolutions presented on the 23rd of February, in which they emphatically denounced the Yazoo sale as an *absolute conveyance* to the Companies of Indian territories amounting, say the Committee, to three-fourths of all the lands held by the Indians under the sanction of National treaties within the limits claimed by Georgia, of which treaties the sale was of course a direct and gross infringement, which the Government of the United States would be bound to resist whenever attempted to be practically carried out. The Committee further declare that the prerogatives over Indian affairs involved such wide, various and serious consequences, and so deeply affected the general good, that they could properly belong only where the Constitution had vested them—in the National Authorities, whose duty they pronounced it to be, to secure the Indians in their rights under the National Treaties; and they call upon the President not to permit infractions of these Treaties by our own citizens or others, and assure him of the full support and co-operation of Congress in all these matters. Still further, they call upon him not to permit treaties for the extinguishment of Indian titles to be held at the instance of individuals or States, even where the property in the lands would, upon such extinguishment, belong to such individuals and States, &c. And they wind up by recommending that all persons who shall be assembled or embodied in arms on lands belonging to the Indians, for the purpose of warring against them, or committing depredations upon them, shall thereby become liable to the rules and articles of war established for the government of the Troops of the United States.

This Report and Resolutions met the full sanction of Congress and the country, which thus stood shoulder to shoulder with Washington in his well known Indian and anti-Yazoo policy. Even before the above mentioned Act of 1793 was passed, and when consequently he had nothing to guide him and point out his duty on this subject, but the broad generalities of the Constitution, he had not hesitated to take on himself the responsibility of effectually oppugning and nullifying the first Yazoo sale by forbidding and arresting all attempts of the beneficiaries under it to occupy the Indian lands. Now, that his sense of duty in the matter and his Executive ability were both abundantly reinforced by appropriate legislation from Congress and by such expressions and resolves as had promptly emanated from that Body in response to his message, nothing could be more certain than the overwhelming discomfiture which awaited the Yazooists at his hands, should they dare to provoke a conflict with him by attempting to wrest their ill-gotten lands from the Indians, either by outright force or by any treaties or arrangements of their own with them, whether open or covert.

The dangers thus impending over the Yazoo purchasers from the national arm, though in the distance and contingent on prior aggressive movements by those purchasers themselves, had been fully foreseen by them all the while, and they saw, too, that they were dangers from which their only mode of escape (to which they were prompt to resort) was to hasten, after their purchase from the State, to sell off their lands and to leave to those, who should purchase of them, to succeed also to all the threatened difficulties and perils of the case, whether coming from the General Government or from Georgia. In the actual event of things, however, it befell not either the original grantees or their sub-purchasers to have this apprehended collision with the General Government. For Georgia, quickly intervening with her rapid, unsparing vengeance, as we shall soon see, crushed the villainy ere it reached the stage at which to incur blows from the Federal arm. And this speedy, clearly foreseen vengeance of Georgia it was, far more than what was remotely feared from the Federal arm, that caused the Companies to be in such a culprit hurry to trade off their wicked landed plunder before another Legislature should meet and have a chance of dealing with their crime. To this end their agents and emissaries were dispersed promptly and widely over the country. They were successful in finding for some two or three millions of acres, an early market in the South at an immense percentage of profit. But it was the North, then as now the home of monied capital and of an intense adventurous love of gain, that was chiefly the buyer and the victim. The Georgia Company dispatched thither, during the summer, a shrewd, plausible, persuasive salesman, who acquitted himself alike to the satisfaction of his employers and to the captivation of quite a number of the solid men of Boston, selling them eleven millions of acres at eleven cents per acre, thereby making a profit of nearly a million of dollars to his Company. These Bostonians subsequently organized under the name of the New England Mississippi Land Company, and proceeded to scatter their lands at greatly increased prices among thousands of beguiled Northern people upon whom soon fell that Tower of Siloam, the Rescinding Act of Georgia, and held them crushed, though not killed, for almost a score of years, until at length the Supreme Court and Congress came to their rescue. They were, or rather were asserted years afterwards by their Congressmen to be, innocent buyers without notice, second purchasers, ignorant and unsuspecting of the fraud that vitiated their title from its very birth. A story not very likely, when we recall how the fraud glared out on the face and in all the facts of the Yazoo legislation, how it resounded through the newspapers all over the United States, how it stuck out obvious in the very deeds (all without any general warranty of title) which were made by the Companies to their under-purchasers, and by these latter to their successors. And then as to the unlawfulness and criminality of the sale by the State in a *national* point of view, who can with decency pretend that Washington's above-noticed message and the action of Congress thereon was not warning enough to put the whole world on notice and on its guard.*

Sales of large amount were also made with the least possible loss of time by the several companies in various other

*Mr. Lucas, of Virginia, in his speech on the Yazoo Claims, in the House of Representatives, January, 1805, adverting to the pretence of the want of notice on the part of the New England purchasers, says: "That they should not have heard of the notorious fraud that had taken place at the passing of the Act of 1795 is a great astonishment to me; that they should have made a purchase of eleven millions of acres without making inquiries sufficient to discover what almost everybody knew throughout the United States, if possible, increases my astonishment. For my part, having never thought of purchasing any land from the Georgia land companies, I made no inquiry about the Acts of the Legislature of Georgia; yet the corruption was so flagrant, the fraud so notorious, that it reached my ears soon after it was passed." Mr Lucas then proceeds to allude to President Washington's message, above quoted, as a proclamation to the whole country against the Yazoo Sale, which must be presumed to have come to everybody's knowledge, and was quite enough to put everybody on notice. He then proceeds to say: "I should rather think that the speculators of New England, sober and discreet, as they style themselves to be, found the bargain so good and tempting, the means of pleading ignorance of fraud committed in the original purchase so easy, the means on the part of the State of Georgia or its vendees to prove the notice so difficult, that the sober and discreet speculators of New England thought it advisable to make a gambling bargain, expecting that the two extremities of the United States being engaged in the same speculation, would combine their influence to press hard upon the centre and save through the conflict their speculation in whole or in part. Other strong circumstances lead still more to the belief that the New England Company were well aware of the danger which did exist in making a purchase from the Georgia Land Companies and that they were taking unusual risks on themselves. This appears clearly from the face of their deeds; not only the covenant of warranty is special instead of being general, but another extraordinary covenant is entered into by which the Georgia Company 'is not liable to the refunding of any money in consequence of any defect in their title from the State of Georgia, if any such there should appear hereafter to be!' Was not such covenant smelling strongly of the fraud which the Georgia Grant was impregnated with? Could the New England Company take more clearly every risk on themselves? Could they more expressly preclude themselves from every remedy in law or equity in case of eviction?"—*Benton's Ab. of Congressional Debates, Vol. III p.* 323, 324.

See also the speech of Mr. Clark and others in the same debate.

parts of the Union, chiefly in the great cities of the North, and to some extent also to foreigners, at prices ranging from eight and ten to twenty cents per acre, resulting in immense aggregate gain. Thus did the original grantees (except the few who took back their money and gave up their interest in the land under the Rescinding Act,) achieve a complete triumph, carrying out successfully their programme, which was neither more nor less than by fraud and corruption to purchase these lands from the State for a mere trifle, and then quickly to shift them off at a huge profit upon others, whom it was their plan to leave to their fate, whatever it might be, of danger, loss or ruin. The Yazoo speculation is seen consequently standing before us bristling with successful fraud, at both ends: Fraud, first, in the purchase from the State, and then fraud again in the sales by the original purchasers to the various secondary buyers.

But it was not merely the above mentioned Report and Resolutions in Congress which Washington's message called forth. The two Houses, incensed at what Georgia had done, felt at the first moment a strong impulse to question her title, and that of the speculating Companies derived from her, and anticipating that the adverse Spanish title would now soon devolve on the United States by treaty for whatever it might be worth, determined to probe to the bottom the right of the State to the territory she had so unpatriotically alienated to a knot of speculators in preference to the United States. To this end, at the very close of the session a joint resolution was adopted directing the Attorney General, Charles Lee, to prepare and present to the next Congress a report on the title of Georgia. That eminent law officer took abundant time and was at the utmost pains, and at length, on the 29th of April, 1796, after more than a year had elapsed from the date of the call upon him, and six months after the Spanish cession to the United States by the treaty of San Lorenzo, he presented his report, which is now to be found in the American State Papers, filling more than thirty great folio pages—forming a fine specimen

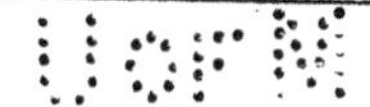

of the thorough and faithful manner in which the public men of that day performed their duty.* Georgia, in particular, is under obligations to Mr. Attorney General Lee for his laborious research and for the great mass of interesting documentary materials relating to her infantine period, which, by ransacking both sides of the Atlantic, he was enabled to bring together. These materials, upon being studied, demonstrated instead of damaging the title of Georgia from Great Britain, and placed it indubitably above that which the United States got from Spain by the treaty of San Lorenzo.

There cannot be a doubt that the call on the Attorney General on this occasion was caused by an opinion prevalent to some extent in Congress that the title of Georgia, derived from Great Britain, and now nefariously conveyed to the Yazooists, would, upon investigation, have to give way before what they supposed would be the better title the United States were expecting soon to acquire from Spain, and that thus the title of the Yazooists, acquired from Georgia, would be superseded. This opinion was not unfrequently expressed in debate and in the reports of committees. Nor was it an opinion merely: With many there was a strong wish to the same effect,—so intense was the resentment against the Yazoo sale, and so powerful the desire to defeat it. But both the opinion and the wish were soon seen by everybody to be utterly inadmissible in the presence of the great diplomatic fact that the title of Georgia constituted the only ground of claim and right advanced by our country in its great territorial strife with Spain, and being thus the banner under which that strife was waged and won on our side, could not now by any possibility be hauled down and set at naught by the United States in the very face of the great territorial victory they had just achieved under it.

**American State Papers, Public Lands, Vol.* 1, *Pages* 34, 69.

SECTION VII.

We have now reached a point in this long and intricate drama, at which the curtain drops for several years on the General Government and Georgia re-enters on the scene, to become this time the fierce assailant and undoer of the monstrous villainy that had been so recently enacted in her Legislature and under her name. Though the hue and cry against the enormity was first raised, as we have seen, at the Federal Capital and by the Federal Executive and Congress, yet here at home, the shock was far the deepest and most violent. It was here the crime struck with its most heinous, deadly effect, despoiling the State at once of a vast public property and her precious public honor,—not only robbing her of invaluable territories, but doing it under circumstances that brought imputation on her national patriotism and magnanimity,—doing it, moreover, by debauching her trusted public servants, whom she had chosen to be the guardians, not betrayers of her high interests and her fair fame. Thus had that crime wounded her in a point dearer than landed or monied wealth, tarnished her reputation, defiled at its young fountain head the eternal stream of her history and polluted the waters mingled with which her name was to go down to future times, and especially to her own children forever.

I design not recounting minutely the oft told, familiar story of the State's strong sovereign action in resentment and redress of this celebrated wrong. That story, at once simple and striking, has ever been so much an attractive theme to writers and talkers as to have become thread bare and to recoil from any thing like a labored handling now. Preliminarily, however, it should be told that the first effect of the sale on the mass of the people was stunning stupefaction and amazement. They found difficulty in believing that the deed had been done. The entire failure of the measure before the preceding Legislature and the entire quietude and silence in regard to it that had ensued, had rendered them unsuspecting and secure, and they had let the subject pass off from their minds and it occurred not to them that it had not been equally dropt by the speculating Companies. They were unaware that these latter had been during the whole interim stealthily, yet industriously, at work every where, both in and out of Georgia, and had really gotten into their hands the complete mastery of the game before they again came out to light and began to take open steps towards their object. It is wonderful what a profound privacy they had succeeded in maintaining in their widely ramified operations, a privacy kept up to the last possible moment. Even after their bill was introduced, there was no notoriety beyond Augusta and its neighborhood that such a measure was on hand. No publicity had been given to it, no announcement made of it by any name or title pointing to its character or contents. A lying title concealed its true nature which consequently was not indicated by anything on the journal of either House or in the newspapers, which were wont to give only lists of the titles of the bills introduced.

The consequence of all which was that the people awoke to find themselves outraged and robbed without having had any notice of the design or warning of their danger or the least chance of outcry and resistance. At first they were likewise ignorant of the turpitude of the means by which the wrong had been effected, or what strangers, or who among themselves except the guilty members of the Legislature and the few grantees named in the act, were concerned in its perpetration. They soon, however, became better and bitterly enlightened. The astounding discovery broke upon them that the cancerous fibres of the monstrous transaction pervaded not only the State but the United States, and embraced they knew not how many powerful and influential names and shrewd, unscrupulous characters. They were especially struck with the successful pains that had been taken to enlist in its interest all the men in Georgia who were prominent enough to attract the base courtship of the

Yazooists and pliant enongh to become their tools and accomplices. Most of those to whom the people would naturally have looked to become their leaders and to champion their cause in this great emergency, were either bought up and subsidized on the side of the enemy by their own interests or paralyzed by their relations to interested parties. Besides, not many men were there, indeed, who were at all competent to such leadership and championship as was wanted. Nothing short of the highest courage and the greatest energy, reputation, talents and self devotion could constitute the necessary qualifications. He who should give himself to the people's service on this occasion had need of a charmed life and an invincible soul, as well as of a concentrated and commanding mind: For assuredly it was a lion's den he would have to enter, a fiery furnance through which he would have to pass. And by universal concession there was but one man in the State, in all respects equal and fitted to the exigency, and who at the same time had kept himself pure and intact, and but for the extraordinary self-abnegation and lofty, patriotic intrepidity and devotion of that one man, the people would have been without a leader and champion, such as the case imperatively required. That man was General James Jackson, the noblest and most admirable name in the history of Georgia, then a member of the United States Senate as Mr. Few's successor and General Gunn's colleague.

I do not know that I can open the part acted by this extraordinary man against the Yazoo Fraud better than by recalling a personal reminiscence of my own full half a century old and more. It was at Hancock Superior Court, at April term, 1823,—a date at which the Governor was still chosen by the Legislature, and as the name of one of those understood to be aspiring to the office was to be found in the old public documents as the owner of a few Yazoo subshares, conversation began to be somewhat turned to the subject of the Yazoo Fraud and young men, especially, were keen inquirers. It was under these circumstances that a number of the junior members of the bar were sitting one night after supper in the large, pleasant room, up stairs, which our good host, William G. Springer, whose soul contended with his body, which should be biggest, had assigned to us across the street,—when we were agreeably startled by Judge Dooly* entering to pay us a visit,—a courtesy on the part of the Judges not uncommon in those days. The Judge, whose mind was a rich treasury of the miscellanies of Georgia, past and present, and whose manner of saying everything was singularly plain, condensed and incisive, was soon drawn out on the Yazoo Fraud. My recollection has ever since been perfectly distinct of the following remark made by him in the course of his conversing: "The people," he said, "were generally against the Yazoo sale, but the rich and leading men were mostly for it, because, in most instances, they or some of their friends or relations were interested in it. The people wanted to get rid of it, but did not know how to do it. They had nobody to lead and contrive for them, and Gen. Jackson resigned his seat in the United States Senate and came home and ran for the Legislature in Chatham county, and was elected to lead and contrive for the people."

Such were the very words of Judge Dooley to us young men about Gen. Jackson—words which struck me greatly and imprinted themselves indelibly, enkindling my mind with a most vivid and exalted conception of the illustrious character, to whom they related and making him from that moment a study and almost an idolatry to me. The annals of mankind teem with the names of heroes, martyrs, self-sacrificers, martial, moral, religious—men who have held their lives and their ease as nothing in the scale against glory, duty, honor; and yet among them all I am unable

*Whoever may feel curious as to what sort of physiognomy belonged to that very striking man, John M. Dooly, long the Judge of the Northern Circuit, the greatest wit as all agreed, and generally conceded to have been also the greatest judicial intellect of his day, may see a wonderfully true likeness of him (Adonised, however,) in the portrait of the celebrated painter, Gilbert Stuart, in the 1st Volume of the American Portrait Gallery.

to recollect any instance parallel and fully up to this conduct of Gen. Jackson so pointedly stated by Judge Dooly, so barely and sleepily mentioned by history. Certainly our own country, vast and diversified as it is, has hitherto furnished nothing equal to it or like it, nor does it promise according to present symptoms ever to do so. Does any man believe that there is now to be found in all the low minded ranks of power and of the public service a single bosom in which even a dormant possibility dwells of such sublime, self-denying, unselfish patriotism? What United States Senator would now resign his seat with yet four years to run and come home and seek the humblest Representative post known to our system of Government,—and all for the sake of the people and their rights and vindication?

Gen. Jackson, however, had given some evidence on a previous occasion in his life of his capability of this *ne plus ultra* of public virtue. In 1788, when but thirty years old, he had been elected to the office of Governor of the State, and declined accepting it upon the ground of lacking age and experience. It was in full keeping with this act of noble, patriotic modesty and humility that he should afterwards in 1795, have so subjugated an ambition of the most ardent and lofty type as to give up the highest and become a candidate for the lowest place in political service, because he beheld his beloved Georgia in a mighty trouble in which she needed the sacrifice from him, and in which by making it he could do so much more and better for her, although at the cost of doing so much less and worse for himself.

For well he knew not only what he was surrendering, but also to what he was exposing himself when he magnanimously resolved to descend from the high round of the political ladder to which he had climbed down to the very bottom, there to scuffle and fight, "lead and contrive for the people," both against all the bad men who had combined, and all the good men who had been misled, to become the State's betrayers and robbers, or the supporters of its betrayers and robbers. He knew what enemies he was necessitating himself to make and how deeply they would be envenomed against him, and that their thirst for his blood would be only less keen than their greed for the prey he was bent on snatching from their grasp. He knew, in fine, that from the first moment to the last of the work on which he was entering, he would have to carry his life in his hand, although the ultimate fate that awaited him lay concealed from human view, and none could foresee that a life so dear and invaluable was destined to pass away, alas! so prematurely—a slow-wasting sacrifice, long offered up on the altar of Georgia's interest and honor.*

From the first Gen. Jackson had been outspoken and vehement in his denunciations of the sale, and had contributed greatly to rousing the popular rage against it. This,—even before he had doffed his Senatorial robes for a candidacy for the State Legislature, and thereby formally entered the lists as the people's leader and champion against a host of powerful and unscrupulous men whose mortal fear and hatred he thenceforward incurred. The people at once hailed him and rallied to him, and it was not long before under his brave

*Col. Benton, in his Abridgement of the Congressional Debates, Vol. III twice comments upon Gen. Jackson and the cause of his death. At p. 338 is the following note at the close of the debate on the Yazoo Claims:

"Mr. Randolph was the great opposer of these claims in Congress and General Jackson their great opposer in Georgia. It was he, who aroused the feeling that overthrew the General Assembly who made the grant, and elected the Legislature which annulled the Act, and burned the record of it. He was in the Senate of the United States with James Gunn, the Senator alluded to in the debate as being engaged in the Fraud, and lost his life in the last of the many duels which his opposition to that measure brought upon him."

And again at page 465, in a note to the proceedings in Congress on the occasion of Gen. Jackson's death, March 19th, 1806, Col. Benton says among other things: "He was a man of marked character, high principle and strong temperament—honest, patriotic, brave, hating tyranny, oppression and meanness in in every form; the bold denouncer of crime in high as well as in low places; a ready speaker, and as ready with his pistol as his tongue, and involved in many duels on account of his hot opposition to criminal measures. The defeat of the Yazoo Fraud was the most signal act of his Legislative life, for which he paid the penalty of his life, dying of wounds received in the last of the many duels, which his undaunted attacks upon that measure brought upon him."

auspices and their fierce enthusiasm the battle into which they had plunged was substantially won. For the storm quickly overspread the State with a violence that appalled the Yazooists and their myrmydons, and they everywhere slunk and cowered before it long before the election day came. But still Jackson's hot and heavy blows were not mitigated, nor did the people's vengeful energy slacken. It was more than even the bravo, Gunn, could brave or bear. He became utterly paralyzed and annihilated, as it were, by the intense, crushing detestation of which he was sensible of having become the object, and we hear no more of him whatever except that he continued to occupy to the last day of his new, basely gotten term, the seat in the National Senate, which he at once obscurely filled and flagrantly dishonored. The bribed Senators and Representatives in the Legislature met from their constituents a fate similar to that of their bribing, bullying chief. The tempest of public indignation against them was such as made not a few of them tremble for their personal safety on their return home. But their fears were groundless. Such was the orderly, law-abiding character of our ancestors, except in cases where society is obliged to resort to the "higher law" for its purgation and protection, that, content with the sort of penalty which God inflicted on Cain, they simply branded their culprit legislators and consigned them to political death and social ostracism and infamy.

In making this statement I am not unaware that a surmise older than my earliest recollection, indeed, older than myself, long existed in some minds, making the case of Roberts Thomas, the recreant Senator from Hancock, whose high-priced vote turned the scale in favor of the Yazoo sale, an exception to this eulogium on the people's moderation. But even on the worst supposition anybody ever entertained (which was that Jonathan Adams, or some other person, whose dark secret was never suspected, followed him from Hancock in his flight and overtook and assassinated him in South Carolina) it was but the crime of an individual to which the public was in no way party or privy. An unconcealed, formal flogging, "hugging a sapling,"* meanwhile, or some other still lighter corporal punishment and disgrace was all he ever had to fear (and it was this fear that made him flee) from his incensed constituents who never dreamed of anything harsher against him than his ignominous expulsion from their midst. Not a man in Hancock ever harbored such a thought as that of pursuing and assassinating him after his flight.† The most probable theory of his murder is that it was procured by some arch fiend among the Yazooists. Thomas' vacilation, timidity and extortion had already excited their displeasure and uneasiness before he gave that vote for them, which they were obliged to have at any price, because if given the other way it would be fatal to them. His vote obtained and the law passed, their uneasiness about him was still kept alive by his indiscretions before he left Augusta and by his coward weakness after he got home. And when soon afterwards he took to flight, thereby proclaiming not only his fears, but, as it was

Sallard's Affidavit, American State Papers, Public Lands, Vol. 1, p. 149.

†Both White in his Statistics of Georgia, page 50, and Gov. Gilmer in his book, entitled "Georgians," take it for granted that Thomas met his fate from the hands of some of his constituents. Gov. Gilmer, though not naming Jonathan Adams, indicates him clearly to every Hancock man as the assassin. The logic which inculpated Adams, ran in this wise: "The Adamses were a strong charactered and very leading, patriotic family in the county and were particularly indignant at Thomas' Yazoo vote and against Thomas himself for it. Thomas fled and was assassinated. After which Jona. Adams fell into bad health and became a great hypochondriac for a number of years. Therefore, some people wondered whether he had not something dreadful on his conscience and whether that something was not the killing of Thomas." Such was the syllogism that I heard occasionally whispered in Hancock in my boyhood,—of which it will be seen that the premises being weak, the conclusion is a mere doubt or wonder. By the time it reached Oglethorpe county it must have become a positive belief or Gov. Gilmer would not have put it in his book as a fact. This sort of reasoning was liable, however, to refutation and was actually refuted by Adams' eventual recovery of his health, mental and physical.

Gov. Troup was in Congress during the Yazoo discussions, and in a speech quoted by Gen. Harden in his Life of him, allndes to the suspicion that Thomas' assassination was contrived by the Yazooists. Such is my recollection, but I have not the book at hand.

argued, his and their guilt also, which they were solicitous should not be noised abroad, at least until they should have time to sell off their ill-acquired lands,—under the impulse of malignant fear, fury and precaution, they contrived his death by the hand of some hired assassin who dogged him from Augusta beyond doubt. For it was the very night after passing through that city that he was killed. And thus was stilled forever that tongue from which alone they had fears of the early betrayal of the yet secret crime of the corruption they had used, and the continued secrecy of which long enough for their purposes they madly hoped might be secured by the prompt taking off of one whom they regarded with suspicion and fear as having it in his power and as being weakly liable to make damaging disclosures against them. So does crime breed crime, the progeny often more hideous than the parent, as all prose and verse, all history and observation have always proclaimed.

But although there was so much popular excitement which found expression through public meetings, the presentments of Grand Juries, the voice of the Press, and by petitions and memorials from every quarter which, numerously signed, were sent up to a Constitutional Convention about to be held at Louisville in the ensuing month of May,* yet the people never fully understood how bad and desperate the state of things was, till after that Body had met and proved itself false to all their expectations. Then it was that the veil was entirely lifted, disclosing a spectacle for which they were unprepared, the spectacle of the Convention itself acting as an accessory to the Yazoo Fraud and playing strongly into its hands. This great and new fangled treachery, more infamous than that of the Yazoo Legislature in proportion as a Constitutional Convention is a Body more exalted and more highly trusted than an ordinary Legislative Assembly, has long since died out of the minds of men. But it becomes necessary even at this late date to disinter it from

Benton's Abridg. Debates, Vol. III, p. 325. *White's Statistics, p.* 51.

its long oblivion as forming a part not less material than repulsive of the odious history through which we are wading.

The Convention, then, of May, 1795, was the child of the Constitution of 1789, a Constitution rather hurriedly gotten up by our forefathers to meet the advent of the newly launched Federal system of the United States which Georgia was among the first to greet and accept. Care, however, was wisely taken by the State's Constitution makers of '89 to insert in their hasty framework of government a provision for its own early revision and emendation. That provision required that at the election of members of the Legislature in 1794, delegates should also be chosen, three from each county, to meet at such time and place as the Legislature should appoint to deliberate and determine what alterations and amendments should be made in the Constitution. It thus happened that this election of members of the Convention took place at the same time and by the same constituencies and under all the same circumstances and influences with the election of the members of the Yazoo Legislature, and the speculators were altogether too shrewd a set of men not to see that it was best to have the Convention as well as the Legislature on their side. They took their measures accordingly. Great though quiet and secret pains were used to pack the Convention with their friends and with persons thought to be accessible to the influences they could bring to bear. They wanted, too, at least one master mind and commanding character there to watch over their interests, to lead and manage for them and to keep things in such a channel as would be for their advantage. They found and returned such a person in George Walker, of Richmond county. This gentleman ranked among the first men in the State for talents, address, popularity and high future promise, and was, by all odds, the very foremost of the Georgians, whom the Yazooists had succeeded in enlisting in their scheme. He was one of their leading partners and his name stands out with those of James Gunn and Matthew McAllister, printed in the Act as one of the original Grantees of the Georgia Company.

Having such advantages as these on their side in the composition of the Convention and perfect concert and understanding among themselves besides, the Yazooists found it not difficult to carry things their own way in that body over the not very small sprinkling of good and true, but not particularly effective men, who were their fellow members. *And their way and wish was to favor and protect the Yazoo speculation and save it from harm.* Ignoring almost entirely the high duty of amending the Constitution for which they had been called together, they devoted themselves to aiding and screening the great Fraud. Their whole doings are distent with internal evidence of this aim. It is apparent in what they *did* and in what they *did not do.* There is nothing which the speculators could have asked or wanted which either through the action or non-action of the Convention they did not get; whilst of all that the people asked for and expected, not a whit was granted or done. What was most desirable for the Yazooists was plenty of undisturbed time for their vast and scattered operations of resale of their lands, and this the Convention secured to them as far as possible by changing the meeting of the Legislature from the old time, the first Monday in November, to the second Tuesday in January, for which change no reason can be imagined except to give the Yazooists more than two full additional months to work off their lands before they could be overtaken and cut down by the dreaded rescinding vengeance of another and purer Legislature. Thus much as to what the Convention *did.* Still more strikingly sinister was the character of what it *refused to do.* To it as the most competent and all-potent Body known to our political system as well as the earliest in point of time to which an appeal could be made, the people had made their loud appeals. Thither they had sent up their complaints and petitions, their protests and fulminations against the sale, accompanied by abundant proofs of the now discovered corrupt means by which it was procured, justly regarding the Convention as clothed with transcendent powers which it was bound to exercise on such an occasion. But these supreme servants of the people literally snubbed their masters, taking no further notice of their views, wishes and demands than to bundle them up and devolve them in a mass on the ensuing Legislature* which they immediately proceeded, as we have just seen, to put off two months longer with no other object than to put this stupendous villainy as much as possible beyond the reach of its arm. But not only did the Convention thus refused to *act* against the Yazoo crime,—it refused even to *speak* against it. Not the slightest whisper of denunciation or disapproval came from its lips; not the slightest opinion was breathed against *it* or the manner of its procurement. So the Yazooists were more than satisfied, having gotten the utmost they wanted,—a friendly inactivity and silence,—a kind refusal to do or say aught against them, and also a lengthened period of time for working out their programme of disposing of their lands at enriching prices.

Having thus extended to the Yazooists all the aid it could give, indeed, all they needed, and refused to say or do aught to their prejudice, the measure of the Convention's shame was full enough, even though it had not been guilty of the further shameless misdoing, of leaving almost untouched the real business for which it had been created, and coolly devolving the same on another Convention, which, for that purpose it ordered to be elected in 1797. But perhaps we ought to be rather thankful for this delinquency of the Convention and the mode it adopted of making amends therefor: Since to this cause we owe a better work than could have been gotten at its hands, namely, the glorious old Constitution of 1798, the time-honored mental product of the illustrious Jackson and his anti-Yazoo compatriots, under which Georgia long grew and prospered, still clinging to it with increasing reverence for nearly seventy years until finally in these evil latter days it was, to her eternal sorrow,

*Benton's *Ab.*, *Vol.* 3, *p.* 325.

overthrown and thrust aside by a conquering despotism and unreasoning bayonets.

When the great disappointment occasioned by the above told gross infidelity of the Convention came upon the people, when they saw what a scurvy, pernicious trick had been played off on them from that high quarter and perceived themselves cheated, wronged, betrayed at every turn, first by their Legislature and then by their Convention, then it was that their fierce indignation rose to its acme. Then it was that enraged and bewildered, they felt intensely the need of somebody on whom they could repose a true and boundless trust, on whom they could fully rely to lead and contrive for them, to conquer and crush in their behalf in this matter. Then it was that they called upon their most idolized man, Gen. James Jackson, to leave his proud seat among the Conscript Fathers of the Union, the constitutional counsellors of Washington, and to come at once to their help and headship. Then it was that with a sublime alacrity and devotion, he instantly responded to a call which his own fiery sentiments and denunciations had largely inspired. Without a moment's hesitation he resigned his Senatorship and dismounting, as it were, from the equestrian rank, trode the ground once more, a private soldier, merging himself with the people as one of themselves and literally fighting on foot in their midst from May to November, to which time the election had been changed by the recent Convention. Behold him there covered with dust, assailed by hatred, the target of the enemy's deadliest aims throughout the long canvass. Behold him, "leading, contriving for the people," toiling with tongue and pen, with mind and body, facing and defying every danger, devoting himself in every way, sparing himself in none: A spectacle, how replete with all that can be conceived of the sublime and beautiful in political conduct! His work was done fearlessly and thoroughly. His spirit pervaded all Georgia and entered like a higher life the souls of her people. The enemy strived at first to make some show of a stand against him and his brave yeomanry, but in vain. In all parts of the State the victory was complete and resulted in returning him and his friends and supporters to the Legislature by an overwhelming majority in both branches.

Of course, in that Legislature he was the master spirit—the dictator and controller. But not much of study or effort was needed from him there. Execution alone was the watchword and work. What had to be done was already prefixed and pronounced by the people at the polls, rendering the duty and action of their Representatives as plain, simple and unobstructed as it was grand, imposing and important. That duty was to repeal the Yazoo Act, to annul and rescind the Yazoo Sale as unconstitutional, fraudulent and void, a huge treachery, a heinous conspiracy of the buyers and sellers against the people, the offspring of bribery and corruption. This duty upon full and convincing proofs laid before them, they unflinchingly performed. Whilst the State was thus asasserting and enforcing her unaltered ownership of the vast territories of which it had been sought to despoil her, she by the same Act disavowed all claim to the vile purchase money that had been thrust into her Treasury and directed it to be restored to those from whom it came or to whom it might belong. Moreover, to give the greater emphasis to her sovreign fiat of condemnation and annulment, she ordered every vestige of the accursed transaction to be obliterated from her records and the huge, pretentious enrollment of the Act itself to be given to the flames, consecrated although it was by accumulated high and solemn signatures and by the great Seal of Georgia pendant in massive wax. The high, unexampled, damnatory sentence was duly carried into execution under the broad, bright sky, on the beautiful State House square, at Louisville, the new seat of Government, in the presence of the Governor and Legislature and a mighty assemblage of the people. And according to a tradition, which cannot de doubted, for it has descended to us uncontradicted in a continuous current from that period to the present day, a holy, religious *eclat*, significant of the Divine displeasure on the great iniquity, was shed over the scene by drawing down the consuming fire from heaven with a sun-glass before that immense and imposing multitude of witnessing eyes.

SECTION VIII.

It was on the 13th of February, 1796, that this crushing blow was struck. After it a long pause ensued, during which the new Yazooists stood still grasping their scrip, awaiting an event which they soon began to foresee,—and which, upon its happening, would at once put a more hopeful face on their now ruined affairs. This event, alike foreseen and wished for by them, was the same that the original speculators had so long deprecated and thwarted, namely, the cession by Georgia to the United States, of all her Western territory, including these very Yazoo lands: A cession which the present claimants very well knew would, whilst carrying the lands over to the Federal Government, carry them at the same time *cum onere*, loaded with any and all claims to which they had previously become subject,—their own, the Yazoo claims, among the rest. An immediate result consequently of the cession would be the thronging of the Yazoo claimants to the Federal capital, and their becoming suitors to the Federal Government for the settlement of their claims.

But although such future cession to the United States undoubtedly became a foregone conclusion in all minds quickly after Georgia's annulment of the Yazoo sale, yet more than two years elapsed before the first step towards it was taken, before any proposal or overture was made from either side. This delay arose from the fact that our Legislature in 1796, among other denunciations of the Yazoo sale, had pronounced it unconstitutional, wholly denying the competency of the Legislature under the then existing Constitution of the State to alienate her Indian domains. It was a clear corrollary from this Legislative pronouncement that no authority existed anywhere among us either to offer or entertain a proposition for such alienation. And not only was there no competent authority for the purpose then existing in the State, but none could be called into existence earlier than the year 1798—at which time the new Constitutional Convention ordered by that faithless one of May, 1795, was to be held: Until the holding of which, therefore, the State had no alternative but to remain silent and inactive on the whole subject of a cession. And Congress also, in deference to the aforesaid disclaimer of power by our Legislature, observed a like silence and inaction, and refrained from any suggestion of a cession until after the Convention had been chosen and was within less than a month of the time of its assemblage. Then it was that Congress spoke, and on the 7th of April, 1798, passed an Act empowering the President of the United States to appoint three Commissioners, whose duty, among other things, it should be to receive from such commissioners as should be appointed on the part of Georgia any proposals for the relinquishment or cession of the whole or any part of the territory claimed by the State lying out of its ordinary jurisdiction.

This act was undoubtedly passed in anticipation of the Convention's soon meeting, and in the confidence that that Body would receive it as an overture for a cession and honor it as such with a suitable response. Nor was this confidence disappointed. How was it possible it should have been? For of that Convention the noble Jackson, although Governor of the State at the time, was a member, master spirit there too as in the anti-Yazoo Legislature of 1796,—surrounded now as he was then, by his most choice, enlightened and pure-minded compatriots. From such men no botched work could come when a great public duty was to be performed. And certainly nothing could be more thorough and perfect than what actually came from their hands in regard both to the Yazoo subject and the State's Western territory. What they did was to erect an express constitutional barrier against the sale of the territory of the State or any part of it to individuals or private companies unless a county or counties should have first been laid off including such territory, and the Indian rights thereto should have been first extinguished also. Anybody can see at a glance how completely this prohibition goes to the bottom of things, exterminating the very roots and all possibility in the future of such crimes and misdoings as the two Yazoo sales had been. It is not in this provision, however, although it was wise and statesman-like in the highest degree, that we find the response that was wanted to the above mentioned Congressional overture. *That* presents itself in another clause which enables the Legislature to sell or contract to the United States all or any part of the State's Western domain lying beyond the Chattahoochee, and then again still further in that third clause which authorizes the Legislature to give its consent to the establishment by the United States of one or more governments westward of that river. Behold here implanted in our long honored Constitution of 1798, by the magnanimous men who then held sway in Georgia, the germ of the memorable cession of April, 1802, and of the two great States of Alabama and Mississippi.

These provisions show that the sense of the Convention was in favor of a cession to the United States. The first Legislature under the new Constitution, being of like opinion, proceeded at once to take measures for carrying out the object. On the 6th of December, 1799, it passed an Act appointing Commissioners to settle with those of the United States the terms of the cession ; to which Act the ensuing Legislature of 1800, made an amendment, adding to the list of Commissioners on the part of the State the name of Gen. Jackson, who was now filling a second gubernatorial term, but had just been chosen by the Legislature to the United States Senate as successor to Gen. Gunn, whose time was to expire on the 3d of March ensuing.

The great business now proceeded at a quickened pace. Assuming it as certain that the ultimate and early event would be a vast territorial cession, embracing the Yazoo lands, Congress had already in May, 1800, amended the aforementioned Act of April, 1798, by imposing on the National Commissioners therein created, a heavy and tedious additional duty which would and could only arise after the cession had been made,—the duty, namely, of investigating all claims against the lands ceded, of receiving from the claimants propositions for the compromise and settlement of their claims, and of laying a full statement of the whole, together with their opinion thereon, before Congress for its decision thereon. Mr. Jefferson upon entering on the Presidency found the appointing of these Commissioners one of the first matters demanding his attention. His sense of the exceeding magnitude and importance of the duties to be devolved on them is strongly attested by the men he selected. They were none other than three of the members of his Cabinet—Mr. Madison, his Secretary of State, Mr. Gallatin, his Secretary of the Treasury, and Mr. Lincoln, his Attorney General. A grander and more imposing set of Commissioners for any object or purpose whatever was never anywhere constituted, whether we regard the illustrious character and ability of the men or their ripe, thorough statesmanship and public experience, or the splendor and importance of the offices they were then actually holding near the President. Their very appointment shows that Mr. Jefferson contemplated that in performing their trust as Commissioners they were to be all the while acting under the responsibility that attached to them as components of his Administration.

Fully worthy of association and conference with such men were the Commissioners on the part of Georgia,—Jackson, Baldwin, and Milledge,—whose functions, however, were to be more simple and of shorter continuance, confined to the single business of negotiating and signing the cession expected to be made by the State—a work which was completed on the 24th day of April, 1802, whereby Georgia conveyed to the United States all the territory stretching from her present Western boundary to the Mississippi river, and lying between the 31st and the 35th parallels of Latitude.

In consideration of which the United States agreed to pay Georgia a million and a quarter of dollars, and to be at the expense of extinguishing for her the Indian occupancy on all the territory still retained by the State.

Long before the great bargain was brought to a close, the Yazoo claimants were astir wherever any of them were to be found in America or Europe. Either in person or by their agents or proxies, they were soon seen swarming around the United States Commissioners and overwhelming them with formal notices of their claims, warning them that if the National Government bought these lands from Georgia, it would have to buy them at its peril, subject to be supplanted and ousted by the older and better title which they asserted they already held from Georgia, the deeds and evidences of which they paraded before and deposited with the Commissioners, *into* the details of whose labors, at once immense and minute, there is no call upon us to enter in this tract. All that we need here is the general result at which they arrived and which, along with their opinion, they reported to Congress on the 16th of February, 1803, with full statements and accompanying documents, all which may be found spreading over many pages of the State Papers.* In their report the Commissioners mention the notorious fact, confirmed by the title papers the claimants had lodged with them, that the lands had all passed out of the original grantees and were now vested in second holders. These secondary holders said that they had bought them without knowledge or notice of the fraud, bribery and corruption that had contaminated the original purchase and, therefore, they claimed immunity for their title from these grounds of attack. The Commissioners, nevertheless, set forth fully all the criminating evidence which had come to their hands, being the same that was before the Rescinding Legislature, and in the body of their report is stated the very significant fact, "that all the deeds given by the Companies, which had been exhibited to the Commissioners, as well as all the sub-

American State Papers, Public Lands, Vol. I, pages 132, 159.

sequent deeds, with only two or three exceptions, not only give a special instead of a general warranty, but have also a special covenant in the following words: 'And lastly, it is covenanted and expressly agreed and understood by and between the parties to these presents, that neither the grantors aforesaid, nor their heirs, executors or administrators, shall be held to any further or other warranty than is herein before expressed, nor liable to the refunding any money in consequence of any defect in their title from the State of Georgia, if any such there should hereafter appear to be.'" Such a phenomenon as this on the very face of their deeds would have been enough in law to charge the claimants with the damning notice they denied, even in the absence of all the other convincing proofs against them that existed. Upon this fact, then, and all the other facts and circumstances which came to their knowledge, the Commissioners were forced to the conclusion that the title of the claimants could not be supported.

But they proceeded, nevertheless, to express their belief that "the interest of the United States, the tranquility of those who may hereafter inhabit that territory, and various equitable considerations which may be urged in favor of most of the present claimants, render it expedient to enter into a compromise on reasonable terms;" and they thereupon proceed to submit to the consideration of Congress two plans of compromise, one proposing compensation to the claimants in land, the other in money—and in case the moneyed plan should be adopted, then that the claimants should be paid $2,500,000 in certificates of the Government, drawing interest, or $5,000,000 in non-interest bearing certificates, payable out of the proceeds of the sale of the lands.

There is a very deep significance in this recommendation of a compromise by the commissioners. It amounts to their saying that, "although the claimants have no title and the Government is under no obligation, legal or equitable, to pay them a cent, yet as they will have a vast and interminable right and faculty of litigation, annoyance and vexation against the future settlers on these lands under titles to be derived from the Government, which, among other huge evils, will have the effect of greatly retarding the sale, settlement and improvement of the lands,—that, therefore, it would be both for the interest of the Government and the interest and tranquility of the future settlers,—to extinguish these claims *now* even at the cost of five millions of dollars, rather than leave all these innumerable acres thus liable to permanent controversy and litigation, and every settler on them thus exposed to law suits, against which the Government would be bound to be at all the trouble and expense of defending him and of making him in the end a full remuneration and imdemnity, in case he should chance unexpectedly lose the land he had bought from the Government.

Such was the view the Commissioners took of this matter, now can the practical sense and wisdom of it be gainsaid.

Yet it prevailed not with Congress. For seven long years from 1803 to 1810, the claimants persisted to little purpose in beseiging and battering that body, which seemed, indeed, rather to harden than to give way under their ceaseless importunity. The terrible Napoleanic wars were all this while raging over Europe, threatening, striving, as it were, to draw our country, too, within their fearful vortex, out of which to keep her was Mr. Jefferson's great study, using to that end all upright and honorable means, even to such harsh and exhausting measures as the Embargo, the Restriction and the Non-Intercourse; in spite of all of which the dreaded engulfment came at last, under Mr. Madison's administration. Yet little recking of the country's troubles or of the mighty and distressful turmoil of the times, the Yazooists haunted Congress every session with their ill-odored, unrelenting claims, backed by the ablest and most influential lobby that had up to that time ever invested Congress; sustained at the same time by a powerful Northern advocacy on the floor. But all would not do. The period had not yet come when the people's Representatives could be gotten to throw a propitiating sop of millions drawn from the sweat of their brow, in order to buy off a vile claim pronounced to be at once the offspring of crime, fraud and corruption, and to be devoid also of all legal quality and character, by which it could demand and coerce support.

If at this remote day any wonder should be felt that the recommendation of a compromise by a Commission composed of such great men and high functionaries as Madison, Gallatin, and Lincoln, should have been so unavailing with the House, where the Bill for the proposed appropriation had to originate,—let it be recalled how lofty and unbending the temper of that House was in those days in maintaining its independence of thought and action, especially on questions of taking money out of the Treasury, that is to say, out of the people's pockets; secondly, how fiercely public and Congressional rage then burned against the monstrous Yazoo crime; and lastly, that that prodigy of parliamentary oratory and debating talent, John Randolph, was there from the outset to the end—in all the pride of young manhood, yet ripe genius and stored, cultivated mind, lashing the House up all the while to its indignant duty with his versatile, unsparing, exhaustless powers of eloquence and argument, persuasion and invective.

Weary of long waiting and continued disappointment, to which they saw no end on their present tack, the Yazooists determined at last on a new departure—on demonstrating to Congress in a manner, at once practical and astounding, that their title was one capable of being supported in law, the opinion of the three Cabinet Commissioners and of the majority of the House to the contrary notwithstanding, and that their claims, in the event of being thrust out of the National Legislature, were sure of finding a favorable reception in the sanctuary of the National Courts. The proceedure instituted and prosecuted to a close with a view to this demonstration long stood out to view as the most erratic and lawless judicial phenomenon ever known in our history.

It was eminently an unprincipled and audacious thing, and nothing but that sort of triumphal palliation which success too often imparts to crime in this world could ever have prevented it from being regarded by everybody as also a mad and disgraceful thing.

The plan was to get up and carry through all the windings and forms of high litigation a *feigned case*, so contrived as to draw out from the Supreme Court of the United States, if entertained there, a solemn, though volunteer, gratuitous pronouncement *ex cathedra* in favor of the claimants on all the points they deemed necessary or advantageous to their title. It was the celebrated case of Fletcher against Peck, reported at great length in the 6th volume of Cranch. No professional man acquainted with the story of the Yazoo Fraud can possibly read that case without seeing in it the unmistakable brands and marks of a *feigned case*, even though one of the Judges, Johnson, had not weakly called attention to the flagrant fact*—I say weakly, because he nevertheless, was not prevented by the fact, from entertaining the case and pronouncing an opinion thereon in favor of the Yazooists. To lawyers it would be neither necessary nor complimentary to enter here into the long and intricate details of the case with its artistically concocted pleadings and laboriously constructed special verdict; for they are to be

---

*Mr. Justice Johnson, in delivering his opinion, made the following remarks at the close: "I have been very unwilling to proceed to the decision of this case at all. It appears to bear strong evidence upon the face of it of being a mere feigned case. It is our duty to decide on the rights but not on the speculation of parties. My confidence, however, in the respectable gentlemen,† who have been engaged for the parties, have induced me to abandon my scruples, in the belief that they would never consent to impose a mere feigned case upon this Court.—*Cranch's Rep.*, 6*th Vol.*, *p.* 147–8.

---

†And yet Robert Goodloe Harper was one of those gentlemen, whose name, as one of the large, original Yazoo partners, was in thousands of Congressional documents with which the country was then flooded. Thirty years ago, in a book store in Washington, I picked up a bound second hand copy of one of them, which I now have, printed by order of Congress in 1809.

supposed acquainted with them already. To the laity such a recital would certainly be alike irksome and unprofitable. Suffice it, then, to say that the Circuit Court of Massachusetts in which the feigned suit was started, gratified fully the wishes of the claimants, deciding every point as they desired, and perfectly validating their title from beginning to end. Nevertheless, they carried the case up to the Supreme Court at Washington, in order that it might be there affirmed and clinched forever. And it was securely clinched by that tribunal. With the exception of poor Johnson, all the Court, from a regard to decency and appearances, made itself voluntarily blind to the staring fact *that it was a feigned case*, and consequently one which it was highly discreditable and criminal for the Court to entertain and decide at all. Moreover, the whole Court persistently shut its eyes to the grand, vital principles on which Washington had so decidedly combated and nullified the first Yazoo Sale, that of 1789, and on which he had equally come forth denouncing and ready, if need there should be, to combat and nullify likewise this second Yazoo Sale of 1795, whenever it should put forth its head so as to be within reach of the National arm. Overlooking all these vast and weighty considerations, so important with the Father of his Country, the Court studiously narrowed its view to the points to which the Yazooists for their own purposes chose to solicit its attention. The result was a judgment delivered at the February term, 1810, going the full length for the title of the Yazoo claimants, pronouncing it just as good as if the Rescinding Act of Georgia had never been passed, invulnerable, indeed, by any act of the State either singly or in combination with the United States, and consequently better than the younger title the State had conveyed to the United States by the cession of April, 1802. In fine, it was a judgment which fully verified and reduced to an absolute certainty all the little credited vaticinations, the possibility of which turning out true had led the Commissioners to recommend the five million compromise as a thing for the interest of the United States and the interest and tranquility of the future settlers on the contested territory.

And now Congress, seeing itself *in vinculis*, and very much at the mercy of the claimants in regard to all the Yazoo lands, upon well revolving the matter thought it best to come to terms with them, and finally, after a moody interval of some four years, passed the Act of 31st of March, 1814, appropriating the sum of five million of dollars to be raised by sales of the lands, to the perpetual quieting and extinguishment all the Yazoo Claims, which being agreed at once to be accepted by the claimants, there was an end at last of a matter which I have essayed to trace from its origin and through all its vicissitudes, and which with a better handling than I have been capable of giving it, would be found forming a chapter in the history of Georgia and of the United States interesting and important, as well as multifarious, complicated and long.

FINIS.

ERRATA IN PART I.

On page 34, 16 line from top, read *post* instead of *past*.

On page 36, 5th line from bottom, read *fury* instead of *fray*

PART III.

GENERAL JAMES JACKSON.

GENERAL ANTHONY WAYNE.

CHAPTER 1.

GEN. JAMES JACKSON—GEN. ANTHONY WAYNE.

As when the laborious husbandman whose daily bread is sweetened by the sweat of his brow and by the holy sense of providing by his toil for his wife and children, has been all the week long, with measured stride and stalwart arms, swinging the scythed cradle here and there over his field wherever the nodding harvest looked ripest and most tempting; wearied at length he pauses from his task at the near approach of the sacred day of rest, surveys his work, eyes gratefully his thick-standing sheaves, and taking note of what there still is for his industrious hands to do, beholds, well pleased, the rich, retiring nooks and deep, fertile hollows that yet await his blade:—so do I, having in an irregular, desultory manner, treated of the development, fortunes and affairs of Georgia during a considerable lapse of time next after the Revolutionary war, now looking back perceive in the period I have thus traversed not a few things which although interesting and well worthy of notice, have as yet remained untouched by my roving pen.

And first—of Gen. Jackson himself it is meet and would be both grateful and rewarding that something further should be said and told, even though it carry us back beyond the Revolutionary era. For it is attended alike with pleasure and profit to follow and observe such a man from his early beginnings and through all his vicissitudes. What we have already had occasion to see and know about him naturally excites curiosity to know more, and we would fain get a full view of one so marked and superior, so much above the world's ordinary standard and requirements, so much a pride and honor to our common nature ;—one whom such a judge as Thos. Spalding, himself assuredly a most noble man and who enjoyed the amplest opportunities, in his long and honorable life, of knowing men of distinction in Europe and America, advisedly pronounced, forty odd years after his death, "the noblest man with whom it had been his lot to be acquainted."*

He landed on our shores from his native England in 1772: a lone lad of fifteen years. Of virtuous and respectable parentage, breeding and connexions, we cannot but suppose that he had at that immature age already strongly evinced safe and superior qualities of mind and character and given evidences of high future promise ;—otherwise his father would hardly have consented, nor would such a man as Mr. Wereat, a name of great note and respect in our Colonial and Revolutionary annals and at one time Acting Governor of the State, have advised him to consent to his son's coming to America under his Mr. Wereat's, auspices, to make his own way and build up his fortunes in this remote and then wild part of the earth. We are told that his father

---

* Bench and Bar of Georgia—vol 2, page 102. Title, John Houston. See there a letter from Mr. Spalding to Maj. Miller, of the 19th October, 1850, from which the following is an extract:

"It gives me pleasure to state that Gen. James Jackson, the noblest man with whom it has been my lot to be acquainted, when I called upon him as Governor to give me a letter to Mr. King, our then Minister in London, kept me to dine with him ; and asked me what were Mr. Gibbons' receipts from his profession." I replied, "Three thousand pounds per annum." "My own were about that amount when I unwisely left my profession for politics. Mr. Gibbons, as a whole, was the greatest lawyer in Georgia." Let me say to you that Gen. Jackson and Mr. Gibbons had exchanged three shots at each other. They were considered the bitterest enemies by the public. A high-minded man knows no enmity."

I had intended to add here a few words of my own about Mr. Spalding, whom I knew, revered and held in the highest honor. But on turning to the notice of him in White's Hirtorical Sketches of Georgia, I prefer it to any thing I can write. It will be found in full as a note at the end of this chapter.

was a strenous lover of freedom and free Government and of the rights of the people as against arbitrary power,—and particularly that he was a warm sympathiser with the Colonies in their as yet bloodless quarrel with the mother country for their rights and liberties. These principles and sentiments young Jackson had deeply imbibed before quitting the paternal roof and indeed they largely influenced his emigration and casting his lot here. Accordingly, it was not long after reaching his new home in Georgia, before they shone out in his warm participation in the feelings and proceedings which were even then beginning to herald the approaching Revolution.

The very pursuit to which his father and Mr. Wereat had destined him in Georgia is proof of their high opinion of his capacity and endowments. For although so young, he was, upon his arrival in Savannah, at once put to the study of law in the office of Samuel Farley, Esq., applying himself at the same time to such other studies as were necessary to the completion of his general education. With what enthusiasm, industry and success he applied himself, some idea may be formed from the fact handed down from his own lips by Mr. Spalding, that after the Revolutionary war and before embarking in politics, he practiced law so prosperously that his professional earnings at their acme reached to the sum of £3,000 per annum—a prodigious amount when we consider the small population and the still smaller wealth, commerce and resources of Georgia in those times.

Before, however, finishing his studies and coming to the Bar, and whilst yet a mere stripling, he, like that other glorious young genius of the day-spring of the Revolution, Alexander Hamilton, betwixt whom and himself there are not wanting strong points of resemblance, obeyed the impulse of courage, ambition, patriotism and a passionate love of liberty and hastened to exchange his books and seclusion for arms and the din of war.

It comports not with my plan to enter into the minute

details of the young soldier's Revolutionary career, and indeed nothing could be more unnecessary. For are they not to be found written in every book of the chronicles of Georgia?—where, among the many things in relation to him, it is recorded that his first feat of arms (a very daring and purely volunteer affair of himself and a little band of other patriots, resulting in their burning several of the enemy's armed vessels which had grounded in proceeding up the river against the city) won for him much applause and a lieutenancy. . Soon a captaincy rewarded his rapidly developing martial merits And so he continued to rise, never failing to justify his promotions by his performances—until at length we see him before the end of the war by Gen. Green's appointment and the confirmation of Congress, the commander, in his 24th year, of a mixed Legion of cavalry and infantry. On every occasion and in every position throughout the long, harsh struggle, he added to his steadily growing reputation. Victory brought him laurels which, so fine was ever his conduct, no adversities or reverses that befel him could take away or dim. For alike in distress and in good fortune he exhibited fertile and brilliant capacity, an unflinching devotion to duty, indefatigable activity and a heroism not to be cowed by wounds, perils, fatigues; nor by hunger, thirst and nakedness, nor all the other nameless discouragements and sufferings of ill-provided war and campaigning in the woods and swamps of lower Georgia and Carolina against an enemy entrenched and under cover in Augusta, Savannah and Charleston, and continually sallying out from these strongholds as assailants, pursuers, marauders, devastators—and then rushing back again to their shelter when routed or endangered or wearied out or sated with spoliation. Such an impression did his extraordinary merits and services in the closing scenes of the war in Georgia make on his General, that renowned soldier and commander, Anthony Wayne, that on the occasion of the final surrender of Savannah by the British to our arms in July, 1782, he honored him by ordering that the formal surrender should be made into his hands. And accordingly it was so done by the keys of the city being delivered up to him by the evacuating British commander in presence of both armies.

One of those remarkable incidents which, by reason of befalling men of celebrity, often become canonized in history, is related to have occurred during the gloomiest period of the Revolution to him and his young friend, John Milledge, the same who afterwards became a Representative and then a Senator in Congress, and Governor also of the State—in honor of whom likewise Milledgeville was named, destined as the permanent capital of the State—a destiny, however, not permitted to stand, but to the mortal shame of Georgia set aside now by her submission thus far to an ephemeral satrap's wanton, dishonoring edict. During the utter prostration of our cause in lower Georgia, consequent on the fall of Savannah, in 1778, these undaunted youthful patriots repaired together to South Carolina to seek service. Whilst on their way to join Gen. Moultrie's standard "barefoot and in rags, these sons of liberty," we are told, "were apprehended as spies by some American soldiers and condemned to be hung. The gallows was actually prepared, and but for the timely arrival of Maj. Devaux, who accidentally heard of the transaction, the two young patriots would have been executed."* Behold here in our own annals an authentic fact which taken in connection with the subsequent eminence and illustriousness of both the men, surpasses any thing in history, nay, even excels that famous antique fiction of Belisarius, old and blind, begging a penny,† victim of Justinian's imperial ingratitude and cruelty after a lifetime of the hardships and dangers of war in his service, and an hundred victories won for him and declining Rome.

The long revolutionary struggle being at last ended and the occupation of arms at an end with it,—peace found Col. Jackson standing amidst the ruins of the recent war like

* White's Statistics of Georgia, page 337. National Portrait Gallery. Title James Jackson.

† "Da Belisario obolum."

thousands of his brother officers and soldiers in utter poverty—houseless, penniless, without means or employment—with no resources but such as existed in his own mind and character, and in the boundless love and admiration of his fellow-citizens, a love and admiration heightened by a sense of gratitude for his services—all which was well attested by legislative resolutions of thanks and honor, and the gift to him by the State of a house and home in the city of Savannah.

But by nothing could he be paralysed or rendered a cypher. It was a necessity of his nature and character that he should cherish and pursue high aims under all circumstances, adverse or prosperous, of peace or of war. He went instantly to work in the arduous, aspiring profession to which he had been early dedicated. As we have already seen, he had stored and trained his mind by juridical and miscellaneous studies before the Revolution, and during it not in arms alone was he developed and exercised. Led by duty and martial ardor to harrangue his commands on many a trying occasion, he found out and cultivated that rare talent of ready, effective, stirring eloquence with which nature, study, self-discipline and practice combined gradually to endow him in a distinguished manner. This bright, crowning talent coming in aid of his general mass of ability and knowledge, and of his great energy, uprightness, industry and enthusiasm, he rose rapidly at the Bar and won the triumphant success there to which allusion has been made. So striking was his success and such the impression he made of possessing qualifications equal to any, the highest, spheres of public service, that his fellow-citizens soon looked forward with pride to his future career and foresaw the honors of the patriot statesman clustering on his brow along with those, already won, of the forum and the field. It was at this stage, in 1788, that the office of Governor was tendered him, but which his modesty declined, on the ground of the want of age and political experience. For though his ambition was high and mettlesome, yet it was far from being prurient and self-blinding, and did not lead him to think that what service he had seen in our Legislature, and which was all the political apprenticeship he had then had, was sufficient to fit one so young for the chief magistracy of the State.

There was, however, another great and interesting political theatre just opening at that time, better suited to his years, his genius, and his training and for which he felt a predilection that may have had some subtle influence, for aught we know, in disinclining him to the Governorship. For the new Federal Constitution had been now adopted, and in apportioning the representation of the States in Congress, there had been given to Georgia three members in the Lower House, and the Legislature at its first meeting afterwards had divided the State into three Congressional Districts for the election of those members. Gen. Jackson became a candidate and a successful one in the First or Eastern District, composed of the counties of Chatham, Liberty, Effingham, Glynn and Camden. In the Second or Middle District, Abraham Baldwin was chosen, and in the Third or Western, George Mathews. All over the United States, likewise, the people rallied in their respective States to make choice of their Representatives in this their First Congress under the new Federal system, and the Legislatures of the several States proceeded also to elect their first National Senators. Slowly and not without a seeming of backwardness and diffidence did the great historic body get together and go about its mighty task of building up from the very bottom, on a plan prefixed and wholly novel, a vast and complex Republican Empire. On the appointed day of meeting, the 4th of March, 1789, only eight Senators and thirteen Representatives were in attendance. Gradually other members came, but so scatteringly that it was as late as the first of April before a quorum appeared in the Lower House, and five days later still before there was one in the Senate, nor was it until the 30th of the month that Washington was installed and the new Government ready to go to work.

In the illustrious assemblage of tried, picked men with whom Gen. Jackson now saw himself associated in the National service, there was not a younger politician to be found than himself. So he himself tells us in one of his speeches. * And yet those who will follow him, as I have done, through the volumes containing the debates of that memorable, three-sessioned Congress, will perceive that he carried with him into that body not only the exalted manly fervor and public-spirit appropriate to his age, temperament and patriotic character, but also such thorough and various preparation of mind and knowledge, such accurate acquaintance with the subjects that had to be discussed, and such sense, talent and readiness in discussing them, in fine, such a judicious activity and such sound, enlightened views, as would have done honor to gray hairs and veteran statesmanship and soon secured to him rank and consideration among his fellow members. Keeping attention closely upon him throughout this, his two-years' Congressional novitiate, we at times cannot help feeling wonder, as in the very parallel case of Alexander Hamilton, that under all the actual circumstances of his whole preceding life he should have been able to make himself what he was in mental culture and discipline, and to have amassed such intellectual stores, especially of the political kind, as he showed himself to possess. Nothing but a very superior constitution of mind and nature combined with high ambition and indefatigable energy, industry and application can explain the rare and interesting phenomenon.

But whilst he was thus devoting himself to his country's service and acquiring a proud name in Congress, intelligence reached him there towards the end of his term, of an event at home for which he was unprepared and which was well calculated to sting him to the quick and rouse all the lion in his nature. The 3d of January, 1791, was the time of the election for the next Representative term. Though

* Gales' Debates of the First Congress, vol. 1, page 1,266.
Benton's Abr. Debates, vol. 1, page 216.

standing again as a candidate, yet with a noble conscientiousness and full of trust in his strength with the people, he stirred not from his distant post of duty, but faithfully remained there—leaving his election to the care of his constituents. That care happened not to be adequate to the needs of the case. It did not prevent frauds and lawless irregularities, the result of which was that he was superseded, and Gen. Anthony Wayne, now become a citizen of Georgia, the famed hero of Stony Point, the recoverer of Savannah and Lower Georgia from the British, the winner also of countless laurels at Brandywine, Germantown, Monmouth, and on other hard fought fields of the Revolution, was returned in his stead.

Perfectly characteristic was Gen. Jackson's dealing with the criminalities of this election, and particularly with the two most conspicuous criminals. His investigations, his denunciations and his vengeance were prompt and severe. The most outrageous villainy was that enacted in Camden county by Osborne, Judge of the Superior Court, who, after the close of the regular election in the day-time, not satisfied with the result, got possession of the legal returns and substituted therefor during the night the forged returns of a sham election. Short breathing time had he to exult over the success of this foul perpetration. The very next Legislature saw him arraigned for the crime, impeached by the House of Representatives, dragged before the Senate, tried, convicted and expelled from office,—the only precedent of the kind in any case higher than that of a Land Lottery Commissioner that has ever occurred in the State. The other worst iniquity was practiced in Effingham county. It consisted of illegal management of the election and some illegal voting besides, under the inimical counsel and influence of Thomas Gibbons, a man of very strong, determined character and great courage and ability, and much noted throughout a long and prosperous after-life, though never engaged in any but private and professional pursuits. He quitted Savannah, where he lived, and repaired to Effingham for the purpose of working there in the election against Gen. Jackson. It was the terrible denunciations which the part he thus acted brought down upon him from Gen. Jackson in his speech before the House of Representatives contesting the election, that, doubtless, led to the duel and 'the three shots' between them of which Mr. Spalding makes mention.*

* For a report of all the facts touching this election and of Gen. Jackson's speech, see Clarke's Book of Congressional Contested elections—p. p. 47–68.

Among the curious things contained in this report is the number of voters in each county. According to the statement furnished to the Committee on Elections by Gen Jackson, the poll, 'if all the returns had been received and had been proper', would have been just 551 votes in the whole district: Chatham county 259 Liberty 69, Effingham 107, Glynn 27, Camden 89. At that time there were in the whole State but eleven counties, and according to the census of 1790, the population was as follows:

	Freee Whites.	Slaves	Total.
Camden	234	70	304
Glynn...............	193	215	408
Liberty...........	1,303	4,025	5,328
Chatham	2,456	8,201	10,657
Effingham........	1,674	750	2,424
Richmond........	7,162	4,116	11,278
Burke.............	7,064	2 392	9,456
Washington....	3,856	694	4,550
Wilkes	24,052	7,268	31,320
Franklin..........	885	156	1,041
Greene	4,020	1,377	5,397
	53,797	29,164	82,163

Columbia county was created out of Richmond by an Act of 10th of December, 1790, but was not organized when the census was taken. Wilkes had then undergone no subdivision, but still retained all her vast pre-revolutionary territory—which accounts for the numerousness of her population.

Mr. Gibbons, in his advanced years, following a fashion formerly not uncommon among Savannah families rich enough to afford it, had a Northern summer residence which was at Elizabethtown, in New Jersey. This circumstance led to a very noted. if not the most noted, thing in his life—a thing which caused his name to become notorious and familiar all over the United States both in conversation and in print. Disbelieving in the constitutionality of the law of New York conferring on a chartered company and its assignees the exclusive right of navigating the waters of that State by steam vessels,—he commenced running in 1818 a line of steamboats of his own between Elizabethtown Point and New York City in violation of the exclusive chartered right. As was foreseen, Ogden, the company's assignee for that route, resorted at once to law to stop Gibbons' boats. He filed a bill before Chancellor Kent for a present and perpetual injunction against Gibbons, which the Chancellor granted, holding the New York law constitutional. Gibbons carried the case

The Congress to which Gen. Wayne was returned assembled on the 24th of October, 1791. At the end of a week from that date we find him in his seat as a member, where he had been but a fortnight when he was disturbed by Gen. Jackson appearing and contesting his right to that seat. The contest lasted several months, Gen. Wayne remaining in his seat and exercising full Representative functions all the while. The investigations were thorough and brought out abundant proof that the General's election was illegal but none whatever implicating the General himself in any of the illegal means by which it had been effected. Nor was there ever any imputation against him personally in connection with the election. It was the not uncommon case of a candidate's partizans without his participation or

up to the highest tribunal in New York, the Court of Errors, where the decision rendered against him in the Court of Chancery was sustained and affirmed. Whereupon an appeal was taken by him to the Supreme Court of the United States which upon full argument and consideration reversed the New York decision and pronounced the New York law unconstitutional, thereby throwing open all the waters of the United States to free navigation by steam. The case throughout its long pendency was regarded as one of immense public, political and commercial importance, and excited, consequently, a strong and unusual interest, and Mr. Gibbons himself, came to be everywhere viewed as the champion of free trade between the States, and indeed somewhat in the light of a great public benefactor by having taken upon himself the burden of this magnificent, costly and finally victorious litigation. In 1824, not long after Mr. Gibbons' triumph in the Supreme Court of the United States, I heard Judge Berrien say in conversing with some gentlemen about it, that Mr. Gibbons, whilst the case was yet pending, made his will and appropriated $40,000 to carrying on the suit in case it should not be ended before his death. Upon some one present expressing surprise, Judge Berrien remarked that Mr. Gibbons was a very able lawyer and felt great pride in having his opinion on the constitutional question sustained. Mr. Spalding, in his letter from which I have already quoted, mentions that he was a law student of Mr. Gibbons, and speaks of him as a great lawyer and a man of most determined character. Cornelius Vanderbilt, more familiarly known as Commodore Vanderbilt, now renowned among the men of New York, great by being rich, was one of Mr. Gibbons' steamboat captains, and was in the course of the litigation actually brought before Chancellor Kent once, charged with a contempt in disobeying the injunction against Gibbons' boats.

In the matter of Vanderbilt, 4 Johnson's Chan. R. 57. Ogden vs Gibbons, Ib. 150. Gibbons vs. Ogden, 17 Johnson's R. 488. Gibbons vs. Ogden, 9. Wheaton's R. 1.

privity doing wrong things and going criminal lengths for him from which he himself would have revolted. No final action was reached by the House till late in March when a decision was pronounced setting aside both the contestants, declaring a vacancy and calling for a new election, at which Mr. Milledge was chosen, neither Gen. Wayne or Gen. Jackson entering the lists as a candidate, and so both these very eminent and meritorious men were sent into retirement.

But their exile was short and more than compensated by their being each soon called to a more exalted and important sphere of public employment. Gen. Wayne, than whom no truer son of Mars ever intensified the splendor of the American arms, being solicited by Washington, almost immediately resumed the sword and went at once to that inveterate theatre of Indian hostilities and British tamperings on the Lake frontier where our armies had for years been so unlucky, and there in August, 1794, at the great battle of the Miami of the Lakes, the greatest and most memorable in all our annals of Indian warfare, repaired the disasters of Harmar and St. Clair and by a bloody arbitrament opened the way to that permanent Indian peace in the North-West which Washington was, as we have seen heretofore,* successful, by peaceful, diplomatic means in bringing about in the South and South-West. This signal and priceless triumph of Wayne's generalship shone the more brilliantly under the dark contrast of the defeat of his predecessors and it may be regarded, too, somewhat as a death-halo settling on his brow, as it was the last fighting exploit of a life that was not to last much longer. For he survived but two years more, dying in the service and at his post on the Indian frontier, Commander-in-Chief of the Army of the United States. So it is inscribed on the monument erected to him at his birthplace in Chester, Pennsylvania, by his brethren of the Society of the Cincinnati.

And he died also still a citizen and a cherished adopted

* In the article on the Oconee War, Part I.

son of Georgia. For in passing from her service into that of the United States, he passed not from her embrace nor lost his domicil, at once tribute of gratitude and memorial of honor, on her soil. He thoroughly won her devotion when as second in command to Gen. Greene* in the South, he had wrought out the full deliverance of the State from the enemy towards the close of the Revolution. And in fact the successes of Greene and Wayne in the extreme South had nearly as much to do in bringing the war to a close as the more impressive and celebrated triumph of Washington over Cornwallis in Virginia. As a consequence of these great Southern services, Wayne as well as Greene was remembered by Georgia when peace came, and she acknowledged her heavy debt to him by bestowing on him a fine estate near Savannah on the soil he had rescued. And hence like Gen. Greene he was led to make Georgia his home. The precise time of his coming I have no means of fixing, but it was certainly later than the year 1787, for we find him in the last months of that year still a citizen of Pennsylvania, and serving as a delegate in her Convention called to ratify the new Federal Constitution. That he should have become Gen. Jackson's opponent for Congress was undoubtedly a circumstance of a nature to inspire regret at the time of its occurrence, and for a long while afterwards. For it was just one of those contests in which our grief over the party that should be defeated was incapable of compensation by any joy that we could feel at the success of his rival. That grief too was in this case not a little exasperated and tinctured with resentment on account of the reprehensible means by which success had been achieved. But here again we take comfort, for that General Wayne was personally untouched by the foul arts employed in his behalf and stands clear of reproach alike from the public and his own conscience and his wronged and irritated competitor. And now at this remote day looking back on the whole affair and seeing how it proved eventually harmless alike to the two

* See his speech on Mrs. Greene's Claims, I. Vol. Benton's Abr. 335-6.

Generals and the country, it cannot be otherwise than that the present generation of the people of Georgia, filially avaricious of every ray of honor that can be counted to her brow, must feel pride at such a spectacle in her history as Anthony Wayne attracted by her generous love and gratitude to become one of her citizens, and as such suing for her suffrages as a candidate for Congress and actually serving her for nearly five months as a Representative in Congress, blameless himself in being there, however great the blame of others for the means used to put him there.

He was born early in the year 1745, which made him older than Gen. Jackson by more than a dozen years. Like Jackson he was of good ancestry, of superior soldierly stock particularly, his grandfather having fought with reputation as the commander of a squadron under King William III at the Battle of the Boyne, in 1690, and his father having been distinguished as well in expeditions against the Indians as in civil affairs in Pennsylvania in the Colonial times. And that he inherited the martial temper and bravery and the strong military bent of his race was manifest not only by all his actions and career, but is strikingly visible in his very looks and lineaments, heroic and spirited in the highest degree, as they have come down to us on canvass. His early advantages were of a high order and were so well improved that we may set him down as having had an education ample for the purposes of a life of activity and distinction either in peace or war. It is not surprising that these advantages aided by family and connexion, by superior endowments of mind and person, by the winning power of a promising, aspiring young manhood and by his noble ardor and forwardness from the very first in the cause of the uprising colonies, should have obtained for him at the beginning of the war a position which the youthful and orphan Jackson with all his merits did not succeed in reaching till near its end,—that of a Colonelcy. In this grade, however, though so honorable to a man of only thirty-one years, Wayne did not linger long. February, 1777, saw him a Brigadier-General, in which rank it was that he made his name resplendent and immortal, covering it with a Revolutionary glory second only to what was earned by Washington himself and by Gen. Greene. He became a Major-General not until 1792, when Washington sent him, as we have just seen, at the head of the army to conquer a peace and which, in the very teeth of British intrusion and instigation, he did most triumphantly succeed in conquering not from one, two or three Indian Nations only, but from all the North-Western tribes combined.

Whilst Gen. Wayne was thus reaping for himself and his country an overflowing recompense for the loss of his seat in the House of Representatives, Gen. Jackson also soon saw himself made more than whole by a proud amends. The very next Legislature after his exclusion from the Lower House conferred upon him a seat in the Senate of the United States for a full term commencing on the 4th of March, 1793. When he had been in that elevation but two years, he heeded the cry of the people calling upon him to disrobe himself and come down at once to their help against the Yazoo Fraud. His ready obedience gave the country example of a resignation the noblest on record, and inculcated a lesson which noble natures only will be ever quick to feel and imbibe, that there are some occasions discernible by such natures which render humility a sublime practical virtue, and make it more glorious to descend with a magnanimous alacrity to the lowlier posts of public service than to cling with tenacious pride and self-love to the higher and more shining ones. What he had to do in the matter for which he resigned and how he acquitted himself therein, we have already sufficiently seen, and seen also how after finishing that task, he otherwise faithfully and ably served Georgia at home until the time came when she sent him once more to represent her in the National Senate contemporaneously with Mr. Jefferson's accession to the Presidency. Death found him in that position and at his post on the 19th of March, 1806. All that was mortal of him is still inhumed at the Federal capital, and the citizen of Georgia who would look upon his grave and the simple stone that marks it can to this day only do so by a pilgrimage to the Congressional burying ground at Washington City. By no monument, statue or even portrait has Georgia ever done homage to the man who from his dawn of youth to his death served her with so much devotion and brought her so much honor and benefit, and whose name on the whole sheds more lustre on her history than any other on its page—a lustre which is destined to brighten under the test of time and contemplation—a man, too, who loved her so intensely as to cause him to exclaim that if, when he died, his heart should be opened and examined, her name would be found imprinted there.* Yet happily his likeness remains to us and those who yearn to know what manner of man he was to the eye, need but to turn to the American Portrait Gallery in order to gaze upon the noble, intellectual, *spirituelle* countenance and the thinking, high-bred, cultured looks and expression that belonged to him.

In estimating Gen. Jackson and awarding him the pre-eminence among the proud names which are the especial growth of Georgia, regard should be had to him as a whole. We must study him in all his elements, qualities and relations, in all his actions and situations. In some particulars there may be named those whom he cannot be said to surpass or even equal. But then there is to be seen belonging to him a signal felicity in which he stands alone,—a felicity consisting in his *tout ensemble* of virtues, talents and merits, moral and intellectual, martial and political, heroic,—civic, chivalrous,—conferring on him a glory composite alike of peace and war, and which rises to the beautiful and sublime in both, though in what it derives from peace it is more fortunate even than in what it owes to war, in that its peaceful part furnishes an impressive, ever-speaking example and lesson to his countrymen, exhorting to purity, rectitude and true wisdom in public affairs, and urging relentlessly to the

* White's Statistics. Title—Jackson County.

undoing, crushing and preventing of all public turpitude and profligacy. Even now in Georgia that example and lesson start up to view and challenge a thoughtful remembrance, warning our people that if they would protect the coffers of the State from legalized robbery, their Legislators from the contaminating approaches of a bribery and corruption outstripping the Yazoo infamy and themselves and their posterity from an iniquitous taxation at once disgraceful, oppressive and blighting,—a taxation to carry out, sanction and reward the villanies of Bullock and his crew, they must pursue the course and act on the principles of Gen. Jackson and his compatriots, and erect an insurmountable constitutional barrier against the payment of Bullock's fraudulent bonds, just as Jackson and his co-workers in the convention of 1798, not leaving such a matter as another possible Yazoo enormity within the Legislative competency, erected an insuperable constitutional barrier against any more sales whatever of Indian lands by the Legislature except to the Government of the United States, and thereby made forever impossible any more Yazoo frauds in Georgia.

Gen. Jackson was not the only one of his blood and name that crossed the ocean to cast his lot in Georgia. Long after him and when he had attained to great eminence, subsequently to the Revolutionary war, a gifted younger brother came, still in his boyhood, who under his fraternal care and guidance grew up to be an admirable, meritorious, accomplished man, useful and honored in his day, though moving in a more confined and unambitous sphere than that illustrated by the General himself. All who are familiar with the history of Franklin College during its slow *renaissance* and hard struggle for a new life after the war of 1812, will know at once that Dr. Henry Jackson, Professor of Natural Philosophy in that Institution fifty-odd years ago, is the person to whom I am now alluding. Among the felicities incidental to my Law studentship in Athens, under Judge Clayton, in 1821, I have always felt it a chief one that by means of it I came to see and know Dr.

Jackson and Dr. Waddell, the then President of the College,—Dr. Jackson having, however, at that time resigned his professorship and gone into retirement, though still continuing to reside in Athens. But quite a number of the brilliant and noble-minded young men who had sat under his instructions were still in the college or otherwise resident in Athens, and I became socially almost as one of themselves. I was struck by the manner in which they invariably spoke of Dr. Jackson. Their conversation about him literally glowed with admiration. They exulted at his talents, character and acquirements and his faculty of winning the interested attention of the young and inspiring their minds. More fortunate than most of the learned men whose destiny it is to fill the chairs of colleges, he was more than a mere man of books and of the closet. He had also seen the world and been a man of the world in the highest, best and most enlarging sense, and the advantages he had enjoyed as such had been to him as seed sown on good ground. It was, according to the published records of the College, as far back as 1811, that he was first called to the Professorship. But he had hardly filled it a twelvemonth when the collapse of the college caused by the war, opened his way, without a resignation, to another and to him a most attractive career. In 1813 he was invited by that great man, William H. Crawford, then just appointed Minister to France, to accompany him in the capacity of Secretary of Legation. He remained in Europe several years, continuing there for some time after Mr. Crawford's return, a studious, enlightened observer of the mighty and tangled mass of events that had in that quarter of the globe been for many years drifting fearfully through seas of blood to a conclusion now in full view—the universal calm of a despotism joyful after the long, convulsive storms through which it had passed. All the while too he was profiting diligently by the splendid opportunities that lay around him for enlarged scientific acquisitions and varied mental culture and enrichment. The result was that he returned home a man of rare and manifold accomplishments and was justly entitled to the extraordinary estimation in which he was immediately held.

But though anxiously expected, as I remember to have read in a Life of President Finley published many years ago and not now within my reach, he did not get back to his Professorial post in time to co-operate, in setting the College anew on its feet, with that greatly-beloved and deeply-lamented gentleman;—who coming from New Jersey a stranger among us, but bringing with him to the headship of the College great advantages of character and prestige, was received with general delight and was successful by his opening labors and exertions in making a most happy impression throughout the State. Public expectation in regard to him rose to a very high pitch, soon to be dashed however, by his premature death in the fall of 1817, filling all Georgia with grief ere the first year of his Presidency had expired. His successor was Dr. Moses Waddell, the father of classical education in our up-country, the schoolmaster of Crawford, Calhoun, McDuffie, Pettigrew, Longstreet, and many others whose after lives and distinction reflected honor on his name. Dr. Jackson returned soon enough to give his valuable aid to this grand, solid, beneficent veteran in finally rehabilitating the college and launching it upon that long career of prosperity which it maintains to this day.

Why, when he saw the college once more securely under way and free from danger of relapse and himself, too, at once an idol and an ornament there, he so soon withdrew from his connection with it and went into absolute retirement, I have never known or heard. I have not, however, been able to help divining somewhat of the cause: — For that conversant during his years of absence with the most distinguished social, scientific and political circles of the world and accustomed, consequently, to high and stimulating intellectual habits, he found himself averse probably after his return, to drudging in a perpetual round of things in science and philosophy familiar and rudimental to him, although ever so new, fresh and interesting to his successive new classes of pupils. His retirement bordered on that of a recluse. Rarely seen abroad, a glimpse of him was sometimes to be had in the cool of a summer evening promenading meditatively the grounds within his own curtilige, conscious of the pure clime that environed him,—the soft, aerial summit of the far off Currihee just not sunken from his view and the fair earth and fairer Heavens serene and sympathetic above and around him.

Note to page 4, from WHITE'S HISTORICAL SKETCHES OF GEORGIA, *page* 634.

Hon. Thomas Spalding was born at Frederica, on the Island of St. Simon's, Glynn county, on the 26th March, 1774, and was of Scottish descent. He was the son of James Spalding, Esq , who married the eldest daughter of Colonel William McIntosh, the latter being the same person who, when a lad, with his younger brother, Lachlan, (afterwards General McIntosh, of the Revolutionary War,) followed their father, John More McIntosh, a Highland chieftain, when, with a band of intrepid Highlanders, he accompanied General Oglethorpe to the wilds of Georgia, in 1736, and from whom sprang many of that name, who periled their all for the independence of their country during our Revolutionary contest.

Mr. Spalding's father was a gentleman of fine abilities, and a great reader of men and of books, the advantages of which he seemed to have early and indelibly impressed upon the mind of his son, who read everything, and whose surprisingly tenacious memory, retaining all that he read, made him as a living book and depositary of literary treasures, especially those of historic interest.

For those gentle and benevolent traits which he so liberally practiced in mature manhood, he was indebted to the influence and example of his excellent and venerated mother, of whom he ever spoke with the most filial tenderness. He was their only child. At the time of his father's decease he was a student of law, in the office of Thomas Gibbons, Esq., of Savannah, whose practice was extensive and profitable; and had circumstances at this period permitted Mr. Spalding to pursue the profession of his choice, he doubtless would have been eminent in it; but his fortune being ample, and requiring his personal attention, he declined to proceed in the practice. He married the daughter and only child of Richard Leake, Esq., which union added much to his already comfortable estate.

About this time, though very young, he was elected to the Legislature, and shortly after, with his family, visited Europe, and took up his residence in London, where he remained two years a regular attendant on, and observer of, the proceedings of Parliament, and in the enjoyment of that society to which his pecuniary means and position among his countrymen abroad entitled him in the British metropolis.

The lady whom he married was of rare accomplishments, good sense, and of singular beauty; yet she alone seemed unconscious of those irresistible fascinations which secured her the respect, admiration and love of all. They had born to them many children, five only of whom survived their parents and are still living. Mr. Spalding had the misfortune to lose his oldest son, James, while a member of the Legislature from McIntosh county, during its session in 1820—an amiable young man, of superior talent, and of great promise. The Legislature erected a monument to his memory in the capital of the State.

On his return from England, Mr. Spalding was elected to Congress, and served two sessions, and was for many years afterwards a prominent and leading member of the Senate of his native State, and until he retired from public life, to superintend his extensive private affairs, and to enjoy the repose and comforts of his attractive home, surrounded by his books, and friends, and strangers visiting our country, to whom he was ever attentive.

For the various measures which he advocated during a long political career, through anxious and perplexing periods of our history, he acted always from a conscientious conviction of being right, and for the interest of his country. There never was a more ardent or a purer patriot. At the close of the war of 1812, in compliance with a commission from the General Government, he proceeded to Bermuda, and negotiated relative to the slaves and other property taken from the South by the British forces.

In 1826, he was appointed Commissioner on the part of the State to meet the Commissioner of the United States, Governor Randolph, of Virginia, to determine on the boundary between Georgia and the Territory of Florida, but which was not conclusively settled, the Commissioners disagreeing as to what should be considered the true source of the St. Marys—the Georgia Commissioner insisting on the Southern and most distant of the two lakes from the mouth of the river discharging its waters into the Atlantic, which lake has since been called after him.

The limit assigned for biographical sketches in this work admits of nothing more than a mere outline of the life of Mr. Spalding. He was a fluent, energetic speaker, and a fine writer. Ease of style and originality characterize the productions of his pen. He was the author of the Life of Oglethorpe, and of many other sketches; and furnished much useful matter for various agricultural journals of the country, was among the earliest cotton planters of the State and introduced the cane, its successful culture, and the manufacture of sugar into Georgia. He was the last surviving member of the Convention that revised the Constitution of the State in 1798.

In personal appearance he was agreeable, of middling stature, of easy, unassuming manners, courteous and affable. His hospitality was boundless, and accessible to all; and it may be truly and emphatically said of him, that he was the friend of the distressed. Kind in all the relations of life, his slaves, of whom he had a large number, felt neither irksome toil or disquiet under his mild and indulgent government.

He felt intensely interested in the Compromise measures of Congress, and, though in delicate health, declared his wish to go as a delegate to the Convention in Milledgeville, even if he should die in the effort. He reached that city in a very feeble state, was elected President of the Convention, and commenced his duties by a neat and appropriate address, remarking in the conclusion, that 'as it would be the last, so it would also be a graceful termination of his public, labors,' After the adjournment, he passed on homeward through Savannah, greatly debilitated, and reached his son's residence, near Darien, where he expired in the midst of his children, calmly relying on his God for a happy futurity, January 4th 1851, in the 77th year of his age, and in sight of that island home in which it is hoped no spoiler will ever be suffered to trespass, but long to remain a sacred memorial of his taste for the sublime beauties of nature. His residence was a massive mansion, of rather unique style, in the midst of a primeval forest of lofty, out-branching oaks, of many centuries, arrayed in the soft and gracefully-flowing drapery of the Southern moss, waving in noiseless unison with the ceaseless surges of the ocean, which break upon the strand of this beautiful and enchanting spot.

www.ingramcontent.com/pod-product-compliance
Lightning Source LLC
LaVergne TN
LVHW050518100826
845148LV00002B/381

* 9 7 8 1 4 2 5 5 2 0 3 4 2 *